# Sɪʀ THOMAS MORE
## AND HIS FRIENDS

*Sir Thomas More*
*by Holbein*

# Sir THOMAS MORE
## AND HIS FRIENDS
## 1477–1535

BY

E. M. G. ROUTH, F.R.Hist.S.

*NEW YORK*

RUSSELL & RUSSELL · INC.

1963

FIRST PUBLISHED IN 1934
REISSUED, 1963, BY RUSSELL & RUSSELL, INC.
L. C. CATALOG CARD NO: 63—15177

PRINTED IN THE UNITED STATES OF AMERICA

'*Ad amicitiam natus factusque videtur, cuius et syncerissimus est cultor et longe tenacissimus est. . . . Si quis absolutum verae amicitiae requirat exemplar, a nemine rectius petierit quam a Moro.*'

ERASMUS

# ERRATUM

Page 87: Latin verses, line 4

*for* Castor Polluxque invicem
*read* Castorque Polluxque invicem

# PREFACE

By THE LATE DAME ELIZABETH WORDSWORTH, D.B.E., HON. D.C.L.

THERE are certain periods, as well as certain personalities in history, which seem to appeal to us in an exceptional way. Among the former, the sixteenth century is undoubtedly prominent. It seems to be half-way between the medieval and the modern world.

Preceded as it was by the Renaissance, the invention of printing, and the discovery of America, it felt the stimulating health of new currents of life. It was, as Shakespeare said of his own generation, a 'growing age'.

Great periods are generally associated with great personalities, and I think no century in English history—not even the age of Cromwell, or the age of Pitt—can boast of such a group of remarkable men as those who cross the stage in the sixteenth century. Among these, if not the most distinguished, yet certainly the most captivating, is that of Sir Thomas More. His life is—if one may coin a phrase—a bundle of antitheses. A devout son of the Church, he amazes us by the freedom of his speculation in the *Utopia*. A strict and conscientious Catholic, a detester of heresy, one who would face, as he did, imprisonment and death rather than be false to the dictates of his own conscience, yet he is the friend of Erasmus, the scholar, the Biblical critic, the satirist of contemporary abuses, and one of the great pioneers of the Reformation. As Lord Chancellor of England we find More, like Daniel, 'doing the King's business', and doing it excellently, and yet, like Daniel, constantly on his knees. Add to this his great personal charm, his family affection—his servants were devoted to him—his fine taste in art and literature, the unquenchable playfulness which did not forsake him, even when he laid his head on the block, his originality and his genial kindliness, and we have before us a figure, which, once seen, never loses its hold on our hearts. We see him once more, as in Holbein's sketch, surrounded by his family, seated in his house at Chelsea; the handsomely panelled room; his old father in the place of honour beside him, his daughter Margaret in front with her book—the clock ticking on the wall, the green plant in a pot, the flagon and the book on a shelf. Above all, there sits the

master of the house, with a calm, dignified, contented face;
yet we feel there is room beneath that broad brow for intelligence, wit, sympathy, originality, and capacity for the highest
things.

It is difficult to resist quoting some of his quaint and brilliant
sayings, but the reader of the following pages will find them
there, and with much more that Miss Routh has in store for us in
her carefully and sympathetically written book, where the results
of a long and careful study are compressed into a modest volume,
which, while it cannot fail to give pleasure, ought to leave us all
the better for enabling us to know more of one of the best, wisest,
wittiest, and most lovable of men.

## AUTHOR'S PREFACE

WHEN Cresacre More, in the reign of Charles I, set himself the task of writing the life of his illustrious great-grandfather, Sir Thomas More, he asked with disarming candour: 'What courage can I have to undertake a work of so great difficulty as this, who know myself a very puny in comparison of so many famous men, that have undergone this business already, finding in the very beginning of this mine enterprise, my small capacity over-whelmed with the plenty and copiousness of this my subject?'

A fellow-feeling with the writer assails me, on the contemplation, not only of the 'plenty and copiousness' of the material which confronted *him*, in his task of selection, but also of the vast quantity of literature which has gathered round the name of Sir Thomas More, from his own day to the present. Many distinguished writers have been attracted by his story (there are at least twenty-four English *Lives* of More of different periods), and nearly all have expressed for him the affectionate regard which is usually reserved for a personal friend, even when their opinions differ widely from his own.

It is a remarkable fact that, at a time when biography was an almost unknown branch of English literature, four or five nearly contemporary writers were inspired to record their knowledge of one who is now recognized as the founder of a school of prose-writing. Only a fragment of the *Life of More* by his nephew, William Rastell, has been found, and the well-known *Life* by William Roper, the son-in-law who lived in More's house for sixteen years, remains the first authority; it is supplemented by the contemporary letters of Erasmus to Ulrich von Hutten, Budé, and other friends, and by many letters and pages of autobiography in More's own writings. The *Life* by Nicholas Harpsfield was compiled from notes given him by Roper, and from some other sources. It has been lately produced for the Early English Text Society. Thomas Stapleton consulted the letters of More's friends, and gathered personally many details from the younger members of his household, for the Latin *Life of More*, of which an English translation has been recently published. The anonymous *Life* published in the *Ecclesiastical Biography* (from a manuscript by 'Ro. Ba.' in the Lambeth Library, attributed to 1599) and the *Life* by Cresacre More were founded upon Roper, Harpsfield, Erasmus, and Stapleton. These, with the *Letters and Papers* for the reign of Henry VIII, are the principal published sources of information.

More's own *English Works*, printed in 1557, are now at last being re-edited by Mr. W. E. Campbell in a worthy form, for modern readers. A much-needed collection of his letters I understand is being prepared by Miss E. F. Rogers. The great revival of interest in this subject leads me to hope that the present essay may serve as an introduction of the life and work of Sir Thomas More to some of the younger generation of students and others to whom they may not be familiar.

A personality so many-sided may be regarded from various aspects. It has been my endeavour to present him as nearly as possible as he is depicted in his own writings and letters and in those of his contemporaries and friends. Many extracts are given from these writings, for they enable us to know him with greater intimacy than is possible—I believe—in the case of any other Englishman of his period. Considerable space has been given to his earlier and less well-known years, to his friendships with scholars of the Renaissance, to his appointments to offices of State, and to his services for education. (It was considered a 'noisome and jeopardous' experiment to educate girls, until More tried it with success.) The religious controversy in which he was deeply engaged, and the question of Henry VIII's marriages, are written of here only so much as seemed necessary in order to indicate More's position in those respects. A number of the Latin letters of More and Erasmus have been translated for me by Miss C. Jamison, and it will be seen that I have also made use of translations by the late F. M. Nichols, J. A. Froude and the Rev. Father T. E. Bridgett, and by Mgr. P. E. Hallett, Mr. G. C. Richards and others; in some instances these translations are abridged, and occasionally slightly altered.

My work has been greatly assisted by researches made at the British Museum and the Public Record Office by Miss C. Jamison, who has brought to light some details of More's official life which were for a long time the subject of conjecture, especially regarding the dates of his appointments as Councillor and as Under Treasurer. Miss Jamison has compiled the index and has helped me by correcting proofs and in innumerable matters in which her accurate scholarship and experienced judgement have been invaluable. My cordial thanks are due to her, to Mrs. C. S. Routh, and Miss E. Blewitt, M.B.E. for their help, and also to Dr. A. F. Pollard, F.B.A., for his kind advice and information, and to the Librarian of the London Library and to Wilfred Merton, Esq., for their frequent courteous assistance. Various notes have been supplied to me by the late Dr. P. S. Allen, Mrs. Fenn, Dr. Elsie Hitchcock, Professor R. W. Chambers, F.B.A., the Rev. Professor N. Sykes, Reginald Blunt, Esq., of the Chelsea Society; Frederick Smith, Esq., Town Clerk of Coventry, and Mr. and Mrs. R. D. West.

I wish also to express my gratitude to all those who have given permission for the reproduction of portraits, and especially to the late Sir Emery Walker, F.S.A., who offered me the use of his photograph of the best portrait of More by Holbein for the photogravure plate, and who collected an interesting set of illustrations, some of them from photographs specially taken at Windsor Castle and the British Museum.

The subject of the book was suggested to me by the late Dame Elizabeth Wordsworth. 'Sir Thomas More is one of the figures of abiding interest in history', she wrote, and in a later letter: 'I am glad you are going on with Sir T. More. I hardly want you to finish it just yet, for I know how dreadfully you will miss him when he is done!'

With affectionate gratitude I recall her ready consent to contribute a preface, and the sympathetic interest which never failed, in the work of one of the former students of Lady Margaret Hall; she was loved by all of those who knew her, as More was loved by his scholars.

E. M. G. R.

# ACKNOWLEDGEMENTS

I have to record my grateful acknowledgement to authors, or their representatives, and publishers for permission to quote from the following books.

P. S. Allen. *Opus Epistolarum Des. Erasmi Roterodami.* 7 vols. published. Clarendon Press, 1906–26.

P. S. and H. M. Allen. *Sir Thomas More. Selections from his English Works and from the Lives by Erasmus and Roper.* Clarendon Press, 1924.

J. S. Brewer. *The Reign of Henry VIII from his Accession to the Death of Wolsey,* edited by James Gairdner. 2 vols. John Murray, 1884.

T. E. Bridgett. *Life and Writings of Sir Thomas More, Lord Chancellor of England and Martyr under Henry VIII.* Burns & Oates, Ltd., 1891.

R. W. Chambers, *On the Continuity of English Prose.* Clarendon Press, 1932.

J. A. Froude. *Life and Letters of Erasmus.* Longmans, Green & Co., 1894.

W. H. Hutton. *Sir Thomas More.* Methuen & Co., 1895.

W. S. Holdsworth. *History of English Law.* Third edition, rewritten. Vols. 1–5. Methuen & Co., 1922–4.

J. H. Lupton. *Life of John Colet.* G. Bell & Sons, Ltd., 1887.

—— *The Utopia of Sir Thomas More.* Clarendon Press, 1895.

R. B. Merriman. *Life and Letters of Thomas Cromwell.* 2 vols. Clarendon Press, 1902.

F. M. Nichols. *The Epistles of Erasmus from his earliest letters to his 51st year.* 3 vols. The Executors of the late Mr. F. M. Nichols and Longmans, Green & Co., 1901, 1904, 1918.

A. F. Pollard *Henry VIII.* Longmans, Green & Co., 1919.

—— *Wolsey.* Longmans, Green & Co., 1929.

G. C. Richards. *More's Utopia.* Translated into modern English. Basil Blackwell, 1923.

T. Stapleton. *The Life and Illustrious Martyrdom of Sir Thomas More.* Translated for the first time into English by Philip E. Hallett, Rector of St. John's Seminary, Wonersh. Burns, Oates, and Washbourne Ltd., 1928.

Foster Watson. *Vives and the Renascence Education of Women.* Edward Arnold & Co., 1912.

E. M. G. R.

# CONTENTS

# LIST OF ILLUSTRATIONS

[1] Names in group, from left to right: Elizabeth Daunce, Margaret Giggs, Sir John More, Anne Cresacre (wife of John More, jun.), Sir Thomas More, John More, jun., Henry Pattison, Cecily Heron, Margaret Roper, Dame Alice More.

# PRINCIPAL AUTHORITIES

*The Works of Sir Thomas More*, Knyght, sometime Lorde Chancellour of England, wrytten by him in the English tonge. Printed at London at the costes and charges of John Cawood, John Waly and Richard Tottel anno 1557. (Referred to as 'English Works', and quoted in the text without alteration of language but with modernized spelling.)

*The English Works of Sir Thomas More*, vol. i. Edited by W. E. Campbell, with introductory essays and notes by A. W. Reed, M.A., D.Lit.: R. W. Chambers, M.A., D.Lit., and W. A. G. Doyle Davidson, B.A. (A reproduction of William Rastell's black-letter edition (see above) with a modernized version.) Eyre & Spottiswoode, Ltd. (1931).

*The dialogue concerning Tyndale*, by Sir Thomas More, edited by W. E. Campbell. Eyre & Spottiswoode, Ltd. (1927).

*The Utopia of Sir Thomas More.*, ed. J. H. Lupton. Clarendon Press (1895).

*More's Utopia*, translated into Modern English by G. C. Richards. Basil Blackwell (1923). (References in the text are to the last-named volume.)

P. S. Allen. *Opus Epistolarum Des. Erasmi Roterodami*, tom. i–vii. Clarendon Press (1906–26).

F. M. Nichols, *The Epistles of Erasmus from his earliest letters to his 51st year*. 3 vols. Longmans, Green & Co. (1901, 1904, 1918).

Public Record Office.
Patent Roll, c. 66, no. 631, m. 12.
Exchequer of Receipt, E. 405, nos. 102, 103, 104 (Tellers' Rolls).
Exchequer of Receipt, E. 405, no. 480 (Rough Entry Book of receipts and issues).
Exchequer of Receipt, E. 405, nos. 192, 193, 196, 202 (Declarations of State of Treasury).
Chancery Inquisition *post mortem*, c. 142, vol. 36.

British Museum, Harleian MS. 6253 (Harpsfield's Life of More).

*Calendar of Letters and Papers, Foreign and Domestic*, of the reign of Henry VIII., ed. Brewer and Gairdner. (Referred to as *Letters and Papers*.)

*State Papers, Henry VIII.* (H.M. Commission for printing and publishing State Papers, 1830), vol. i.

*Calendar of State Papers, Venetian*, vols. ii and iv.

*Calendar of State Papers, Spanish, 1530–1535.*

P. S. and H. M. Allen, *Sir Thomas More. Selections from his English Works and from the Lives by Erasmus and Roper*.) Clarendon Press (1924).

L. E. Bins, *Erasmus the Reformer*. Methuen (1923).

J. S. Brewer, *The Reign of Henry VIII*, 2 vols., ed. J. Gairdner. John Murray (1884).

Rev. T. E. Bridgett, *The Life and Writings of Sir Thomas More.* Burns & Oates Ltd. (1891).

—— *Life of Blessed John Fisher* (Bishop of Rochester). Burns & Oates Ltd. (1888).

Rawdon Brown, *Four Years at the Court of Henry VIII.* Smith, Elder & Co. (1854). (Giustiniani's dispatches.)

*Cambridge Modern History,* vol. i. Cambridge University Press (1902).

John, Lord Campbell, *The Lives of the Lord Chancellors* (3 vols.), vol. i. John Murray (1845).

W. E. Campbell, *More's Utopia and his Social Teaching.* Eyre & Spottiswoode, Ltd. (1930).

R. W. Chambers, *On the Continuity of English Prose, from Alfred to More and his school.* Published for the E.E.T.S. by Humphrey Milford, Oxford University Press (1932).

*The Fame of Blessed Thomas More,* by Professor R. W. Chambers and other writers. Sheed and Ward (1929).

*The Coventry Leet Book and Mayor's Register 1420–1555,* edited by Mary Dormer Harris. Published for the E.E.T.S. by Humphrey Milford, Oxford University Press (1913).

Joseph Delcourt, *Essai sur la langue de Sir Thomas More.* Paris, H. Didier (1914).

Rev. R. Demaus, *William Tyndale.* Religious Tract Society (1871).

*Ecclesiastical Biography,* 6 vols., vol. ii, edited by Dr. Christopher Wordsworth, containing an anonymous *Life of Sir Thomas More,* by 'Ro. Ba.' (Lambeth MS. no. 179). F. C. and J. Rivington (1810).

Sir Thomas Elyot, *The Boke named the Gouernour,* 2 vols., edited by H. H. S. Croft. Kegan Paul (1880).

*English Historical Review,* 1922, vol. xxxvii. 'The Council under the Tudors', by Professor A. F. Pollard, and 'A Calendar of the Correspondence of Sir Thomas More', by Miss E. F. Rogers.

Erasmus, *The Lives of Vitrier and Colet.* Translated by J. H. Lupton. G. Bell & Sons (1883).

H. A. L. Fisher, *The Political History of England,* vol. v. Longmans, Green & Co. (1928).

H. Fishwick, *Proceedings in the Court of Duchy Chamber 1485–1558* (Pleadings and Depositions in the Duchy Court of Lancaster, vol. i.) Lancashire and Cheshire Record Society, vol. xxxii (1896).

Major Benton Fletcher, *Royal Homes near London.* John Lane (1931).

Edward Foss, *Judges of England,* vol. v. Longman, Brown, Green, Longman & Roberts (1857).

J. A. Froude, *Life and Letters of Erasmus.* Longmans, Green & Co. (1894).

James Gairdner, *The English Church in the Sixteenth Century.* Macmillan & Co. (1902).

D. Gardiner, *The Story of Lambeth Palace.* Constable & Co (1930).

Charles W. F. Goss, *Crosby Hall.* Crowther & Goodman (1908).

Hall's *Chronicle.* J. Johnson, F. C. and J. Rivington, &c. (1809).

H. Hall, *Antiquities of the Exchequer.* Camden Library (1891).

Nicholas Harpsfield, *The Life and Death of S͏ʳ. Thomas Moore, knight, sometymes Lord High Chancellor of England.* Edited by Elsie Vaughan Hitchcock, Ph.D., D.Lit., and R. W. Chambers, M.A., D.Lit., F.B.A. Published for the E.E.T.S. by Humphrey Milford, Oxford University Press (1932).

J. C. Hearnshaw, *The Social and Political Ideas of some Great Thinkers of the Renaissance* (Sir Thomas More by Prof. A. W. Reed). G. C. Harrap & Co (1925).

J. O. Hertzler, *The History of Utopian Thought.* George Allen & Unwin (1923).

W. S. Holdsworth, *The History of English Law,* vols. i–v. Methuen, (1922, 1923, 1924).

W. F. Hook, *Lives of the Archbishops,* vols. v and vi. Richard Bentley (1867).

W. H. Hutton, *Sir Thomas More.* Methuen (1895).

Karl Kautsky, *Thomas More and his Utopia.* Translated by H. J. Stenning. A. & C. Black (1927).

J. S. Leadam, *Select Cases in the Court of Requests, 1497–1569.* Selden Society, vol. xii (1898).

—— *Select Cases before the King's Council in the Star Chamber,* vol. ii, 1509–44. Selden Society, vol. xxv (1911).

Sir Sidney Lee, *Great Englishmen of the Sixteenth Century.* Constable & Co. (1904).

Thomas M. Lindsay, *A History of the Reformation,* 2 vols. T. & T. Clark, Edinburgh (1906, 1907).

J. H. Lupton, *Life of John Colet.* George Bell & Sons (1887).

Sir James Mackintosh, *Sir Thomas More.* (Lives of Eminent British Statesmen, vol. i, in Lardner's Cabinet of Biography.) Longman, Rees, Orme, Brown & Green & John Taylor (1831).

R. B. Merriman, *Life and Letters of Thomas Cromwell,* 2 vols. Clarendon Press (1902).

Cresacre More, *The Life of Sir Thomas More,* edited by Rev. J. Hunter. William Pickering (1828).

D. Nisard, *Renaissance et Réforme.* (Érasme, Thomas Morus, Mélancthon.) 2 vols. Calmann Lévy, Paris (1877).

*North British Review,* xxx (1859). 'Sir Thomas More and the Reformation.'

*Philomorus.* (Notes on the Latin poems of Sir Thomas More.) 2nd ed. Longmans, Green & Co. (1878).

A. F. Pollard, *Henry VIII.* Longmans, Green & Co. (1919).

—— *Wolsey.* Longmans, Green &. Co. (1929).

*Proceedings of the British Academy,* xii. 'The Saga and the Myth of Sir Thomas More', by Professor R. W. Chambers. Humphrey Milford (1926).

*Records of the Society of Lincoln's Inn,* Black Books, vol. i. Lincoln's Inn (1897).

A. W. Reed, *The Beginnings of the English Secular and Romantic Drama*. Published for the Shakespeare Association by Humphrey Milford, Oxford University Press (1922).

—— *Early Tudor Drama*. Methuen & Co. (1926).

William Roper, *The Life of Thomas More*, edited by S. W. Singer. From the Press of C. Whittingham, for R. Triphook, Old Bond Street, London (1822).

Frederic Seebohm, *The Oxford Reformers* (Colet, Erasmus, and More). Longmans, Green & Co., 3rd edn. (1887).

Thomas Stapleton, *Tres Thomae*. John Bogard, Douai (1588).

—— *The Life and Illustrious Martyrdom of Sir Thomas More*, translated into English by the Rev. P. E. Hallett. Burns, Oates, & Washbourne (1928).

A. B. Teetgen, *The Footsteps of Sir Thomas More*. Sands & Co. (1930).

Foster Watson, *Vives and the Renascence Education of Women*. Arnold's Educational Classics (1912).

## CHAPTER I

## EARLY YEARS

### 1477–1494

AT the time of Thomas More's birth, his parents were living in Milk Street, Cheapside. Their marriage had been made in the Parish Church of Saint Giles without the Cripplegate, on the 24th of April 1474. John More, a man well known in the City of London, was born probably in 1453, of a family described by his son as 'worthy, though not famous'; he owned property in Hertfordshire, including the Manor of Gobions or 'Gubbins' near North Mimms, but lived chiefly in London, having entered the profession of the law. He became butler, steward, and reader of Lincoln's Inn; barrister, and in 1503, serjeant-at-law; later in life he was knighted; by 1518 he had been made a Judge of the Common Pleas, and finally, by November 1523, a Justice of the Court of King's Bench.[1]

His wife, Agnes Granger, died while her son Thomas was a child. Her eldest daughter, Jane, became the wife of Richard Stafferton; the second child was Thomas, born probably on the 7th of February 1477.[2] A younger boy, John, died in 1512.

[1] Edward Foss, *Judges of England* (1857), v. 196–8, 200.

[2] The date of Thomas More's birth has been the subject of considerable discussion. Sir James Mackintosh and other early biographers put it at 1480; but some correspondence in *Notes and Queries*, October 1868 (quoted by Seebohm in *The Oxford Reformers* (1887), app. C), shows it to have been at least two years earlier than this. An apparently contemporary family register, discovered in the library of Trinity College, Cambridge, gives the date as *Friday*, the 7th of February, in the seventeenth year of the reign of King Edward IV (1478) between two and three in the morning. Professor Seebohm and the late Dean Hutton have accepted this as conclusive evidence, but Mr. F. M. Nichols disputes the point (*Proceedings of the Society of Antiquaries*, 2nd series, vol. xvi, pp. 231–7). The question arises from an error in the MS. entry; for, in 1478, the 7th of February was a *Saturday*. Seebohm assumes that a mistake was made in the day of the week. Mr. Nichols, however, considers that as the regnal year of Edward IV changed on the 5th of March, a mistake in the *year* was not improbably made in the entry, and would put the date of More's birth as Friday the 7th of February 1477.

He supports his opinion by several reasons, including the indirect evidence of Erasmus, in his letter to Ulrich von Hutten (F. M. Nichols, *The Epistles of Erasmus*, iii, p. 402). The late Dr. P. S. Allen was inclined to accept this view, though he suggested that another possibility might be the *6th* of February 1478, by the substitution of *sexto* for *septimo* (*die Februarii*), (*Opus Epistolarum Des. Erasmi Roterodami*, i, pp. 265–6). Professor R. W. Chambers considers the year 1477 to be more probable (*The English Works of Sir Thomas More*, edited by W. E. Campbell (1931), i. 35, 39).

The manuscript mentioned above contains the record of the marriage of Thomas More's parents, i.e. John More, gent: to Agnes, daughter of Thomas Graunger, in the Parish of St. Giles without the Cripplegate, London, 24th April 1474. The dates of birth of six children follow. Jane, 11th March 1475;

Elizabeth, the youngest child, married John Rastell; two other children did not live to grow up.

There is little record of Thomas More's childhood, but in the last year of his life, he looked back with the eyes of memory to see an old nurse sitting by the fire, surrounded by a group of four or five small children, all listening intently to her stories. He wrote of 'Mother Maud, the good old woman that his Mother had that took heed to her children'; in her fables of wonderful talking animals and other 'fond childish tales' he found a pointed moral, which he kept in mind to retell in later years to his own children, with the reflection that 'there is almost no tale so foolish but that yet in one matter or other, to some purpose or other it may hap to serve'.[1]

One of his earliest childish recollections was the conversation of his father with a friend, who related that a neighbour, on hearing of the death of King Edward IV, had exclaimed: 'By my troth, man, then will my Master, the Duke of Gloucester, be King!' At this time—April 1483—Thomas was not more than five or six years old, but already his mind was quick and his memory retentive; the incident was impressed on his imagination and never forgotten. Soon after this he must have heard of the murder of the Princes in the Tower, by order of their uncle, the Duke of Gloucester; the news was received with such general horror that no one could speak of it without tears. In later life More described with dramatic force the tragic scene in the Tower of London, and the dreadful events of Richard's reign, in his *History of King Richard III*.

While the reign of terror of Richard III passed on, to end in the Battle of Bosworth in 1485, John More found that his elder son showed more than ordinary intelligence; he sent him at an early age to Saint Anthony's School in Threadneedle Street, under the mastership of Nicholas Holt. This school, endowed by King Henry VI, was one of the best two in London in the last quarter of the fifteenth century, though even in these the schoolboy's life was very rough and hard.[2]

Thomas, 7th February 1477 (see above); Agatha, 31st January 1479; John, 6th June 1480; Edward, 3rd September 1481; Elizabeth, 22nd September 1482.

According to the above record Cresacre More was mistaken in stating that Thomas More's mother was 'Handcombe of Holliwell' in Bedfordshire. Possibly Agnes Granger, or Graunger, was John More's first wife (and the mother of his children), Jane Handcombe the second, Mrs. Bowes (*née* Barton) the third, and Mrs. Alice Clarke (*née* More of Loseby) the fourth. (Erasmus to Hutten; Allen, iv, p. 19, and note, p. 15.) Erasmus spoke of Thomas More's three stepmothers (ibid.).

[1] Cf. More's *English Works* (1557), p. 1183; P. S. Allen, *Sir Thomas More. Selections from his English Works, etc.* (1922), p. 126.

[2] J. H. Lupton, *Life of John Colet* (1887), p. 18. The other was the hospital school of St. Thomas Acons which in 1524 became the Mercers' school. Ibid., p. 17.

'The interior of the school-room is familiar to us from the many wood-cuts on the title-pages of old books. There we see the awe-inspiring Orbilius seated, with birch erect in one hand, and the fore-finger of the other tracing a line of the open book upon his knee. Beside him is the biggest boy, reading from it, while the rest of the flock are seated on the floor, or, it may be, on little three-legged stools, gazing up with looks of admiration at the performance. Sometimes, but rarely, they sit at desks with stiff high backs, as though for writing. But in general the lesson was oral. Boys learnt by hearing what the master said. The attentive ones would go over it again mentally at home, marking by a note in the margin of their text-book what they had thought most worthy of being remembered.'[1]

This method of learning improved a naturally good memory; Thomas More acquired at school at least a good foundation of Latin, and a capacity for great application.

One of his early verses describes the ideal of the small school-boy of his day.

> I am called Chyldhod, in play is all my mynde
> To cast a coyte, a cokstele[2] and a ball.
> A toppe can I set, and dryve it in his kynde.
> But would to God these hatefull bookes all,
> Were in a fyre brent [burnt] to pouder small.
> Than myght I lede my lyfe alwayes in play :
> Which lyfe God send me to myne endyng day.

This earnest aspiration can hardly have been his own; though he loved play, books were never 'hateful' to him; his mental powers developed rapidly, and before long his father thought it advisable to give him a more advanced and general training.

Although Winchester and Eton were already founded, the fame of the great public schools was still in the future; John More followed a usual custom in sending his son, between the ages of twelve and fourteen—the date is uncertain—to serve in one of the great houses of the day.

He was fortunate in opportunity and wise in choice when he arranged that Thomas should enter the service of John Morton, Archbishop of Canterbury and Lord Chancellor of England.[3] Morton was by training a lawyer and a scholar, by profession a Churchman, and by experience a diplomatist and a statesman. He had taken part in the troubles and excitements of four reigns;

---

[1] Ibid., pp. 20–1.
[2] This was a horrid game, in which a live cock, buried up to the neck in sand, tried to evade the 'steels' thrown at it by the boys. Cock-fighting was forbidden by Colet at his school of Saint Paul, and no doubt this game also.
[3] Created Cardinal in 1493; Chancellor of the University of Oxford, 1495.

he had been one of the strongest supporters of the Lancastrian
cause, and it was he who concerted with the Countess of Richmond the plan to unite by marriage the rival houses of York and
Lancaster, which brought Henry VII to the throne in 1485. He
now held the greatest offices in the Church and State and was
respected as one of the most powerful men in England.

It was recorded by More that 'the King placed great confidence
in his advice and the State seemed to depend on him'. He was a
loyal servant to Henry VII and by his supposed support of the
King's money-making propensities, he gained some unpopularity
among unwilling taxpayers.

To those who knew him personally, Morton showed a more
attractive aspect. More wrote of him:

'The Bishop was a man of great natural wit, very well learned, and
honourable in behaviour, lacking in no wise ways to win favour. He had
been fast upon the part of King Henry [VI] while that part was in wealth
and natheless left it not nor forsook it in woe. . . . This man . . . by the
long and often alternate proof, as well of prosperity as adverse fortune,
had gotten by great experience (the very mother and mistress of wisdom)
a deep insight in politic worldly drifts.'[1]

More felt for the Cardinal a lasting admiration and gratitude.
Describing him in the introductory book of *Utopia*, he wrote:

'He deserved respect as much for his wisdom and virtue as for his
authority. He was of middle stature, and showed no sign of his advanced
age; his countenance inspired respect rather than fear; in intercourse he
was agreeable, though serious and dignified. By rough address he sometimes made trial of those who made suit to him, but in a harmless way,
to see what ability in answering, and presence of mind a man possessed,
which virtue, provided it did not amount to impudence, gave him
pleasure, as akin to his own disposition, and excited his admiration, as
suited to those holding public office. His speech was polished, and to the
point. His knowledge was profound, his ability incomparable and his
memory wonderfully retentive, for by learning and practice he improved
his natural qualities. . . . He had spent his whole life in important public
affairs and had had many vicissitudes of fortune, so that by many and
great dangers he had acquired his sagacity, which, when thus learned, is
not easily forgotten.'[2]

The Archbishop's manor house at Lambeth—rebuilt about
sixty years earlier by Archbishop Chichele, with the great
entrance gates lately added by Morton—stood in lovely surroundings of green fields, looking towards the Surrey hills in one

[1] More's *English Works* (1557), p. 70.
[2] *More's Utopia*, translated into modern English, by G. C. Richards (1923),
p. 9.

direction, with a view from the windows of its hall across the Thames to the Royal Palace at Westminster. From the river, the great highway of London, rose the sound of music from passing boats at evening, while the gilded barges of the nobility and the painted boats of the middle classes presented to the eye a gay and animated scene.[1]

In Morton's household Thomas More was given an orthodox religious training, and was taught to entertain that spirit of reverence for the authority and precepts of the Church, which he never lost. Here he first began to understand the terrible social evils which he described with pointed eloquence in his *Utopia*, and to feel that deep sympathy with the poor and oppressed which became one of the guiding motives of his life. Here too he received a training for public life which helped to develop his natural readiness of wit and of speech, as well as the sympathetic tact and endearing charm of manner which won him the affection of a host of friends.

He found himself in a large and busy community; a great prelate's 'family' included numbers of officials of all degrees— steward, treasurer, comptroller, almoner, clerks, gentlemen ushers, yeomen of the chamber and the wardrobe, yeomen of the horse, porters, butlers, grooms, cooks, pantlers, 'daily waiters in the great chamber', and many others. Lambeth Palace was ever a centre of learning, of business, and of hospitality. To Morton's table came men of letters, nobles, statesmen, lawyers, priests and friars, and travellers from foreign parts; their host directed the conversation but encouraged the free expression of opinion. The boys serving in the great dining-hall, as they waited silently behind their masters' seats, handing dishes or pouring wine, and eating, as they stood, whatever might be given them from the table, had the opportunity of hearing discussions on all the topics of the hour. Religion, politics, literature—the latest editions produced by the venerable printer, Caxton, at his press in the almonry at Westminster—the appearance in Ireland of a new pretender to the throne—the inexpediency of capital punishment for theft—all the social and economic problems that followed a period of civil war and unrest—from all these subjects they might gain an insight into the world of affairs, and the pages themselves were sometimes drawn into talk by their elders, who took this means to test their readiness and wit.

Morton felt a great interest in More, the intelligent amusing boy 'in whose wit and towardness the Cardinal much delighting',

[1] W. F. Hook, *Lives of the Archbishops*, vi. 310. More may sometimes have accompanied Morton to Knowle, or other manors.

wrote William Roper,[1] 'would often say of him unto the nobles that divers times dined with him: "This child here waiting at the table, whosoever shall live to see it, shall prove a marvellous man." '

The same writer says: 'Though he was young of years, yet would he at Christmastide suddenly sometimes step in among the players, and never studying for the matter, make a part of his own there presently among them, which made the lookers on more sport than all the players beside.'

It is interesting to note that Dr. W. A. Reed sees in Morton's household at this period 'a school of renaissance culture and homely blunt wit' and has traced to it the beginning of a movement towards a freer kind of imaginative drama, 'the spirit of which is one of liberation, romance and variety, looking abroad for new dramatic material and finding it in Italy, France and Spain'.

The Archbishop's chaplain, Henry Medwall, shows an instance of this movement in his play *Fulgens and Lucres* for he took his romance of Roman life from an English translation (printed by Caxton in 1481) of a French version of the Latin work of Bonaccorso, an Italian. In this play was a comic under-plot for two boys, who made love to the maid while the hero paid court to the mistress; Dr. Reed hazards the attractive suggestion that the parts of these two boys may have been played by Thomas More and John Rastell, whose family was associated with that of More, and who in later life produced and printed a series of early secular plays which 'pointed the way to the Romantic Drama of Shakespeare'.[2]

Surrounded by these influences, More acquired a sense of rhythm and a feeling for dramatic expression, as well as an unusual command of language; in his youth he wrote and acted in some small comedies, now lost.[3] His earliest known attempt at verse-making was entitled *A mery gest how a sergeant would learn to play the Frere* (friar)—a rollicking, spontaneous rhyme, often passed over with scornful criticism, but admirably suited to its purpose as prelude to some Tudor revelry or Christmas play. With some elaboration of dialogue, it might have served as the plot of a comedy or 'interlude'. The theme of the 'jest' is that a man should stick to his own business, or ill may befall him if he

---

[1] *The Life of Sir Thomas More*, by his son-in-law William Roper. S. W. Singer's edition (1822), p. 4.

[2] *The Beginnings of the English Secular and Romantic Drama*, a paper read before the Shakespeare Association, 29 Feb. 1920, by A. W. Reed, M.A., D.Litt.; and *Early Tudor Drama*, by the same author (Methuen, 1926).

[3] 'Adolescens comoediolas et scripsit et egit.' Erasmus to Hutten, Allen, iv, no. 999, p. 16.

attempt to play another's part. One of the introductory verses
runs as follows:

| | |
|---|---|
| Whan an hatter | All that ensue |
| Wyll go smatter | Suche craftes new |
| In philosophy, | They drive so farre a cast |
| Or a pedlar | That euermore |
| Waxe a medlar | They do therfore |
| In theology | Beshrewe themselfe at last. |

The rhyme goes on to relate that a 'thrifty man' died, leaving
to his son 'an hundred pound of nobles round, for to beginne
withal'. 'But to suffice his chylde, well thrise that money was
too smal.' The young man borrowed more money from his
neighbours, never paid it back, but bought extravagant clothes,
and

| | |
|---|---|
| With lusty sporte | There spent he fast |
| And with resort | Till all was past |
| Of joly company | And to him came there meny |
| In mirth and play | To ask theyr det |
| Full many a day | But none could get |
| He liued merely[1] | The valour[2] of a peny. |

His creditors then set the law upon his track, but he evaded
arrest by feigning illness in a friend's house, refusing to stir out
of doors.

| | |
|---|---|
| It happed than | Of an officere |
| A marchant man | Than gan enquere |
| That he ought money to | What him was best to do. |

The 'officere', a serjeant-at-law, undertook to arrest the
miscreant, saying boldly 'and for your sake, let me be bake, but
yf I do this cure'. He then borrowed for a day the habit of a
friar.

| | |
|---|---|
| So was he dight | He dopped and dooked |
| That no man might | He spake and looked |
| Hym for a frere deny | So religiously. |

So disguised, the pretended friar was admitted to the pretended
invalid's bedside.

| | |
|---|---|
| Whan there was none | Thou shalt obay |
| But they alone, | Come on thy way |
| The frere with euyll grace | I have the in my clouche[3] |
| Sayd 'I 'rest the, | Thou goest not hence |
| Come on with me'. | For all the pense |
| And out he toke his mace. | The mayre hath in his pouche. |

[1] merrily     [2] value     [3] clutch

The two then came to blows and a terrific battle ensued.

| | |
|---|---|
| And so there goth | With many a sadde stroke |
| Betwene them both | They roll and rumble |
| Many a lusty cloute | They turne and tumble |
| They rent and tere | As pygges do in a poke. |
| Eche other's here | So long aboue |
| And clave togyder fast | They heue and shoue |
| Tyll with luggyng | Togider, that at last |
| And with tuggyng | The mayd and wyfe |
| They fell downe bothe at last | To breake the strife |
| Than on the grounde | Hyed them upward fast. |
| Togyder rounde | |

The two women fall upon the false friar, in defence of their guest, 'with a great batyll dore', and when they have the unlucky man 'full-nigh slayne',

| | |
|---|---|
| Up they hym lift | Downe they hym threwe |
| And with yll thrift | And said 'adewe |
| Hedlyng along the stayre | Commaunde us to the mayre'. |

The rhyme concludes:

| | |
|---|---|
| Now masters all | His owne craft use |
| Here now I shall | All new refuse |
| Ende there as I began | And lyghtly let them gone. |
| In any wyse | Play not the frere. |
| I would auyse | Now make good chere |
| And counsayle every man. | And welcome every chone.[1] |

If it cannot be considered good poetry, the jovial rhyme must at least have seemed good fun to those who heard young More recite it with his own inimitable drollery, giving point to that ironic touch 'Commend us to the Mayor'; and so it seemed to his nephew, William Rastell, who included it, as an afterthought, in the 'great volume' of More's *English Works*, collected by him and printed in 1557.

The Archbishop's household was a good school for many purposes, but Morton showed wise judgement when he sent his favourite scholar from this over-stimulating atmosphere to the more serious and austere conditions of a university life, and 'for his better furtherance in learning', placed More at Oxford. Here, probably in 1492, he entered Canterbury College, and apparently occupied for a time a room in St. Mary Hall.[2]

Undergraduates at that time were given no material comfort; often they lived four in a room, and 'in the chilly squalor of

---

[1] *chone* = one.
[2] W. H. Hutton, *Sir Thomas More* (1895), p. 14. Canterbury College was absorbed in Wolsey's foundation of Christ Church.

uncarpeted and unwarmed chambers, by the light of narrow and unglazed casements, or the gleam of flickering oil-lamps, they pored over dusty manuscripts'.[1] A penny a day was thought to be enough for 'commons' which in consequence were 'short' indeed; the fare provided was scanty and rough. More, always ready to make the best of things, found ample opportunity to acquire that liking for coarse salt beef which surprised his friend Erasmus in his more prosperous days. Perhaps John More shared with Bishop Fisher a prevalent idea that good meals were detrimental to good learning; at any rate he gave his son an allowance too small to provide for any but the barest necessaries. Young More had to account to his father for every penny he spent, and had not even enough money in hand to pay for the mending of his shoes. 'Thus it came to pass', he would say, later in life, 'that I indulged in no vice or vain pleasure, that I did not spend my time in dangerous or idle pastimes, that I did not even know the meaning of extravagance and luxury, that I did not learn to put money to evil uses, that, in fine, I had no love, or even thought, of anything beyond my studies.'[2] Though he praised his father's parsimony, he took care, nevertheless, to treat his own children in a very different way.

Towards the end of the fifteenth century, the universities were but just emerging from a period of inertia, consequent upon the long civil wars. Many members of the powerful noble families— the traditional patrons of learning—had fallen on the battle-field or on the scaffold; some of the survivors were almost ruined; some despised learning; there were fewer helpers for men of letters. The old conventional teaching became stereotyped and out of date; Erasmus wrote that little was taught either at Oxford or Cambridge except 'antiquated and artificial studies'.

Yet, in the midst of a general depression, fresh forces were at work. In all directions the narrow bounds of medieval life were breaking down; new vistas of thought were opening out in the spreading light of the Renaissance. While explorers were discovering the existence of countries hitherto unknown, bringing to knowledge a veritable New World, in England great social changes were taking place. The monasteries—once great homes of learning and culture—were losing their power and repute; in the middle classes now rising on the ruins of feudalism, there were many families whose sons were to become distinguished in the

---

[1] Lupton, *Life of John Colet*, pp. 35–6 (from Brodrick's *Memorials of Merton College*).
[2] Thomas Stapleton, *Life of Sir Thomas More*, edited by the Rev. P. E. Hallett (1928), p. 3.

history of their country as men of letters, statesmen, lawyers, and divines.

At Oxford, More found a little group of men who brought to his ardent mind the conception of a wider intellectual life than any he had yet dreamed of; he threw himself eagerly into the 'New Learning' which ultimately transformed the universities, and changed the tendency of thought in all Europe.

Not many years earlier, William Grocyn had learned a little Greek from the Italian Praelector at New College, Cornelio Vitelli, and Thomas Linacre had heard from Selling of rare Greek manuscripts brought from Italy.[1] Before this, the Greek language had been almost unknown in England, and its study was still regarded with suspicion by the older 'Schoolmen' who thought it 'next door to heresy'. But when More was at Oxford, both Grocyn and Linacre had returned from Italy, where alone teachers of Greek could be found, and were making known to a few students the wonderful tongue which was proving the key to untold treasures of classical knowledge. They had rediscovered the existence of an ancient and rich civilization. 'The poetry of Homer, the drama of Sophocles, the philosophy of Aristotle and Plato woke again to life.' A new world of thought and literature, science and art, opened out before More's delighted mind. While he attended lectures on the orthodox subjects of logic, rhetoric, and scholastic philosophy, and acquired a remarkable facility in writing and speaking Latin, at the same time he began to gain his wide acquaintance with authors of both the classical languages. His great-grandson remarked: 'He profited exceedingly in rhetoric, logic and philosophy, and showed evidently what wonders wit and diligence can perform, when joined, as they seldom are, in one painful student.' It is clear that study was anything but painful to More, except in the sense of 'taking pains'.

His unusual ability attracted the notice of the best scholars of his time, who welcomed him to their company, young though he was, as one of their most brilliant students.[2] William Latimer, a Fellow of All Souls, tutor of Reginald Pole, the future Cardinal, and well known for his learning, became More's friend. Grocyn, whose lectures he attended, had spent some time in Florence, where the Platonic Academy met in the villa of Lorenzo de' Medici on the heights of Fiesole; he had studied under both

---

[1] 'William Tilly of Selling' often alluded to as 'Selling (or Celling) of Canterbury'. (*Cambridge Modern History*, i. 643.)

[2] The friendships begun in More's early life continued later, in London; it is doubtful how far they developed while he was at Oxford.

Chalcondylas, the Greek exile, and Poliziano, renowned for his
wide scholarship and his eloquence.[1]

More learned Greek also from Linacre, studying with him the
works of Aristotle. Linacre, famous for his medical studies, and
destined to become the founder of the Royal College of Physicians,
had taken a degree at Padua, and, after a long stay in Italy, could
tell his pupil of rare manuscripts in the Vatican Library, and of
Rome, the 'bright and glorious city', spoilt indeed by vice and corruption, but still to be described by Erasmus as 'a rich treasure-
house of literature and art, the centre of polite society, refined
luxury and learned intercourse'. He could speak, from personal
knowledge, of Savonarola, the ardent preacher of reform, just
beginning to attract attention by his fiery eloquence; of Pico della
Mirandola, who became one of More's heroes, and of Aldo Manu-
cio, who settled in Venice in 1490, and who was planning to print
the masterpieces of Greek literature, which by his means would
be accessible for the first time in convenient form to English
students.

The influence of Linacre and Grocyn over More in his early life
was surpassed only by that of Colet, the future Dean of St. Paul's,
and founder of St. Paul's School. John Colet was the son of a
rich merchant of London no doubt well known to John More.
A man who loved youth, he was greatly attracted to the brilliant
young student, and the friendship between the two continued till
Colet's death in 1519.

'There seems always to have been a fascination about More which no
cultured man could resist,' writes Dean Hutton.[2] 'It was the union of
simplicity of manner and purity of soul with a swift appreciation of the
thoughts and a true sympathy with the sorrows of others—of a keen
intellect and deep earnestness of purpose, softened by a bright and continual humour.'

Like his friends Linacre and Grocyn, Colet went to Italy in
search of treasures of Christian learning, 'a merchant seeking
goodly pearls', as Erasmus said. More, inspired by the example of
these friends, was turning eagerly to the study of 'good letters'
(*bonae litterae*) when suddenly a heavy paternal hand cut short the
most promising University career of his day. After scarcely two
brilliant years, he was hurried away from Oxford without taking
a degree, and bidden to study law in London.

The universities taught only civil and canon law; for the study
of the common law of England it was necessary to go to one of

[1] *Cambridge Modern History*, i. 555, 559.
[2] Hutton, *Sir Thomas More*, p. 15.

the Inns of Court or of Chancery.[1] Sir John More himself was a successful lawyer and a man of the old school; he was willing to give his son a good education, but only as a prelude to earning a good income at the Bar. Naturally he thought it waste of time for a practical lawyer to spend seven or eight years in the usual course of study for a degree at the University; he could not wish his son to become one of the moneyless scholars who wandered about Europe seeking wealthy patrons; he despised the learning of Greek; there was no fortune to be looked for in a knowledge of 'good letters'. In short, as More once observed, 'a father would sooner have his son wealthy than learned'—*nummatum malle quam literatum.*

Rebellion would have been useless in any case, and he was always the most affectionate and dutiful of sons. He made no protest and bore no grudge, but cheerfully left the learning and the friends that he loved, to apply himself industriously to an uncongenial profession. Only to his dearest intimates, Colet and Erasmus, did he reveal how distasteful to him were the 'noisy wranglings of the law courts', and the sordid surroundings of a city life.

Towards the end of his Oxford days, More first fell in love. He was sixteen—the lady, two years younger. The attraction was mutual, but unkind parents intervened.

> Then the duenna and the guarded door
> Baffled the stars and bade us meet no more.[2]

Twenty-five years later they met again, and in Latin verse More recalled that among a bevy of girls none had seemed to him so fair as his lost love; her bright eyes and complexion of milk and roses he had never forgotten, and in his memory, if not in reality, her charms were ever unfaded and fresh. These lines were described by Sir James Mackintosh as the most poetical of his poems.

A few more harmless love passages[3] followed the first romance; More was a favourite among women and enjoyed their company, but no scandals were attached to his name.

Probably at about this period, he designed, for his father's house in London, nine painted 'pageants', with appropriate verses of his own composition. The first verse is quoted above on page 3.

[1] W. S. Holdsworth, *History of English Law* (1923), ii, pp. 141, 494.
[2] *Philomorus* (1878 edition), p. 54. From Archdeacon Wrangham's translation.
[3] *citra infamiam*, Erasmus to Hutten, Allen, iv, no. 999, p. 17.

These nine tableaux were depicted on a 'goodly hanging of fine painted cloth'; the first five represented the ages of man— Childhood, Young Manhood, the Triumph of Cupid, Old Age, Death. The next three typified Fame, Time, and Eternity; the last, accompanied by Latin verses, 'the Poet'.

# CHAPTER II

## SOME FRIENDSHIPS

### 1494–1500

ON his return to London, More began his legal training, and was 'for the study of the law of the Realm put to an Inn of Chancery called New Inn, where for his time he very well prospered'.[1]

After about two years, however, he was transferred to Lincoln's Inn, following in the steps of his father and grandfather, and on his admission in February 1496, he was pardoned four vacations through John More's influence. His brother-in-law, Richard Stafferton, was admitted on the same day and received the same privilege.[2]

The four great Inns of Court—Lincoln's Inn, Gray's Inn, the Inner and the Middle Temple—with the connected lesser Inns of Chancery, ten in number, formed a legal University of the best type, combining the advantages of a collegiate life with an excellent practical training in the common law. In each of the greater Inns there were about two hundred students; they had obtained, before More's time, a great reputation as 'an university or school of all commendable qualities'. The training given was intensely practical, consisting in lectures and argument; 'a constant rehearsal and preparation for the life of advocate and Judge'.[3]

At Lincoln's Inn, Thomas More studied industriously till he was called to the Outer Bar, probably in 1501, 'being made and accounted a worthy utter barrister'.[4]

[1] Roper, p. 5.

[2] Records of the Society of Lincoln's Inn. *Black Books*, i. 105. (11 Hen. VII, 12 Feb. 1496.) Cf. Foss, *Judges of England*, v. 198. Thomas More's father and grandfather appear to have held successively the offices of Butler and Steward of Lincoln's Inn, and to have become members of the Society. (*Transactions of the London and Middlesex Archaeological Society* (1875), pp. 434–5; and note in J. H. Lupton's edition of *The Utopia of Sir Thomas More* (1895), Introd. xvii.)

[3] W. S. Holdsworth, *Hist. of Eng. Law*, ii. 494, 508; iv. 262.

[4] The dates of calls to the bar are not given in the books of Lincoln's Inn. Dr. P. S. Allen gives 1501 as the probable date (Chron. table in *Sir Thomas More. Selections*). An 'utter barrister' was one accustomed to plead *without* the Bar, as distinguished from a bencher, who was permitted to plead *within* the Bar (*Black Books of Lincoln's Inn*, i. x).

Sir W. S. Holdsworth (*Hist. of Eng. Law*, ii. 504) quotes another possible explanation. Utter barristers 'for their learning and continuance are called by the Readers to plead and argue doubtful cases and questions . . . when they argue . . . sit uttermost on the forms which they call the Bar . . . of these be chosen and made the Readers'.

He applied himself, according to Stapleton, to 'the study of municipal law, i.e. to English law', and so distinguished himself that the governors of the Society of Lincoln's Inn appointed him 'Reader' or lecturer on the science of law at Furnival's Inn, one of the Inns of Chancery dependent on their house, and his appointment was renewed in three successive years.[1]

While More was reading for the Bar, a memorable event took place in his life, when for the first time he met Erasmus.

The great scholar of Rotterdam, 'herald of humanism in the North', was still on the road to fame, though many learned men already knew him well. Longing to go to Italy, the home of culture, to study theology and Greek, for want of means he was struggling on as a teacher in Paris, when, in the summer of 1499, his friend and pupil William Blount, fourth Baron Mountjoy, persuaded him to visit England. He came with some apprehension as to the welcome he might find in the foggy island of reputed barbarians, yet with the hope of enlarging that circle of correspondents which in later years grew to enormous proportions. Soon after his arrival in England, he was invited to the London house of a friend—perhaps Sir William Say, Mountjoy's father-in-law, or Sir Henry Colet, both of whom were acquainted with the More family;[2] at the same table, unknown to him except by name, was young More, of whom John Colet spoke as 'England's one genius'.[3]

After the fashion of the day, a discussion arose between the two, when Erasmus, himself brilliant in debate, was so much impressed by the wit and readiness of his unknown young opponent, that at last he exclaimed: 'You are no one if not More!' To this More instantly retorted: 'And *you* are Erasmus—or the Devil!' ('Aut tu es Morus, aut nullus.' 'Aut tu es Erasmus, aut

---

[1] Stapleton (Hallett's ed.), p. 16, and Rev. T. E. Bridgett, *Life and Writings of Sir Thomas More* (1891), p. 22. The Reader or lecturer, having prepared his theme, was subjected to the arguments of one of the younger utter barristers, who 'laboured to prove the Reader's opinion to be against the law'. The case would be debated by the rest of the utter barristers and readers and a verdict given by the serjeants or judges, if any were present. The governing bodies of the Inns were the Benchers, while the Readers were responsible for the education of the members (Holdsworth, *Hist. of Eng. Law*, ii. 506, 508).

[2] In a settlement of Sir William Say's property, 20 May 1515, both John and Thomas More were appointed trustees (F. M. Nichols, *The Epistles of Erasmus* (1901), i, p. 200). Seebohm (*Oxford Reformers* (1887), p. 113) suggests that the host may have been Sir Henry Colet.

[3] The date of this meeting has been very doubtful; cf. Allen, iv, p. 14, note. It was probably in the autumn of 1499 when More (if he was born in February 1477, see note, p. 1, *supra*) would have been in his twenty-third year. Erasmus said More was not more than twenty-three when they first met.

diabolus.') The remark was taken as it was meant—a compliment to Erasmus's skill and subtlety in argument; not, as Cresacre More naïvely supposed, as a reproof, 'because he sought to defend impious positions and had a delight to scoff at religious matters, and find fault with all sorts of clergymen'.

Erasmus 'fell in love' with More at first sight, and the friendship begun on this occasion was to them both one of the greatest delights in life. Their letters amply prove their mutual affection, even though some allowance should be made for the language of extravagant compliment which was the current coin of Renaissance friendships. Twenty years later Erasmus wrote to Ulrich von Hutten his well-known account of More, saying that he had been ever the most perfect of friends.[1]

'He seems born and made for friendship, and is a most faithful and enduring friend. He so delights in the company and conversation of those whom he likes and trusts, that in this he finds the principal charm of life. . . . Though he is rather too negligent of his own interests, no one is more diligent in those of his friends. . . . He is so kind, so sweet-mannered, that he cheers the dullest spirit and lightens every misfortune. Since his boyhood he has so delighted in merriment that he seems to have been born to make jokes, yet he never carries this to the point of vulgarity, nor has he ever liked bitter pleasantries. If a retort is made against himself, even if it is ill-grounded, he likes it, from the pleasure he finds in witty repartees. He extracts enjoyment from everything, even from things that are most serious. If he converses with the learned and wise he delights in their talent; if with the ignorant and foolish, he enjoys their stupidity! With wonderful dexterity he accommodates himself to every disposition. His face is in harmony with his character, being always expressive of a pleasant and friendly cheerfulness and ready to break into smiles. To speak candidly, he is better adapted to merriment than to gravity or dignity, but he is never in the least degree tactless or coarse.'

In the personal description of his friend, Erasmus is not quite so happy. He speaks a little confusedly of 'hair darkish-light—or rather, lightish-dark—a complexion fair rather than pale—not at all ruddy but with a slight colour—eyes a sort of bluish-grey, and speckled—a well-proportioned figure, not tall, but not very short either—hands, a trifle awkward'. In fact, there was nothing very distinctive in More's appearance, except the sweetness and intelligence of his expression; his was the charm of mind and manner, not depending upon outward things.

To complete the portrait, one turns to the admirable drawings of Holbein, only to be struck by the thoughtful sadness shown by

---

[1] Erasmus to Hutten, 23 July 1519, Allen, iv, no. 999; cf. Nichols, iii, p. 387, who gives the date as 1517.

the face in repose, quite at variance with the impression of happiness made on his friends by his vivacity and gaiety in speaking. The painter, with his keen insight into character, has indicated the depth, rather than the sparkle, of More's nature. It is true that Holbein knew him only when the cares and anxieties of life had begun to overshadow his natural gaiety, yet even in the days of his deepest troubles he never lost this altogether. In great things, as in small, he maintained usually a steadiness and serenity of mind unattained by the more brilliant and mercurial Erasmus, whose sensitive nature would never allow him to 'suffer fools gladly'.

In Erasmus, More found with delight an intelligence 'brilliant, clear, lucid, witty'; a love of intellectual truth, a deep and accurate scholarship, a wide experience of men and books, allied to a power of observation and description unrivalled even by his own.

Above a rising tide of national feeling, there still stood in Western Europe a cosmopolitan brotherhood of learning, which found in the restoration of ancient literature a common fund of thought and knowledge, and in the printing press, a new means of communication. The Latin language, still generally used in the monasteries, the universities, and the courts of Europe, assumed under the facile pen of Erasmus, an unorthodox flexibility and liveliness which made it seem a fresh and living speech. 'Il parlait à une république universelle dans une langue encore maîtresse du monde.'[1] In this language, More too was completely at home; he could converse with Erasmus with the facility and sympathetic understanding usually so difficult for a foreigner to command. They had many points in common and their friends traced both a mental and a physical likeness between them. 'You know how quick More is', said William Latimer to Erasmus, 'how eager his intellect and with what energy he pursues any work that he has begun—in short, how like he is to yourself.'[2]

They both were earnest and deep thinkers, with a current of playful humour running through their intercourse. They loved the same books and laughed at the same absurdities; both were masters of the art of ridicule, disliking and deriding insincerity, vanity, avarice, and pride. Both were men of thought, rather than of action; they worked for peaceful reform, never for rebellion; essentially the apostles of moderation, they fought only against ignorance and excess. In furthering the revival of Christian learning, Erasmus, Colet, Fisher, and More helped to set

---

[1] D. Nizard, *Renaissance et Réforme* (Paris, 1877), i. 62.
[2] 30 Jan. 1517, Allen, ii, no. 520; Nichols, iii, ep. 734; cf. Allen, iv, p. 14, note (Beatus Rhenanus' description of Erasmus).

in motion the English Reformation, though it flowed eventually in a direction far away from their hopes. Their ideal of Christianity was that it should transform life without subverting authority.

Intimacy was begun by a request from More that Erasmus would help him to polish the style of his Latin verses, and very soon they were writing to each other in the most affectionate terms. 'My dearest, sweetest More'—'More charissime, melitis-sime'—writes Erasmus, begging for more frequent letters. 'Erasme omnium dulcissime' responds More. 'I love the man so much that I would jump about in a dance if he told me to', says Erasmus. His ten or more years seniority seemed of little account. Not long after their first meeting he wrote to More from Oxford:

'I cannot find any malediction sufficiently strong to hurl at the head of the messenger, to whose carelessness or perfidy I attribute it that I am defrauded of that letter which I so certainly expected from my More. For I cannot suppose for a moment, that the fault is yours, though I was a little vehement in my expostulations in that former letter—but I am not afraid of my freedom giving offence to you, who are not ignorant of that Spartan fashion of fighting . . . jesting aside, I do beg, sweetest Thomas, that you will cure the sickness which I have contracted from the long want of you and your handwriting, by a payment with interest —not a mere letter, but a huge packet—and it will be a kindness, if you will incite any persons within your reach, who are cultivators of Good Letters, to write to me, that my circle of friends may be complete. As for you, I reckon you will not care in what fashion I write to the best-natured of men, who, I am persuaded, has no little love for me. Farewell, dearest More.'[1]

In the same year there occurred an incident described by Erasmus. 'I was staying at Lord Mountjoy's country house',[2] he wrote, 'when Thomas More came to see me, and took me out with him for a walk as far as the next village [Eltham], where all the King's children, except Prince Arthur, who was then the eldest son, were being educated.'

The beautiful palace of Eltham had been a royal residence since the time of Edward II; it was the prison and afterwards the refuge of King John of France in the reign of Edward III. Froissart wrote there:

> Betwixt Eltham and Westminster
> Yestreen I saw a meddow fair

[1] Erasmus to More (abridged), Oxford, 28 Oct. 1499, Allen, i, p. 266; cf. Nichols, i, pp. 212–13.
[2] Sir William Say appears to have had a house at Greenwich in the neighbourhood of the Court, which was occupied in the autumn of 1499 by his son-in-law, Mountjoy. Nichols, i, p. 200, note.

Wherein a band of shepherds were
In merry guise and debonheur.
And therewith many a shepherd maid
Went dancing as the pipe was played.

At the end of their walk, Erasmus and More came to the stone bridge across the moat by which the palace was approached, and it was apparent that they were at the entrance to a place of great importance 'for beyond the silent moat there appear the stone traceried double-lighted windows of . . . the historic hall where councils assembled for the making of English history in the middle ages'. On entering a beautiful stone doorway directly facing the bridge they found themselves in the great hall—which still exists—with its mullioned windows and splendid open oak-timbered roof.[1]

To continue the narrative of Erasmus.

'When we came into the hall, the attendants not only of the Palace but also of Mountjoy's household were all assembled. In the midst stood Prince Henry, then nine years old, and having already something of royalty in his demeanour, in which there was a certain dignity combined with singular courtesy. . . . More, with his companion Arnold,[2] after paying his respects to the boy Henry (the same that is now King of England)[3] presented him with some writing. For my part not having expected anything of the sort, I had nothing to offer. . . . I was angry with More for not having warned me, especially as the boy sent me a little note, while we were at dinner, to challenge something from my pen.'

Erasmus goes on to complain that, having written no verses for some years, it took him three days to hammer out a poem in praise of King Henry VII, his children, and his country, which he sent to the young Prince.[4] But there was no malice in the little plot concerted by More with Mountjoy, who was a favourite at the Tudor Court. In those days of patronage, it was all to the advantage of an impecunious scholar to make friends at Court; the acquaintance thus begun with the future Henry VIII might, but for unforeseen mischance, have turned to the benefit of Erasmus, and this no doubt he recognized.

Critical though he was, his early letters show that at first he was

[1] The above details are taken from *Royal Homes Near London*, by Major Benton Fletcher (John Lane, 1931). A beautiful drawing by the author shows the interior of the great hall; others show the moat and bridge, the entrance, exterior of the palace, and the Chancellor's lodging.

[2] References to Nicholas Arnold may be found in the *Black Books of Lincoln's Inn* (publ. 1897), e.g. i. 222; 'All Saints Day 20 Henry VIII (1528) Master of the Revels, Arnold—if not, More.'

[3] Henry VIII, who entered his ninth year on 28 June 1499.

[4] *Prosopopœia Britanniae*. Nichols, i, pp. 201, 202 (from Erasmus's catalogue of Lucubrations).

delighted with his welcome to England. Writing to Robert Fisher, he says:

'But how do you like our England? you will ask. Believe me, dear Robert, when I answer that I never liked anything so much before. I have met with so much kindness and so much learning—not superficial either, but intelligent and accurate—both Latin and Greek, that but for the curiosity of seeing it, I do not now so much care for Italy. When I hear my Colet, I seem to be listening to Plato himself. In Grocyn, who does not marvel at such perfection of learning? What can be more acute, profound and delicate than the judgement of Linacre? What has nature ever created more sweet, more endearing, more happy than the genius of Thomas More? It is marvellous how general and abundant is the harvest of ancient learning in this country.'[1]

Erasmus, staying in Oxford with Prior Charnock of the Augustinian Canons, met at his table John Colet, who held the whole company as if spellbound by the fascination of his talk, which seemed inspired by a divine power.

In their admiration for Colet, More and Erasmus found a further ground for sympathy. His earnest character and practical Christianity, his mingled austerity and tenderness, made an instant appeal to them both; his influence showed itself in the writings of Erasmus and fortified the already strong religious feeling of More, whose spiritual director he became.

To Erasmus, all learning was of some worth; he approved every literary pursuit and thought that nothing conducive to a good life should be called profane. But to Colet, the whole value of the revival of learning lay in its religious and moral aspect; his enthusiasm was roused by the discovery of the ancient records of Christianity in their original languages. He longed for a reform in Christian life and in the religious teaching which, in the hands of medieval churchmen, had tended to become a 'huge and be-wildering mass of dreary and lifeless subtlety'. His visit to Italy left him untouched alike by the art of the Florentine school and by the spirit of Paganism which held some of the Italian humanists. Influenced apparently by the teaching of Savonarola, Colet re-turned from his travels to give his famous lectures on the Epistles of Saint Paul, which inaugurated in England a movement of practical Christian reform. The whole University crowded to hear him with unusual interest, for he broke new ground by treating the Epistles as a whole, not merely as 'an arsenal of texts', but seeking their true meaning and making them real and living to

---

[1] 5 Dec. 1499, Nichols, i, ep. 110, p. 226 (abridged). Robert Fisher, a relative of the Bishop of Rochester, studied Latin under Erasmus in Paris. He was employed in diplomacy as English agent in Italy. Ibid. i, pp. 115, 165.

PLATE 2

JOHN COLET. Dean of St. Paul's

his hearers. If More could not attend these lectures—though he may have ridden to Oxford on occasion—yet he knew Colet's advice to his students, perplexed by the minute discussions and hypotheses of Scholastic theologians, to 'keep firmly to the Holy Scriptures and the Apostles Creed, and let Divines, if they like, dispute about the rest'.[1]

[1] Seebohm, *The Oxford Reformers* (1887), p. 111; cf. also Lupton, *Life of John Colet*, p. 52, and ch. v, *passim*.

# CHAPTER III

# THE CHOICE OF A PROFESSION

## 1500–1504

IT is not surprising that Thomas More, the youngest of such a group of friends, should turn with longing eyes to the light of Renaissance learning, while his father urged him on in the dusty by-ways of the law. Dutifully he gave up a great part of his time to the distasteful—though successful—pursuit of legal knowledge, but in his leisure hours he read Greek philosophy under the direction of Linacre. He worked hard to improve his style in Latin prose and verse, making experiments in different kinds of writing and practising Latin declamations and arguments on disputable subjects. He studied the works of Plato and Aristotle, the laws of Lycurgus, the dialogues of Lucian, as well as Latin poets and historians, and the writings of the early Christian fathers. Boëtius was one of his favourite authors.

His constant companion in this voracious reading was William Lily, a noted classical scholar and grammarian, who had travelled in Italy and the Near East, and had made a pilgrimage to Jerusalem. Lily, an Oxford graduate, was associated with More's older friends; Grocyn was his godfather, and Colet appointed him, in 1512, the first High-Master of his school of St. Paul's. He was a congenial friend to More, and together they translated epigrams from the Greek anthology into Latin elegiacs.[1]

More composed also some original Latin epigrams expressing in verse his observations on the life and manners of his day, with pointed mockery of folly or of vice.[2] His verses were inspired by a variety of subjects and marked by the love of contrast which is found so often in his writings. In many of them he criticizes the ambition of princely tyrants; in others he satirizes the folly of misers or of spendthrifts; he laughs at the superstition of astrologers, the ignorance of women, and the ineptitude of monks. He makes fun of the fop who imitates French fashions, and speaks every language with a French accent—except French, which he speaks with an English accent. He tells of a preacher who announced to his congregation: 'To-day being the festival of

---

[1] *Philomorus* (1878), p. 30.
[2] The term 'Epigramma' is used to denote 'a fugitive composition springing out of the more salient topics of everyday life; terse in diction and steady in its pursuit of one subject. . . . Many of them might be classed under the modern designation of *vers de société*.' Ibid., p. 6.

Saint Andrew, all present must observe *yesterday* as a solemn fast.'

More had not intended to publish these verses, written for the amusement of his own circle; they were, however, so much admired by his friends, that Erasmus collected the scattered manuscript copies, and Beatus Rhenanus supervised their printing at Basel by Froben.[1] Rhenanus spoke with high compliment of the eloquence, the wit, the clarity and musical rhythm they displayed, and said that he 'preferred them to the verses of Marullus and Pontanus'.

'Thomas More is in every way admirable', he wrote. 'How sweetly and easily flow his verses! He writes the purest and clearest Latin, and everything is welded together with so happy a wit that I never read anything with greater pleasure. The Muses must have showered on this man all their gifts of humour, elegance and wit. He jokes, but never with malice, he laughs, but always without offence.'[2]

More's return to classical studies so greatly exasperated his father that he cut off entirely his son's already very small allowance, and all but disowned him, because he seemed to be deserting his hereditary study of the law,[3] although John More, as Erasmus drily observed, 'in other respects was a sensible and upright man'. Erasmus held no high opinion of the legal profession, which he declared to be 'quite incompatible with true learning', though he admitted that its luminaries were held in great esteem by the English people.[4] With his own absorbing passion for 'good letters', he longed to attract his friend wholly to the company of scholars whose learning shone like a beacon in an ignorant and superstitious world. It seemed to him a dreadful waste to force into so arid a field this bright intelligence which was fitted to take a place among the foremost minds of Europe in his day. 'What would not such marvellous natural gifts have accomplished', he asked, 'if his intellect had been trained in Italy? If it were wholly devoted to literature; if it had had time to ripen for its proper harvest, its own autumn?'[5]

Erasmus had not imagined the development of a national literature; he could not know that, if More had given himself up

[1] Published under the title of *Progymnasmata* in 1518. More wrote also some English verses, and on the death of Queen Elizabeth in 1503, he composed *A ruefull Lamentation*.

[2] Stapleton (Hallett's ed.), p. 7 (abridged). Beatus of Rheinau (1485–1547) became intimate with Erasmus and edited his works; he shared the publishing activities of Froben for some years.

[3] Stapleton, op. cit., p. 16; cf. Roper, p. 5.

[4] Erasmus to Hutten, Allen, iv, no. 999, p. 17.

[5] Erasmus to Froben, 25 Aug. 1517, ibid. iii, no. 635; cf. Nichols, iii, ep. 610.

to classical learning, a great loss to English prose literature would have been sustained.

It may have been to avoid reproaches at home that More left his father's house, and took a lodging, shared with his friend Lily, near the Charterhouse. He was resolved not to quarrel, and in spite of all differences of opinion, he remained on cordial terms with his family.

His reputation in London was steadily growing; not only did he lecture in Furnival's Inn, but he gave also a course of addresses in the Church of Saint Lawrence in the Old Jewry, where Grocyn was Rector.[1]

The subject was Saint Augustine's *de Civitate Dei*—the City of God in which all things would be used for the common good; in which they who provide for the welfare of others bear rule, 'and yet even those who rule are the servants of those over whom they seem to rule'. More is said to have treated his subject on philosophical and historical lines, dealing with the connexion between the character and religion of the Romans, and the history of Rome.[2] This series of addresses had a remarkable success. They were given, no doubt, on the invitation of Grocyn, and they proved even more popular than the Rector's own sermons, for 'all the chief learned of the City of London' came to hear the young lawyer, who attracted and pleased a diverse audience by his charm and eloquence, by the quick turns of his humour from grave to gay, his use of startling contrast, his readiness in apt and homely illustration of his point, and his art in the vivid pictorial description of a scene or an incident, whereby he caught the attention of his audience and brought home to them the good principles and solid learning which made the basis of his philosophy.

All records of these addresses have been lost, but it may be that More startled and amused his hearers by advancing some of those surprising suggestions for the ruling of an ideal state, afterwards set forth in his *Utopia*.

At a period when the art of public speaking was but little practised,[3] More—so Erasmus affirms—had all the qualities most needed in an orator. His voice was not loud, but clear and penetrating, and he spoke without either hesitation or haste.

'It would be difficult to find anyone more successful in speaking extempore, the happiest thoughts being attended by the happiest language, while a mind that catches and anticipates all that passes, and

---

[1] From 1496. Grocyn did not reside in London till three years later. *D.N.B.*
[2] Cf. J. H. Lupton's introduction to More's *Utopia* (ed. 1895), lxxviii; Seebohm, p. 143; Stapleton, (Hallett's ed.), p. 9.
[3] Erasmus to R. Whitford, 1 May 1506, Nichols, i, p. 407.

a ready memory, having everything as it were, in stock, promptly supply whatever the time or the occasion demands.'[1]

His fame as an orator probably contributed to his return as a member of Parliament, while still a young man, when he is said to have spoken so ably and boldly against the financial aids demanded by Henry VII, though all others were silent through fear, that the subsequent grant made by the House fell far short of the King's demands.[2]

While he delighted London with his lectures, More was passing through a period of anxious consideration for the future. His chief confidence was given to Colet, to whom he wrote the following letter, preserved by Stapleton.[3]

'While I was walking in the law courts, I happened to meet your servant (*puer*); I was delighted to see him, both because I have always liked him, and especially because I thought he would not be here without you. But when I learnt from him, not only that you had not returned, but that you were not coming for a long time—I cannot tell you from how much joy I was thrown, into how much sadness! For what could be worse to me than to be deprived of your delightful company? I ever relied on your wise counsel, enjoyed your pleasant companionship, was roused by your earnest sermons and helped by your example, so that I used to depend on your very look or nod. Fortified by these defences, I felt myself strong, deprived of them I seem to be weakened and undone.

In the city, what can incite a man to a good life, and does not rather, by a thousand devices call back him who is struggling to climb the hard tracks of virtue? One sees nothing but false affection and flattery on the one hand; hatred, quarrelling, and the wranglings of the law courts on the other. Wherever you look you see nothing but caterers, fishmongers, butchers, cooks, confectioners, poultrymen, all occupied in serving the body, the world and the devil! Even the houses block out a great part

[1] Erasmus to Hutten, Allen, iv, no. 999; cf. Nichols, iii, p. 398.

[2] Roper (Singer's ed. 1822, pp. 7–8) gives a circumstantial account of the occurrence, saying that More 'ere ever he had been reader in Court' was 'in the latter time of King Henry VII made a Burgess of the Parliament, wherein there were by the King demanded, as I have heard reported, about three-fifteenths for the marriage of his eldest daughter, that then should be Scottish Queen. At the last debating whereof, he made such arguments and reasons there against, that the King's demands thereby were clean overthrown, so that one of the King's privy chamber, named Master Tiler, being present thereat, brought word to the King out of the Parliament House that a beardless boy had disappointed all his purpose.' Roper adds that the King retaliated by imprisoning More's father in the Tower, till he paid a fine of a hundred pounds. Roper must have had the story from More, but he gives no dates. Dean Hutton, in his *Sir Thomas More*, pp. 24–5, points out that the Parliament of 1504 was the first to be held for seven years and that there is no record of any opposition to a money grant. The Princess Margaret was married to the Scottish King, James IV, in 1503.

[3] Thomas Stapleton, *Tres Thomae* (Douai, 1588), ii. 20–3; (Hallett's ed.), p. 11 (abridged). The letter was probably written in Latin, as given by Stapleton. Cresacre More gives a translation, *The Life of Sir Thomas More* (1828), pp. 29–34.

of the light, so that one cannot freely see the heavens; it is not the arc of the horizon that bounds the view, but the roofs of the houses.

I cannot blame you if you are not tired of the country, where you see simple people, ignorant of the wiles of town, and wherever you turn your eyes, the beautiful face of the country refreshes you, the soft air exhilarates you, and the sight of the sky delights you.

Yet your country parish of Stepney may afford you the same attractions, and from it, moreover, you can sometimes reach the city.

There come sometimes to the pulpit at St. Paul's some who promise men health, but when they seem to have preached a fine sermon, they irritate rather than soothe us, for their life is so contrary to their words; they cannot persuade men that they are fit to cure others when themselves are more ill than any. But if the physician in whom the patient has the greatest faith, is the one most likely to cure him, then there is no one more fit than yourself to remedy the ills of all this city, for all are ready to trust and obey you, and are longing for your return.

Come then, my dear Colet, for the sake of your Stepney, which laments your absence, as a child its mother's; come for the sake of your native city, to which you owe the care due to a parent, and lastly—though this be your least motive—for my sake, who have given myself up wholly to you, and anxiously await your coming. Meanwhile I pass my time with Grocyn, Linacre, and our friend Lily; the first, as you know, the director of my life in your absence; the second, the master of my studies; the third, my most dear companion. Farewell, and continue to love me. From London, the 10th November.'[1]

The letter to Colet shows something of More's dissatisfaction with his daily life. The time was not long past when a thoughtful man had turned naturally to the cloister as the only hope of escape from a turbulent world to a peaceful life of learning and religion. The old traditions and ideals of monastic life made a strong appeal to More; he had many an earnest discussion with Lily on the question of taking Holy Orders. For some time he thought of becoming a Franciscan friar, and for four years he lodged near the Charterhouse, observing as far as possible the strict rule of discipline followed by the Carthusian Brotherhood, pondering the question with 'vigils, fasting and prayers' and 'applying his whole mind to exercises of piety', yet without binding himself by any vow.[2]

'In the which thing', said Erasmus, 'he proved himself far more prudent than most candidates, who thrust themselves rashly into that

---

[1] Probably 1503 or 1504. Colet was Dean of St. Paul's from 1504–19, and must have returned to London soon after this letter was written. He resigned the living of Stepney on 21 Sept. 1505 (Lupton, Life of John Colet, p. 145, note). More's Latin letters are of course translated into modern English.

[2] Cf. F. A. Gasquet, English Monastic Life, pp. 221, 222, note; Roper, p. 6. The period in question seems to have been somewhere about 1500, at all events

arduous profession, without any trial of their powers. The one thing that prevented him from giving himself to that kind of life was that he could not shake off his desire for the married state, and therefore he chose rather to be a chaste husband than an impure priest.'[1]

It was characteristic of More to mistrust his own strength of will, and to fear that 'even with the help of his practices of penance, he would not be able to conquer the temptations of the flesh that come to a man in the vigour and ardour of his youth'.[2] Besides this, there is no doubt that the awakening spirit of the age, working against the older monastic ideals, provided a thousand interests to call him to the open world. He was eagerly alive to new discoveries and inventions; literature and music, art, astronomy, natural history; the story of strange lands and uncharted seas even then becoming known—all these attracted him, and above all, the joys of friendship. The spirit of the new learning and the influence, either tacit or expressed, of the chief of his friends, combined to draw him from a cloistered life. His father, it has been seen, urged him to follow the profession of the law. Lily gave up his own thoughts of the priesthood, married, and devoted himself to teaching. John Fisher, More's friend from youth to death, urged his patroness, the Lady Margaret, to found colleges rather than to endow convents.[3] Colet, More's own confessor, gave little money to monasteries and thought that the best way in which he could promote Christian learning was by the foundation of his school at St. Paul's, taking, for its governors, not priests but married laymen, because, 'though nothing was certain in human affairs, he had found the least corruption among these'.[4] Erasmus, after the unhappy experiences of his youth, spoke with bitterness of decadent houses of so-called religion, in which a life of virtue and chastity was no longer required, and where the revival of learning was derided and feared.

'Obedience', he said, 'is so taught as to hide that any obedience is due to God. It may happen that an abbot is a fool or a drunkard. He issues an order to the brotherhood in the name of holy obedience. And what will such an order be? An order to observe chastity? An order to be sober? An order to tell no lies? Not one of these things. It will be that a brother is not to learn Greek; he is not to seek to instruct himself. He may be a sot. He may go with prostitutes. He may be full of hatred and

prior to 1504. Erasmus spoke of him as resident in Lincoln's Inn in April 1500 (Erasmus to Batt, Paris, 2 Apr. 1500, Nichols, i, p. 235).
   [1] Allen, iv, no. 999, p. 18.
   [2] Stapleton (Hallett's ed.), p. 10.
   [3] Bishop of Rochester in 1504. The colleges were Christ's and St. John's, Cambridge.
   [4] Erasmus, *Lives of Vitrier and Colet*, J. H. Lupton, trans. (1883), pp. 28, 34.

malice. He may never look inside the Scriptures. No matter. He has not broken any oath. He is an excellent member of the community.'[1]

The Church was indeed a recognized road to wealth and worldly honours; the law of celibacy was not strictly observed; many of the clergy had wives, forbidden but acknowledged—but More had no desire to combine the privileges of the world, the flesh, and the Church; such a life as Erasmus and Colet could reprove had no attraction for him. As monk or as parish priest he could have been satisfied only with the strictest life of self-sacrifice and holiness, and to this, with genuine humility, he decided that he dared not aspire.

'Perhaps', said Stapleton, 'the circumstances of the time were not propitious to his desire of embracing a stricter life, for our religious communities had become lax, as the utter destruction and desolation of the monastic state, which followed so soon afterwards, showed with sufficient clearness. . . . Certainly, when he came to the conclusion that it was not for him to aspire to the more perfect state of life, he at least earnestly resolved never to cease throughout the whole course of his life, to worship God with the most sincere devotion.'[2]

From time to time in later years, a fleeting regret for this decision came to his mind. In his prison cell, a little before his death, he said to his daughter Margaret:

'I believe Meg, that they that have put me here ween they have done me a high displeasure. But I assure thee on my faith, mine own good daughter, if it had not been for my wife and you that be my children, whom I account the chief part of my charge, I would not have failed long ere this to have closed myself in as straight a room, and a straighter too.'[3]

And again, at his prison window, seeing some of the Charterhouse monks going from the Tower to their execution, he said to his daughter, standing beside him:

'Lo, dost thou not see Meg, that these blessed fathers be now as cheerfully going to their deaths as bridegrooms to their marriages? Wherefore thereby mayest thou see, mine own good daughter, what a great difference there is between such as have spent in effect all their days in a straight, hard, penitential and painful life, religiously, and such as have in the world, like worldly wretches, as thy poor father hath done, consumed all their time in pleasure and ease licentially!'[4]

It was about the year 1504 that More decided to remain in the world, 'neverthemore discontinuing his study at Lincoln's Inn, but applying still the same until he was called to the Bench, and

---

[1] J. A. Froude, *Life and Letters of Erasmus* (1894), p. 64 (abridged).
[2] Stapleton (Hallett's ed.), p. 10.       [3] Roper, p. 73.
[4] Ibid., pp. 76–7.

had read there twice'.[1]  He adopted, as his ideal of a Christian
life in the world, the example of Pico della Mirandola.  His
translation of Pico's life, probably published first in 1510, may
be ascribed to the years 1504–5.[2]

'In that fascinating hero of the Renaissance', wrote the late Dean of
Winchester, 'there was every beauty to attract, every virtue to secure,
and every talent to confirm the admiration of such a man as More.

'In him no keen eye could detect the subtle flavour of a Pagan life, nor
was his Christianity cold, unsympathetic or unreal.  His abilities were
remarkable even among his contemporaries, and his energy and devotion
were as extraordinary. . . . The favourite of Lorenzo de Medici, he was
also the friend and disciple of Savonarola. . . . There is much similarity
between Pico and More.  Both were keen classical scholars, tinged with
the mysticism of Renaissance imaginings, men of wide human interests,
bent on bringing the Divine Spirit into every sphere of human thought.
The Italian humanist was penetrated with the sense of the beauty and the
mystery of life.  To him it did not seem that Christianity was less true
because Paganism was so beautiful, and the same thought was never
absent from the mind of More. . . . The whole story of his life, of its fair
hopes, bitter disappointments, and calm peaceful ending, sounds like
one of the poetic legends which the fancy of the age so freely created and
cherished.'[3]

This was the story chosen by More for his first serious essay in
English prose.  In it he broke away from the tradition that Latin
was the sole worthy means of literary expression.  By his flow-
ing and facile English, expressive phrases and comprehensive
vocabulary, he justified his own defence of the use of his mother-
tongue, of which he wrote at a later period:

'For as for that our tongue is called barbarous, is but a fantasy.  For
so is, as every learned man knoweth, every strange language to other.
And if they would call it barren of words, there is no doubt but it is
plenteous enough to express our minds in any thing whereof one man
hath used to speak with another.'[4]

Certainly More was never at a loss for words, either in speech
or writing.

The preface to his book took the form of a charming letter
addressed 'Unto his right entirely beloved sister in Christ,

[1] Roper, p. 6.
[2] Translated by More from the Latin of Pico's nephew, Giovanni Francesco
Pico (More's *English Works* (1557), p. 1 et seq.).  The *Life of John Picus* is
included in W. E. Campbell's edition of More's *English Works*, vol. i (1931)
with some original verses by More based on Pico's twelve points of a perfect
lover.  Professor A. W. Reed (introd. to above, p. 18) places the date of composition as early as 1504–5.  It was printed by John Rastell probably about
1510, and also by Wynkyn de Worde.
[3] Hutton, *Sir Thomas More*, pp. 28, 30, 34, 35.
[4] More's *English Works* (1557), p. 243.

Joyeuce Leigh'. He sent his little book as a New Year's gift, with the following explanation.

'But commonly all those presents, that are used customably all in this manner between friends to be sent: be such things as pertain only unto the body, either to be fed, or to be clad, or some otherwise delighted: . . . . But forasmuch as the love and amity of Christian folk should be rather ghostly friendship than bodily. . . . I therefore mine heartily beloved sister, in good luck of this New Year, have sent you such a present, as may bear witness of my tender love and zeal to the happy continuance and gracious increase of virtue in your soul. And whereas the gifts of other folk declare that they wish their friends to be worldly fortunate: mine testifieth, that I desire to have you godly prosperous.'[1]

It has been discovered lately that More dedicated his translation of Pico's life to the sister of his friend, Edward Lee, afterwards Archbishop of York; the different spelling of the name having previously obscured the fact. The Lees appear to have been friends from childhood with the Mores and Rastells; Joyce Leigh, the recipient of More's gift, became a nun of the Order of the Minoresses, and her mother was allowed to live with her in the precincts of their House at Aldgate.[2]

At the end of his translation, More added some original verses based on Pico's 'twelve points of a perfect lover'; the following are specimens of his *Twelve properties or conditions of a lover.*

> The first point is to love but one alone,
> And for that one all other to forsake,
> For whoso loveth many, loveth none:
> The flood that is in many channels take,
> In each of them shall feeble streamès make,
> The love that is divided among many,
> Unneth [hardly] sufficeth that every part have any.

> So thou that hast thy love set unto God,
> In thy remembrance this imprint and grave,
> As he in sovereign dignity is odd [unique],
> So will he in love no parting fellows have:
> Love him therefore with all that he thee gave,
> For body, soul, wit, cunning, mind and thought
> Part will he none, but either all or nought.[3]

[1] More's *English Works* (1557), p. 1.
[2] Reed, Introduction to More's *English Works* (1931), i. 20; and Reed, *Early Tudor Drama*, p. 74. See also More's *Giovanni Pico della Mirandola, his life*, etc., edited by J. M. Rigg (1890), p. 81, note. The will of Richard Lee or Leigh, Joyce's eldest brother, was drawn up by John Rastell and written by William Rastell.
[3] More's *English Works* (1557), p. 28.

# CHAPTER IV

# A POPULAR BARRISTER

## 1504–1509

HAVING decided that he could be a good husband, while he feared to become a bad priest, More embarked upon his first courtship, towards the end of the year 1504.

Riding out of the clatter and smoke of London streets, through green lanes to the quiet fields of Essex, he began to pay frequent visits to the stately house called Netherhall, built some thirty years earlier, the home of Mr. John Colt and his wife, Elizabeth Eldrington.[1] The amusing talk and merry banter of young More made him a welcome guest to the daughters of the house—a trio of fresh country girls, who had seen nothing of the world—while his sterling qualities won him the lifelong confidence of their father.

The story of his wooing has been told pleasantly by William Roper:

'He resorted to the house of one Master Colte, a gentleman of Essex, that had oft invited him thither, having three daughters whose honest conversation and virtuous education provoked him there specially to set his affection. And albeit his mind most served him to the second daughter, for that he thought her the fairest and best favoured, yet when he considered that it would be both great grief and some shame also to the eldest to see her younger sister preferred before her in marriage, he then of a certain pity, framed his fancy toward her and soon after married her.'[2]

'She was very young', said Erasmus, who stayed with More soon after his marriage, 'of good family, with a mind somewhat uncultivated, having always resided in the country with her parents and sisters, but she was all the more apt to be moulded according to his habits. He took care to have her instructed in learning, and especially in all musical accomplishments, and had made her such that he could willingly have passed his whole life with her, but her premature death separated them.'

Early in the year 1505 the wedding of Thomas More and Jane Colt was celebrated, probably in the Parish Church of Royden, Essex, where some brasses of the Colt family still lie.[3] More took

---

[1] A. B. Teetgen, *The Footsteps of Sir Thomas More* (Sands & Co., 1930), pp. 57–60. John Colt was twice married, and had eighteen children in all.

[2] Roper, p. 6. The little story has been taken too seriously. 'Family jokes' were apt to flourish vigorously in More's house, and this is just the kind of remark he might have made to his young wife if he wished to discourage in her any sign of conceit.

[3] Described by A. B. Teetgen, op. cit., p. 60.

his bride home to a comfortable house known as the Barge, in Bucklersbury, near Wallbrook, which he had taken in order to live near his father. Here they spent six happy years together, and here were born the four children, Margaret, Elizabeth, Cecily, and John, whom More loved with a deep and tender affection.

An amusing anecdote, told by Erasmus, has been thought on good authority to refer to Thomas More and his wife Jane.[1]

'A young gentleman married a maiden of seventeen years who had been educated in the country, and who, being inexperienced, he trusted to form easily in manners to his own humour. He began to instruct her in literature and music and by degrees to repeat the heads of sermons which she heard and generally to acquire the accomplishments he wished her to possess. Used at home to nothing but gossip and play, she at length refused to submit to further training, and when pressed about it, threw herself down and beat her head on the ground as though she wished for death.

'Her husband concealed his vexation and carried her off for a holiday to her home. Out hunting with his father-in-law, he told his troubles and was urged to "use his authority and beat her!" He replied that he knew his power, but would much rather that she were persuaded, than come to these extremities. The father seized a proper moment, and looking severely on the girl, told her how homely she was, how disagreeable and how lucky to have a husband at all; yet he had found her the best-natured man in the world and she disobeyed him! She returned to her husband and threw herself on the ground, saying: "From this time forward you shall find me a different sort of person!" She kept her resolution and to her dying day, went readily and cheerfully about any duty, however simple, if her husband would have it so.'

With the responsibility of a family on his hands—or, as Cresacre More put it, 'when he began to be clogged with wife and children'—More applied himself unremittingly to his professional work. Though he greatly enjoyed a leisure hour, no one could be more patiently industrious when duty required it. He gave to all his clients the most disinterested and friendly counsel, generally advising them to settle their differences out of court, himself acting as mediator. If they refused to do this, he would show them how to bring their action at the least expense. He would never undertake to defend a case unless he could first satisfy himself of its justice; if it seemed to him that his clients were in the wrong, he would tell them so plainly, and beg them to

[1] It is retold (from the *Colloquies* of Erasmus) by A. W. Reed in *Social and Political Ideas of Some Great Thinkers of the Renaissance* (J. C. Hearnshaw), p. 128, confirming the opinion of Dr. P. S. Allen. The only discrepancy is that More disliked hunting and disapproved of it, but he may nevertheless have accompanied his father-in-law in a hunting expedition.

give up the case, saying that it was not right either for him or for
them to go on with it. If they still persisted, he would resign the
case and refer them to other lawyers. From widows and orphans
whom he defended, he would take no payment.[1] Before long he
became the most popular barrister in London. Almost in spite of
himself, he made a large income by his legal practice. His ability
and integrity won the confidence of the merchant citizens of
London so that 'there was at that time in none of the King's
courts of the laws of this realm, any matter of importance in
controversy, wherein he was not with the one party of counsel'.[2]

In his life at Bucklersbury, More had the happiness of being
surrounded by his best friends, and of sharing their affection with
his 'other self', Erasmus, who visited him from time to time and
encouraged him to continue his literary studies.

Although Colet was inclined to share the view that only
Christian writers should be read by Christian men, More, with
Erasmus, was ready to take advantage of all good learning. With
him he translated into Latin some of the dialogues of Lucian, the
greatest writer of the second century outside the Christian church.
By no means tempted to disbelief by a Pagan philosophy, he yet
found much to admire in the arguments and raillery against vice
and superstition. He composed a Latin declamation in the same
style. Erasmus wrote of their joint work to a friend:[3]

'For several years, dearest Richard, I have been occupied entirely with
Greek literature, but lately, in order to resume my intimacy with Latin,
I have begun to declaim in that language. In so doing, I have yielded to
the influence of Thomas More, whose eloquence, as you know, is such
that he could persuade even an enemy to do whatever he pleased, while
my own affection for the man is so great, that if he bade me dance a horn-
pipe I should do at once just as he bade me! He is writing on the same
subject and in such a way as to thresh out and sift every part of it. I
do not think that nature ever formed a mind more ready, clear-sighted
and subtle; or with greater ability of every kind than his. Add to this
a power of expression equal to his intellect, a singular cheerfulness of
character and an abundance of wit, and you miss nothing that should be
found in a perfect advocate. I have therefore undertaken this task, not
in rivalry, but only to break a lance, as it were, in this tourney of wits
with the sweetest of all my friends, with whom I am always pleased to
join in any employment, grave or gay. I have done this all the more
willingly, because I very much wish this sort of exercise to be introduced
into our schools, where it would be of the greatest utility in improving the

---

[1] Stapleton (Hallett's ed.), pp. 17, 73.      [2] Roper, p. 9.
[3] Erasmus to Richard Whitford, inscribing to him the translation of Lucian's
*Tyrannicida* (cf. Nichols, i, ep. 191, p. 406), 1 May 1506. Whitford had been
with Mountjoy to Paris, and afterwards was chaplain to Bishop Foxe of Winchester (Allen, i, no. 191, p. 423).

art of oratory—there are many eloquent writers, but few scholars are even passable orators. . . . You may compare my declamation with More's, and so decide if there is any difference in style between those whom you used to declare to be so much alike in genius, character, taste and studies, that no twin brothers could be found more closely resembling one another! I am sure you love them both alike and are in turn equally dear to both.'

More inscribed his Latin versions of the *Dialogues* to Dr. Thomas Ruthall; in an introductory letter he displayed his enlightened view of the superstition which defaced so much of the religion of his day.[1]

'It does not much disturb me', he wrote, 'to find that the writer was not sure of immortality. Why indeed should I care for the opinion of a Pagan upon matters which are among the chief mysteries of the Christian faith ? At any rate the Dialogue teaches us to keep our minds clear of the superstition which creeps in under the guise of religion. We shall lead a happier life when we are less terrified by these dismal and superstitious lies which are often repeated with so much confidence and authority . . . by those who think they have done a lasting service to Christ when they have invented a fable about some Saint, or a tragic description of hell, which either melts an old woman to tears, or makes her blood run cold! An act of piety, no doubt, considering the risk that truth would be insufficient, unless propped up by lies! They have not scrupled to stain with fiction that religion which was founded by truth itself and ought to consist of naked truth. They have failed to see that such fables are so far from aiding religion, that nothing can be more injurious to it.'

More's observant eyes found many subjects for satire in the world around him, and his well-trained memory stored up many scenes to illustrate his philosophical writings.

Probably about the year 1507, he journeyed to Coventry to visit his sister, Elizabeth Rastell.[2] On his arrival an incident took place which he described some years later, in his *Letter to a Monk*, in a vivid and characteristic narrative.

'There was at Coventry', he wrote, 'a Franciscan of the unreformed sort. The man preached in the city, the neighbourhood and villages

---

[1] Cf. Nichols, i, ep. 190 (abridged), p. 403. Dr. Ruthall was Dean of Lincoln and secretary to the King. He became Bishop of Durham in 1509. The dialogues in question were *Cynicus*, *Necromantia*, and *Philopseudes*.

[2] This visit has been assigned to the year 1519, when the *Letter to a Monk* was published, but it appears that More was then recalling an incident of earlier date. Father Bridgett (*Life of More*, p. 97) says: 'As Rastell's wife lived in London this [sister] must have been Jane Stafferton'; but the Staffertons also lived in London, and Dr. A. W. Reed has ascertained that John Rastell (husband of Elizabeth More) lived in Coventry, where he was Coroner, till about 1508 or 1509 (Reed's article in *The Social and Political Ideas of Thinkers of the Renaissance etc.*, F. J. C. Hearnshaw, ed.) ; and cf. *Coventry Leet Book and Mayor's Register* (1420–1555), pp. 605, 619, edited by Mary Dormer Harris for E.E.T.S. (1907–13).

about, that whoever should say daily the Psalter of the Blessed Virgin, could never be lost. The Pastor there, an excellent and learned man, then began to warn his flock not to trust too much in the Rosary, even though they said it ten times a day.

'When the matter was at its hottest, it happened that I arrived at Coventry on a visit to my sister. I had scarcely got off my horse when the question was put to me: "Could anyone be damned who should daily recite the Rosary?" I laughed at the foolish question but was at once warned that I was doing a dangerous thing.

'Being invited to a dinner, I accepted the invitation and went. There entered also an old friar, with head bent, grave and grim: a boy followed him with books. I saw that I was in for a quarrel. We sat down; no time was lost, the question was at once proposed by the host. The friar answered just as he had preached. I said nothing; I do not care to meddle in provoking and fruitless disputes. At last they asked my opinion. As I was obliged to answer, I told them what I thought, but only in a few words and without emphasis. Then the friar poured out a long prepared speech which might have made two sermons.'

More replied by an analogy, saying that though a King, on the intercession of his mother, might pardon a rebel, yet he would not pass a law promising immunity to traitors, on the sole condition of their paying homage to her.

'Much was said on both sides, but I only succeeded in getting laughed at as a fool, while he was extolled to the skies.

'I have not told this in order to impute crime to any religious body, since the same ground produces herbs both wholesome and poisonous, nor do I wish to find fault with the custom of those who salute Our Lady, which is most beneficial, but because some trust so much in their devotions that they draw from them boldness to sin.'[1]

About a year after this visit to Coventry, More made his first journey to the Continent, and greatly interested himself in visiting the famous Universities of Louvain and Paris. He took pains to ascertain their subjects and methods of teaching, but came to the conclusion that as good an education could be obtained at Oxford and Cambridge.

According to Stapleton, he travelled in France merely 'to see the country as was customary with young Englishmen of rank', and to perfect his already fluent conversational French. Roper, on the other hand, suggests that he had some thought of taking refuge abroad from the displeasure of Henry VII, incurred by his bold speeches in Parliament, and this view has been widely accepted.[2] The danger may have been partly imaginary, for More

---

[1] More's *Letter to a Monk* (abridged), cf. Bridgett, op. cit., pp. 96–8 and *North British Review* (1859), no. xxx, p. 112, 'Sir Thomas More and the Reformation'.
[2] Roper says: 'Had not the King soon after died, he was determined to have gone over the sea, thinking that being in the King's indignation, he could not

was on excellent terms with several men who were in favour at the Royal Court—notably so with Mountjoy, companion to Prince Henry; with Ruthall, secretary to the King; and with Fisher, Confessor to the King's mother.

However that may be, the position was changed by the death of the King in 1509, and the accession of his son as Henry VIII.

live in England without great danger.' Roper no doubt took this statement seriously. It is not so certain that More made it in the same spirit.

# CHAPTER V

# A BUSY LIFE

## 1509–1512

IN the light of later events it is difficult to realize how great was the enthusiasm that greeted the young king, who was welcomed as the liberator of his people from the oppressions of the last reign, and as the personification of the new spirit of enlightenment and progress.

At the age of eighteen, Henry had all the qualities apt to win popularity. A jovial laugh, a gay blue eye, immense physical strength, skill, and courage, were combined with quick intelligence and great ability of mind. The gross crafty visage made familiar by his portraits was described in his youth as 'so very beautiful that it would become a pretty woman'. 'His face is angelic and his person of singular beauty', reported the Venetian ambassador. He could outride all others in the hunting-field; at tennis, archery, and tourney he was tireless and unexcelled. All these things endeared him to his people, and he had other qualities which raised great hopes in such men as Erasmus and More. He was well read in theology; interested in literature and science; a student of astronomy; a good linguist; he sang; he played with skill the organ, lute, and harpsichord; his musical compositions are among the best productions of his time. His generous impulses were not yet smothered by his overwhelming egotism; he said with sincerity that his actions were guided by his conscience; it was not yet evident that justice, in him, was that princely virtue which, 'as it is more august than that of ordinary folk, is also far freer, so that everything is permitted to it except that which it does not want'.[1] He had very evidently the courage, the force, and the cleverness of his race—time had yet to reveal him as the most heartless Tudor of them all.

More himself joined in the chorus of rejoicing. He had known Prince Henry from his childhood, and with some Latin verses he hailed the accession as the beginning of a golden age. Virtue and learning were to reign supreme; liberality was to expel avarice, darkness to give way to light.[2]

---

[1] *Utopia*, p. 92. For Henry VIII, see the biography by A. F. Pollard. 'For all the strange and violent things that he did, he obtained the sanction of his conscience, but his imperious egotism made conscience his humble slave and blinded to his own sins a judgment so keen to detect and chastise the failings of others' (A. F. Pollard, *Henry VIII* (London, 1919), p. 243).

[2] *Carmen gratulatorium*, and other Latin poems.

Letters were sent in haste to Erasmus, telling him of a monarch who declared that life without men of letters would be merely useless existence, and who was ready to offer him honours and riches equal to his deserts.

'Oh Erasmus!' exclaimed Mountjoy: 'if you could see how all the world is rejoicing in the possession of so great a Prince! When you know how nobly he bears himself, how wisely he behaves, what a lover he is of all that is good and right, what affection he feels for men of letters, I will venture to swear that you will need no wings to make you fly to behold this new and auspicious star!'[1]

Erasmus then came hurrying back from Italy to England, full of the brightest hopes. This time his fame had preceded him. A new edition of his *Adagia* had lately appeared. This collection of popular sayings, quotations from the classics, epigrams, proverbs, and anecdotes, with his own amusing reflections, was extolled on all sides. 'The Archbishop (Warham) is so delighted with it that I cannot tear the book out of his hands', said Mountjoy.

Arrived in England, Erasmus soon made his way to Bucklers-bury to stay with More.[2] There, a sharp attack of lumbago kept him in the house for some days. His books had not yet arrived; he began to amuse himself by putting into writing the crowd of ideas and reflections which had arisen in the course of many conversations. The result was the *Praise of Folly* (*Encomium Moriae*)—written with the encouragement of More, who delightedly urged him on, 'making the camel frisk'. It was part of More's charm for his friends that he was as keenly interested in their work as in his own.

This mordant satire met with immense success. In it, Folly personified, in cap and bells, mounts to a pulpit and makes merciless fun of people in every rank of society, from Pope to beggar. Armed with the witty pen of Erasmus, she ridicules popular superstitions and attacks abuses in society and in the Church; the quibblings of theologians, ignorance in monastic orders, scandals among the clergy, the lazy vagabondage of mendicant friars who thought themselves above criticism—none were immune from scornful attack.

It was by monks and friars that the sting of ridicule was most sharply felt and fiercely resented. A shriek of protest arose;

---

[1] 27 May 1509. It has been conjectured that Mountjoy's letter was written for him by Ammonius, Latin secretary to the King, and friend of Erasmus. Cf. Nichols, i, p. 457

[2] Erasmus never saw the house that More built at Chelsea, though he has been often pictured there. He described it from hearsay some time after his last visit to England.

Erasmus was surprised by the anger he had excited; the Pope himself, he said, had read the book through and laughed over it, only remarking: 'I am glad our friend Erasmus has a place for himself in his Folly!'[1]

The preface to the book, written a little later, took the form of a letter to More. On his way back from Italy, said Erasmus, he fell to thinking of his friend:

'for when you are absent from me, I enjoy my memories of you, just as, when you are present, I enjoy your company, for I protest I never in my life met with anything more delightful.' Then, to beguile the tediousness of travel, 'I chose to amuse myself with the Praise of Folly. "What Pallas" you will say, "put that idea into your head?" Well, the first thing was your name of More, which is as near to the name of Folly (*Moria*) as *you* are far from the thing. Next, I surmised that this playful production would please you, disposed as you are to enjoy jests of this kind, and to play in society the part of a sort of Democritus. . . . Some critics may complain that these trifles are too frivolous for a theologian and too aggressive for a Christian—but when we allow every department of life to have its amusements, how unfair it would be to deny to study any relaxation at all, especially if the pastime may lead to something serious.'[2]

Erasmus knew that his point of view was shared by More, to whom it seemed that the weapon of mockery was not pointed against true religion, but adroitly used in the best interests of Christian learning. The 'Moria', by its bold criticism and sharp edged satire, called attention to the evils of the time, and to the need for reform which was engaging the serious minds of Colet, Fisher, and Warham. With these men More was in complete sympathy; he did not yet foresee any danger to the mighty structure of the Medieval Church.

Meanwhile his legal practice increased year by year, as he became a prominent and well-liked personality in London life. In September 1510, he was given the important and remunerative post—as it then was—of Under-Sheriff of the City of London, and this he held until 1518.[3] It was his business to act as expert adviser to the Mayor and two sheriffs, who were usually without technical legal knowledge, and to represent them as judge for the city.[4] Erasmus described the office as that of 'Judge in civil causes, not onerous but honourable', and added: 'No one ever

---

[1] Erasmus to John of Louvain, 2 Jan. 1518, Allen, iii, no. 749; cf. Nichols, iii, ep. 720.
[2] 9 June 1510 (?), Allen, i, pp. 460–2; cf. Nichols, ii, ep. 212, p. 1.
[3] His successor in this office, John Pakington, was appointed on 23 July 1518.
[4] Stapleton (Hallett's ed.), p. 18. Foss, *Judges of England*, v. 209. 'On the

concluded more cases or decided them with greater integrity.
He often remits the fees which it is customary for the suitors to
pay. Before the opening of the case each party pays in three
groats, nor is it allowed to demand anything further. By his
way of acting, he has become very popular with the citizens of
London.'[1]

'I have heard him say', writes Roper, 'he gained without grief
not so little as four hundred pounds by the year.'[2]

In the following year, having become a Bencher, he was made
Reader at Lincoln's Inn. This post of distinction he held in the
autumn of 1511 and again in the Lent term of 1514–15.[3] He was
appointed Marshall, but paid a fine in lieu of service.[4]

From time to time he undertook other public duties which gave
him an insight into municipal and economic questions, and a
perception of the great need for sanitary rules, then very little
understood, and practised only in *Utopia*.[5]

More cared for riches less than most men, but for two things
he valued them: they afforded opportunities for helping his
poorer neighbours, and they enabled him to exercise the hospitality
in which he delighted. No splendid banquets were given at his
table, but his greatest pleasure was to surround himself with
chosen friends. At More's house—whether among the herbsellers
shops of Bucklersbury, or in the stately Hall at Crosby Place, or
later still at Chelsea—they loved to meet and talk, and listen and

Under Sheriff in those days, not only devolved the duties which that officer now
has to perform, but he acted also as the judicial representative of the Sheriff in
all those cases which came under his jurisdiction, part of which have since been
decided by a regularly constituted judge of the Sheriff's Court.'

[1] Erasmus to Hutten, Allen, iv, p. 20. The passage is translated by Bridgett
in his *Life of More*, p. 66. A groat equalled fourpence.

[2] Roper, p. 9. An income of £400 in 1510 has been estimated as equalling
£4,000 in 1910. 'Without grief', i.e. without difficulty.

[3] *Black Books of Lincoln's Inn* (ed. 1897), i. 162, 175. Bridgett (*Life of More*,
p. 65) says: 'The Office of Reader at an Inn of Court demanded much higher
learning and ability [than that of Reader at an Inn of Chancery] and was
reserved for the Benchers. The Chancery Reader had for his audience young
students, clerks, and attorneys; the Reader at the Inn of Court, his brother
barristers and even the Judges.'

[4] In the *Black Books of Lincoln's Inn*, i. 163, is an entry for 4 Feb. 1511:
'M[d] that it is agreed by the Rewlers and others of the Bench that for that
Tho[s] More was ij tymes appoynted to be Marshall and lettid by divers
casualtees, and for other causes them movyng, the seid Tho[s] shall paie to the
seid Companie vli, and therfor to be discharged of the kepyng of the Blak Boke
and also of the Marschalshippe for euer; the which he paid to Will[m] Machall,
Tresorer, in the presence of the seid Rewlers.'

[5] In 1514 More was one of the Commissioners of the Peace for Hampshire and
Middlesex, an office which he held more than once. In the same year he was
appointed one of the Commissioners of Sewers along Thames bank, between
East Greenwich and Lambeth (*Letters and Papers for the Reign of Henry VIII*,
i, no. 4701, 1 Feb. 1514).

talk again. Endlessly the stream of intercourse flowed on, devout, or learned, or merry ('merry' was a favourite term of More's), and the one attribute did not preclude the others, for sacred themes were so familiar that pleasantries were not thought anomalous to the most solemn subjects. He did not think it amiss to introduce amusing passages into a treatise on the Passion of Christ; the next world was never far from his thoughts; his prayers were real, and uttered from his heart. 'He talks with his friends about a future life', said Erasmus, 'in such a way as to make you feel that he believes what he says, and does not speak without the brightest hope.'

Colet could rarely be persuaded to dine at the house of a friend, but More had not far to go, to find the tall, commanding figure in a dark gown, always neat and precise, among the boys of 'Paul's', or at his frugal dinner-table at the Deanery, whence the guests would depart, refreshed in mind and 'better men at leaving than when they came, though with no over-loaded stomachs'.[1]

In planning his new school, for specially chosen scholars, Colet could rely on the sympathy of More. He was determined that only good literature should be taught there, both Latin and Greek, but 'specially Christian authors that wrote their wisdom with clean and chaste Latin'. 'Filthiness and abusion', he declared, 'which more rather may be called blotterature than literature, I utterly abanish and exclude out of this school.' Colet took pains to render the parts of grammar 'a lytel more easy to yonge wittes . . . considering the tendernes and small capacyte of lytel myndes', trusting that his boys might 'of this begynnynge procede and growe to parfyte lyterature and come at the last to be gret clarkes'.[2] More, with his growing family, was deeply interested in the education of children, and applied many of Colet's *Preceptes of Lyvynge* in the guidance of his own household. A small selection shows how closely the two men were allied in thought and principle.

'Thrust down pride; forget trespasses; forgive gladly; dispend measurably. Reverence thine elders; obey thy superiors; be felow to thine equals; be benign and loving to thine inferiors; love all men in God. Love peace and equity. Think of death; dread the judgment of God. Trust in God's mercy. Be alway well occupied; lose no time. Stand in grace. Falling down, despair not. Wash clean. Sorrow for thy sins. Ask often mercy. Learn diligently. Teach that thou has learned lovingly.'[3]

All these precepts were put into practice in More's house.

[1] Erasmus, *Lives of Vitrier and Colet* (1883), p. 26.
[2] Lupton, *Life of John Colet*, pp. 169, 290, 291 (Appendix B). Linacre's *Latin Grammar* he thought too difficult, ibid., p. 25.
[3] Lupton, *Life of John Colet*, p. 289 (Appendix B).

The letters of Erasmus afford glimpses of the coming and going of many guests in a large and busy household. Writing from Cambridge to his Italian friend Ammonius, he says:

'On my first arrival [in London] I had not the least suspicion that you were still at More's house . . . the following morning I knocked at the door of your room, but you were not within. After my return from Church, I heard a noise of horses, and asked Linacre to look out, as I was writing. He told me it was you going off, but by that time you were already gone.'

More liked to keep open house, and his table was always amply provided for his guests, though his own tastes were simple. He was indifferent about food, did not care for elaborate or highly spiced dishes, but liked salt beef and coarse bread, and was fond of eggs, milk, and fruit. Water was his principal beverage, or very light ale, but he would use a pewter cup in order to disguise his temperance from his guests.

Many notable men were entertained by him; his old friends, Fisher, Latimer, Grocyn, Lily, and Linacre; Edward Lee, who became Archbishop of York; Stephen Gardiner, later on Bishop of Winchester; Richard Pace, diplomatist and author; Reginald Pole, destined to be Archbishop of Canterbury and Cardinal; Richard Croke, Thomas Lupset, young Miles Coverdale, and many another were attracted to his house.

Many of these friends from time to time shared the hospitality of Warham, kindly, cultivated, and urbane, who became Archbishop of Canterbury in 1504; they would take boat and make their way to Lambeth, and in the scene of More's boyish days, would find in Warham the perfect host whose modest geniality brought out the best in his guests. Warham was no favourite at a Court in which Wolsey was the rising star; though he held the office of Lord Chancellor till 1515, and was therefore counted as 'the King's eye, the King's mouth and his right hand, and the supreme judge of the whole realm', he found greater pleasure in the quiet life of a scholar. He was the kindest patron of Erasmus, and was greatly respected by More.[1]

With his own relations More lived on most friendly terms. His younger brother John acted at times as his amanuensis, transcribing manuscripts for him and for Erasmus, until his death

[1] Dr. J. S. Brewer (*Reign of Henry VIII* (1884), i. 55) says: 'With the solitary exception of Erasmus and perhaps of the unhappy Duke of Buckingham . . . it would be hard to point out a single person with whom Warham lived on terms of friendship. Yet the correspondence of Erasmus and More, and More's letter to Warham on his retirement, indicate that More and Warham were on terms which might be described as friendship.

PLATE 3

WILLIAM WARHAM. Archbishop of Canterbury. *By* HOLBEIN

early in 1512.[1] His two sisters found in him the best of friends, always ready to be helpful, but never intrusive or exacting in his affection. Jane, the elder, was married to Richard Stafferton, his own contemporary at Lincoln's Inn; her son Richard was in his turn admitted to Lincoln's Inn at the instance of his uncle Thomas.[2]

Closely connected with the More circle were the Rastells. John Rastell, Thomas More's brother-in-law, was a lawyer of the Middle Temple, whose father was a Justice of the Peace for Warwickshire. After his marriage to Elizabeth More, Rastell returned with his wife to Coventry, where he served as Coroner, until in, or about, 1509, they came back to live in London.

Rastell was distinguished as a printer of law-books, and from his press and from that of his son William, came also the most interesting and original plays printed during the reign of Henry VIII.[3] He was a famous deviser of pageants, and he designed the roofs of the great banqueting halls at the Field of the Cloth of Gold. He was a writer as well as a producer of plays; his name is associated with those of Medwall and John Heywood in the development of early secular drama, which included the plays *Gentleness and Nobility, The Four Elements, The Pardonere and the Frere*, and *Johan and Tib*. Dr. A. W. Reed has suggested that the t vo last-named plays, which were published anonymously, may have been actually written, or at least inspired, by More, though attributed to Heywood or Cornyshe. 'To many', he says, 'it will seem bold to give More a place in the development of this drama, but I am confident that my suggestion is not lightly to be set aside.'[4]

John Rastell had a pleasant country-house at Monken Hadley, a mile or two from Sir John More's Manor House at Gobions;

[1] Stapleton stated that Thomas More had no brothers, but allusions to his brother John are found in the letters of Erasmus, e.g. Nichols, ii, pp. 43–4, 50 (Nov. 1511), also *Letters and Papers*, no. 1998. He was probably the 'John' whose illness is referred to by Erasmus on 16 Feb. 1512 (Nichols, ii, p. 62).

[2] *Black Books of Lincoln's Inn*, i. 194, 24 June 1520. 'Richard Stafferton, one of the Prenotaries of the Sheriffs Court of London, son of Master Stafferton, was admitted at the instance of M^r Thomas More of the King's Bench, and George Treheyron, the Reader.'

[3] John Rastell printed Fitzherbert's *Grand Abridgement* (Holdsworth, op. cit. iv. 311); Linacre's *Latin Grammar*; and the *Hundred Merry Tales* (the first Tudor jest book). The plays *Gentleness and Nobility* and the *Four Elements* are attributed to him.

[4] A. W. Reed, *The Beginnings of the English Secular and Romantic Drama* (1922), p. 28; cf. also *Early Tudor Drama* (1926), by the same writer, and also his Introduction to *The English Works of Sir Thomas More* (W. E. Campbell ed.), vol. i (1931), for an account of the Rastells and the 'More Circle'. Another play in this group was *The four P's, a mery interlude of a Palmer, a Pardoner, a Potecary and a Pedlar*, almost certainly by John Heywood. The 'boyish comedies' written by More have never been actually identified.

the young Rastells were about the same ages as More's children, and the two families must have been often associated in the dramatic and musical entertainments which lightened the atmosphere of learning in More's house. The versatile John Rastell was a man of action as well as of literature; in the service of Sir Edward Belknap, he acted as transport and artillery officer in the war in France, 1512–14, and was a 'trench-maker' in the campaign of 1523. He was caught by the spirit of discovery of his day, and was the hero of an adventure which is perhaps worth a further digression. In 1517, having received letters of recommendation from the King, he set out to sail to the New Found Lands, with two small vessels and a mixed cargo including flour, baysalt, friezes, canvas, silks, feather beds, napery, pans, pots, salt, hides, tallow, and divers other wares. Both John and Thomas More were guarantors. Unfortunately, the master mariner and purser were thorough-going rogues, and, having reached Falmouth, they proposed to Rastell to give up his voyage and 'fall to robbing upon the sea'. As he refused to turn pirate, they stole the cargo (which they sold at Bordeaux) and put Rastell ashore in Ireland. After some time he succeeded in returning home, and initiated a lawsuit against the mutineers. He gave up the attempt to reach the New World, and consoled himself for his failure by composing the Interlude of *The Four Elements*, in which occur the lines:

> But they that were the venterers
> Have cause to curse their maryners
> Fals of promys and dissemblers
> That falsly them betrayed.
> Whiche wold take no paine to saile farther
> Than their owne lyst and pleasure
> Wherfore that vyage and dyvers other
> Such kaytyffes have destroyed.

Many years later, Rastell's son John, inheriting his father's adventurous spirit, sailed with Hore to Labrador, encountering many hardships.

When More lived at Chelsea, Rastell built a house in Finsbury Fields, with an open-air stage for the performance of plays. The two families remained on intimate terms until the shadow of religious differences fell between them with the coming of the Reformation. In the beginning of the controversy, Rastell supported More, but he learned to sympathize with the reformers, and became absorbed into the service of Thomas Cromwell, the implacable enemy of More. Rastell was very frequently engaged in litigation, and his vehement nature led him into further troubles, on account of his expression of unorthodox ideas. He suggested the revolutionary measure that judges should be 'removable' after four or five years in office, that they should answer all complaints of extortion and injustice, and he urged that tithes ought to be abolished and the clergy made to work for a living.

One cannot but feel that poor Rastell's enterprising and versatile spirit would have fitted him better for the Elizabethan era than for his own. In spite of all his talents and his industry, his life ended in failure. He lost the confidence of his nearest relatives and died unhappily in prison in 1536, a year after the execution of More, 'forsaken of his kinsmen, destitute of his friends, comfortless and succourless' His wife Elizabeth, More's sister, died in the same year.

In the midst of a busy and prosperous life, sorrow fell upon the cheerful home of the More's. In May 1511, Ammonius, who had a lodging there for some time, wrote to Erasmus: 'Our charming friend More, and his very good-natured wife, who never speaks of you without wishing you well, with his children and whole household, are in the best of health'[1]—but very soon after this, suddenly death took away the young mother of More's four surviving children, after six years of happy marriage.

Very little is known of Jane More, except that she became a delightful companion to her husband. He wrote for her epitaph 'Dear Jane lies here, the little wife of Thomas More'[2]—one loving line more expressive than many praises. We have no portrait of Jane More, but possibly there may be a resemblance to her in the attractive face of her youngest daughter Cecily.[3]

The death of his wife left More with the cares of a large household and the responsibility of his four dearly-loved children. Margaret, the eldest—his 'dear Meg'—so deeply devoted to her father, was only five years old; Elizabeth and Cecily, four, and three; John, a baby scarcely two. For their sake rather than his own, their father resolved at once to marry again. Though sentiment had little part in most marriages of the time, it was rather to the dismay of his friends that he paid his court with extreme haste to a plain and middle-aged widow: 'No great beauty, nor yet young', said Erasmus, 'but an active and careful housewife.'

---

[1] 19 May 1511, Allen, ii, no. 221; Nichols, ii, ep. 217. This letter is wrongly given under 1515, in *Letters and Papers*, ii, no. 477. More was in Bruges on 18 May 1515 (ibid. ii, no. 473. Spinelly to Henry VIII).

[2] *Chara Thomae iacet hic, Ioanna uxorcula Mori* (More's *English Works* (1557), pp. 1420–1).

[3] See Holbein's drawing, reproduced on p. 136.

The same writer states that the marriage took place within a few months of Jane's burial; a letter written many years later by More's parish priest and confessor assigns an even earlier date to the ceremony.[1]

More, at the time, was about thirty-four, his bride, Alice Middleton, several years older. Doubtless she was an old friend of the family and was a woman of many excellent qualities, though she has been greatly disparaged by several writers—'Aged, blunt, rude and barren'; 'spareful and given to niggardliness'; 'harsh and very worldly'; 'one of the most loquacious, ignorant, and narrow-minded of women'—these are some of the unkind things written of her. Yet in spite of her quick temper and sharp tongue, her vanity and ambition, More's choice was justified, if his chief desire was for the welfare of his children. In practical ways his wife seconded his own educational ideas, and he declared more than once that no mother could have brought up his family more carefully and kindly. Her own daughter, Alice, a handsome, pleasant, and intelligent girl, loved More as a father;[2] an adopted daughter, Margaret Giggs, whom he took into his family as a child, was equally devoted and dear to him. His household became a noted example of domestic happiness. He married in haste indeed, but there is little foundation for the assertion that he repented at leisure; though he met with difficulties, he surmounted them with tact and good-humour. After some years of marriage he wrote to a friend: 'I am so far of your opinion, that I do not think it possible to live even with the best of wives, without some discomfort . . . this I would say with all the more confidence were it not that generally we make our wives worse by our own fault.'[3] Asked why he chose little women for his wives, he replied: 'if women were necessary evils, was it not wise to choose the smallest evil possible?' Mistress Alice's sharpness of temper became something of a joke between them, and she bade him one day 'be merry', for she had been to confession and was well shriven; 'and I purpose now therefore to leave off mine

[1] *English Historical Review* (1892), vii. 714 (Notes and documents contributed by Dr. H. Gairdner). John Bouge, of the Charterhouse of Axholme, who christened two of More's children and officiated at the funeral of his first wife, wrote after More's death in 1535, to Dame Katherine Mann, 'Within a month after [the burial of Jane More] he came to me on a Sunday at night late, and there brought me a dispensation to be married the next Monday, without any banns asking. This Mr More was my ghostly child, in his confession to be so pure, so clean, with great study, deliberation and devotion, I never heard many such. A gentleman of great learning both in law and divinity, having no man like now alive, of a layman.'
[2] She was brought up as one of his own daughters until her marriage in 1515 to Thomas Elryngton. Her second husband was Sir Giles Alington.
[3] 10 Aug. 1524, More to Cranefeld, Stapleton (Hallet's ed.), p. 60.

old shrewdness and begin even afresh'.[1] It was spoken in jest,
though More averred the 'beginning again' was in earnest. Yet
he was never so happy as when he was at home; with wonderful
adaptability he 'set himself to love what he could not change',
and after twenty years he could say, perhaps with truth, that he
did not know which of his two wives had been dearer to him. But
it surely would have occurred to no one except More, to inscribe
on a tombstone (in the lifetime of the second wife) the wish that
they might *all three* live united in Heaven—'a happiness which
the rules of custom and religion had denied to them on earth!'[2]

Erasmus wrote:

'He lives with his wife on as sweet and pleasant terms as if she had
all the charms of youth. You will scarcely find a husband who by
authority or severity has gained such compliance as More by playful
flattery. What indeed would he not obtain, when he has prevailed on a
woman already elderly, by no means of a pliable disposition and intent
on domestic affairs, to learn to play the harp, the viol, the monochord,
and the lute, and by the appointment of her husband to devote to
this task a fixed time every day?[3]

With the same address he guides his whole household, in which there
are no disturbances or quarrels. If any such arise, he immediately
appeases it and sets all right again, never conceiving enmity himself nor
making an enemy. Indeed there seems to be a kind of fateful happiness
in this house, so that no-one has lived in it without rising to higher
fortune; no member of it has ever incurred any stain on his reputation.'[4]

Stapleton relates:

'When anyone committed a fault, More would administer reproof with
such gentleness that afterwards the offender would love him all the more.
Margaret Giggs used to relate that sometimes she would deliberately
commit some fault that she might enjoy More's sweet and loving reproof.
Twice only in his life was he ever known to be angry.'[5]

William Roper lived for sixteen years in his house and 'could
never perceive him as much as once in a fume'.

Several passages in More's *English Works* are accepted as
references to his own family life. It may be that he had his own
wife in mind when he reflected on the vast amount of trouble
people will give themselves for trivial objects. They are, he said,

'as sore panged and pained therein... that it maketh me think upon a good
worshipful man, which when he divers times beheld his wife what pain

---

[1] More's *English Works* (1557), p. 1184; and Allen's *Selections*, p. 129. *shrewdness*=shrewishness.      [2] More's *English Works* (1557), p. 1420.
[3] The words of Erasmus—*cithara, testudine, monochordo, tibiis canere*—have
been variously translated. It is said that More played duets with his wife.
[4] Erasmus to Hutten, Allen, iv, no. 999.
[5] Stapleton (Hallett's ed.), p. 96. Stapleton does not give any details of these
two remarkable occasions.

she took in straight binding up her hair to make her a fair large forehead, and with straight bracing in her body to make her middle small, both twain to her great pain, for the pride of a little foolish praise, he said unto her: "Forsooth, Madame, if God give you not hell, he shall do you great wrong. For it must needs be your own of very right, for you buy it very dear, and take very great pain therefore"!'[1]

On such occasions as this, More would remind his wife, with his quizzical smile, that she was 'hardly a beautiful young girl!'

Mistress Alice was talkative as well as vain, and More—who himself liked talking—is thought to have referred to himself and his wife, when he wrote:

'Her husband had much pleasure in the manner and behaviour of another honest man, and kept him therefore much company; by the reason whereof, he was at his meal time the more ofte from home. So happed it on a time that his wife and he together dined or supped with that neighbour of theirs, and then she made a merry quarrel to him, for making her husband so good cheer out a-door that she could not have him at home.

' "Forsooth, Mistress", quoth he (as he was a dry merry man), "in my company nothing keepeth him but one; serve you him with the same and he will never be from you." "What gay thing may that be?" quoth our cousin then. "Forsooth, Mistress", quoth he, "your husband loveth well to talk, and when he sitteth with me, I let him have all the words." "All the words", quoth she, "Marry, that am I content, he shall have all the words with goodwill, as he hath ever had. But I speak them all myself, and give them all to him, and for ought I care for them, so shall he have them still: but otherwise to say that he shall have them all, you shall keep him still, rather than he get the half." '[2]

Possibly the 'dry merry man' was Antonio Bonvisi, a merchant of Lucca living in London, for forty years a faithful friend to More. He bought the lease of Crosby Place from More in 1524.[3]

During the early years of his second marriage, More occupied his leisure hours with a work which—though it was never finished —placed him among the foremost writers of English prose literature in the sixteenth century.

In the fragmentary *History of King Richard the Thirde*[4] are displayed a skill in narrative and description, a freshness of style,

[1] More's *English Works* (1557), p. 1205 (*sic*) (Second book of *A Dialogue of Comfort against Tribulation*). The pagination is wrong and the number should be 1203.
[2] More's *English Works* (1557), p. 1170 (*Dialogue of Comfort against Tribulation*).    [3] Charles W. F. Goss, *Crosby Hall* (1908), pp. 47, 52.
[4] '*The History of King Richard the Thirde*, Written by Master Thomas More, then one of the Undersheriffes of London, about the yeare of our Lord 1513.' More's *English Works* (1557), pp. 35–71. Reprinted in Grafton's Chronicle, and newly edited by W. E. Campbell in the *English Works of Sir Thomas More*, vol. i (1931).

a keen appreciation of human character, an easy handling of dramatic situations, all combining to produce a moving and readable story, carrying on the interest from one point to the next. The characters are shown as living people; their speeches—though extremely long—are probable; their actions consistent; every detail contributes to form a convincing picture.

There is, for example, the vivid portrayal of the scene of hurry and confusion, when the widowed Queen of Edward IV hastens in alarm from the Palace of Westminster into the Sanctuary, 'lodging herself and her company there in the abbot's place'.

The Archbishop of York, roused by a messenger at midnight,

'caused in all the haste all his servants to be called up, and so, with his own household about him, and every man weaponed, he took the Great Seal with him, and came yet before day unto the Queen. About whom he found much heaviness, rumble, haste and business, carriage and conveyance of her stuff into Sanctuary; chests, coffers, packs, fardels, trusses, all on men's backs, no man unoccupied; some lading, some going, some discharging, some coming for more; some breaking down the walls to bring in the next [nearest] way, and some yet drew to them that holp to carry a wrong way.

'The Queen herself sat alone, alow on the rushes, all desolate and dismayed: whom the Archbishop comforted in the best manner he could . . . and departed home again, yet in the dawning of the day. By which time he might in his chamber window see all the Thames full of boats of the Duke of Gloucester's servants, watching that no man should go to Sanctuary, nor none could pass unsearched.'[1]

The dramatic scene at the Council summoned to discuss the proposed coronation of Edward V, is better known in Shakespeare's version, but it is well worth reading in More's own pages.[2]

With sympathy and pity More drew an unforgettable portrait of pretty, merry, unfortunate Jane Shore—loved by one king, and put to public shame by another. The passage is one of the most memorable in the literature of the period.

'Proper was she and fair, nothing in her body that you would have changed, but if you would have wished her somewhat higher. . . . Yet delighted not men so much in her beauty as in her pleasant behaviour. For a proper wit had she, and could both read well and write; merry in company, ready and quick of answer, neither mute nor full of babble, taunting without displeasure and not without disport.'

Of all the women favoured by Edward IV,

'the merriest was this Shore's wife, in whom the king therefore took

[1] More's *English Works* (1557), p. 43; cf. Campbell's ed., i. 410; Allen, *Selections*, p. 53.
[2] Shakespeare's *Richard III*, iii. iv; More's *English Works* (1557), pp. 53–5; Campbell's ed., i. 425–7.

special pleasure. For many he had but her he loved, whose favour, to say the truth (for sin it were to belie the devil), she never abused to any man's hurt, but to many a man's comfort and relief; where the king took displeasure, she would mitigate and appease his mind; where men were out of favour, she would bring them in his grace. For many that had highly offended, she obtained pardon, of great forfeitures, she gat men remission. And finally in many weighty suits she stood many men in great stead, either for none or very small rewards, and those rather gay than rich. . . . I doubt not some shall think this woman too slight a thing to be written of and set among the remembrances of great matters. . . . For men use, if they have an evil turn, to write it in marble, and whoso doth us a good turn, we write it in dust, which is not worst proved by her, for at this day she beggeth of many at this day living, that at this day had begged, if she had not been.'

Admirable too, in its restrained pathos, is More's account of the young princes in the Tower, done to death by order of Richard of Gloucester. His description of Richard's remorse is well known:

'after this abominable deed done, he never had quiet in his mind, he never thought himself sure. Where he went abroad, his eyen whirled about, his hand ever on his dagger . . . he took ill rest a nights, lay long waking and musing . . . rather slumbered than slept, troubled with fearful dreams . . . so was his restless heart continually tossed and tumbled with the tedious impression and stormy remembrance of his abominable deed.'[1]

The materials for More's *History of King Richard III* must have been obtained by him from Cardinal Morton, who could speak from personal knowledge of some of the events described, which took place during More's early childhood. For some time it was thought probable that Morton was the author of the Latin version of this history; it is now generally agreed that the English version at any rate is More's alone.[2] The unfinished work was rescued by his nephew, William Rastell, who found the copy in More's own hand and included it in the 'Great Volume' of his *English Works* in 1557.

This historical fragment seems to have been little thought of by More's friends, and still less by himself, yet in its English prose he had found his best medium of expression, and had

[1] More's *English Works* (1557), p. 57 (abridged), 68–9; Campbell's ed., i. 431–2, 450–2.

[2] Sir Sidney Lee (*D.N.B.*) and Dr. Lindsay (*Cambridge Hist. of Eng. Lit.*) considered the evidence in More's favour insufficient, but Professor R. W. Chambers, supported by Mr. W. A. G. Doyle-Davidson, has demonstrated that both the Latin and English versions may be accepted as More's own compositions (Essays in the *English Works of Sir Thomas More*, Campbell's ed., i. 24–41, 42–53.)

created a link between the medieval chroniclers, and a later school
of writers of modern history.[1] His work, however, is not historically
accurate; it is as much a moral treatise, as a record of events.
The art of brevity is not to be found in his prose writing; in
developing an argument, he leaves no point unstated.

[1] Cf. Joseph Delcourt, *Essai sur la langue de Sir Thomas More* (Paris, 1914):
'Il fut bien le premier maître qu'aît eu la prose anglaise et en un sens le
fondateur de la littérature anglaise moderne' (p. 311). 'Il n'est peut-être pas
exagéré de dire que c'est More qui légua à son pays le goût et un peu le secret
de l'art de conter en prose' (p. 302). M. Delcourt sees in *Richard III* 'les qualités
maîtresses . . . le besoin de clarté, l'éloquence, le goût anglais du détail et de
l'image, l'humour, les artifices littéraires . . . le souci de la composition et de
la forme' (p. 294). Cf. also Professor R. W. Chambers *On the Continuity of
English Prose, from Alfred to More and his school* (1932).

# CHAPTER VI

## ERASMUS, COLET, AND MORE

MEANWHILE Erasmus came and went, always restless and a little discontented. In London he stayed sometimes with Mountjoy, more often with Grocyn or with Colet. Rushing off to Paris, he returned to make a long stay in Cambridge, on the invitation of Bishop Fisher, Chancellor of the University—but always, it appears, there was a room ready for him when he chose to visit More's house. He was not quite so happy there after his friend's second marriage, and at the end of one of his visits, he confided to Ammonius: 'I am tired of England, and More's wife is tired of *me*!' He was perhaps a difficult guest; often out of health and spirits; a connoisseur of wine, he could not drink English beer; he could not bear the smell of fish; he wanted fresh salads mixed with oil and vinegar in the French fashion (Stephen Gardiner mixed them the most to his liking of any one)—worst of all, he never troubled to speak English; it must have been irritating to the hostess to hear a flow of jests and quick repartee in Latin which she did not well understand. Nevertheless, compliments passed between her and her guest by the hand of More, who wrote to Erasmus, then in Brussels; 'My wife bids me give you a thousand greetings and thank you for your kind salutation, in which you wish her a long life. She says she is all the more desirous of this, that she may plague me the longer.'

This message might have been invented by More, but it is by no means out of keeping with his wife's own trenchant humour. Ammonius too, after her arrival, found things not to his taste, and removed himself to other quarters, where, as he told Erasmus, he did not see 'the hooked beak of the harpy!'

Erasmus could have had a post at Court in the service of Queen Catherine; the exercise of diplomacy might have won him ecclesiastical preferment, but he refused to sell his liberty either to the Crown or the Church, though he was always in need of money in spite of many gifts from his admirers and friends.

He had looked for a philosopher's paradise at the Court of Henry VIII; a golden dream of learned leisure, liberty, wealth, and honour had filled his mind—but he found the King and Wolsey absorbed in French and Scottish wars, or else engaged in hunting expeditions.

In October 1511, an alliance had been formed between Aragon,

Venice, and the Pope; on the invitation of Julius II, Henry joined the 'Holy League' and pledged his country to join the war against France; he was young and ardent, and in attacking the hereditary enemy of England, he felt himself to be at the same time the chivalrous defender of the Church.

More shared with Erasmus and Colet a deep hatred of war; they approved of the maxim that 'the most disastrous peace is preferable to the most just war'.

'I often wonder', said Erasmus, 'what it is that drives—I will not say Christians, but men, to such a degree of madness as to rush with so much pains, cost and risk, to the destruction of one another! For us who glory in the name of Christ, how can anything in the world be important enough to provoke us to war, a thing so calamitous and so hateful, that even when it is most righteous, no truly good man can approve of it!'

He lamented that preparations for war had changed the spirit of England; prices rose daily; liberality decreased as public demands increased. 'While every island is to some extent a place of banishment', he wrote, 'we are now confined more closely than ever by war; it is difficult even to get a letter sent out.'[1]

Mountjoy and other friends at Court were absorbed by military claims; it was left to Warham and More to try to compensate Erasmus for his disappointment. 'The Archbishop of Canterbury is one of the best of men', he said, 'he has been father and mother to me!'

Warham was indeed his most generous helper. Besides a number of private gifts, he presented him in 1512 to the benefice of Aldington in Kent. When Erasmus demurred that he could not preach in English, the archbishop replied:

'What great good would you do, if you preached to one little country congregation? You now teach the preachers themselves by your books, and so do much more service; does it seem wrong that you should receive some small portion of the revenue of the Church? I myself will take care that your church is duly provided.'

Warham afterwards charged a pension of £20 a year on the tithes in his favour.[2] It became More's business to see that he received this pension, wherever he might be, for no one was ever more helpless than Erasmus in managing his money, though he was miserable without the leisure, the books, and the comforts

---

[1] Erasmus to the Abbot of St. Bertin, 14 Mar. 1514, Nichols, ii, ep. 281.

[2] Nichols, ii, pp. 64, 146. The living of about £50 was bestowed on Warham's suffragan, Dr. John Thornton, and afterwards on Richard Master, who was sworn (18 Nov. 1514) to pay the allotted pension for Erasmus of £20 (about £200 in modern money).

which money alone could provide. The practical help of More in
extracting payments from the slippery Italian money-broker
employed by the Archbishop was of great benefit to his friend.
He described one day with glee how he tricked the wily Maruffo
by surreptitiously exchanging one letter for another, to the
advantage of Erasmus, and how the next day Maruffo came back
frantic, exclaiming: 'Master More, you have made the worst of
blunders; you have kept back the letter which you ought to have
shown the Archbishop, and sent him one which specially ought to
have been kept back!'

To this More replied solemnly: 'See what comes of employing
a one-eyed messenger! Doubtless the mistake was his.' This was
an allusion to the Flemish scribe Peter Meghen, who carried many
letters for More and his friends, and was known among them as
Peter One-eye.[1]

English admirers of Erasmus—Colet, Fisher, Warham, More,
and others—were eager that he should settle in England, and
devote his genius to promoting the revival of Christian learning,
and the reform of Christian practice so dear to their hearts.

The need for a higher standard of life in the Church was
acknowledged. It was by command of the Archbishop that Colet
preached his memorable sermon before the Convocation of 1512,
when four or five hundred clergy listened to his burning words.
With fiery eloquence he denounced the unworthy lives of priests
and rebuked the venal spirit which condoned offences in return
for money, and sold bishoprics and benefices to evil or ignorant
men.

'How much greediness and appetite of honour and dignity is nowadays
in men of the Church!' he exclaimed. 'How run they, yea, almost out of
breath, from one benefice to another, from the less to the more, from the
lower to the higher! Who seeth not this? Who seeing it sorroweth not?
They give themselves to feasts and banqueting, they spend themselves
in vain babbling, they give themselves to sports and plays, they apply
themselves to hunting and hawking, they drown themselves in the
delights of this world. What other thing seek we nowadays in the Church
than fat benefices and high promotions? We care not how many, how
changeful, how great benefices we take, so that they be of great value.
All corruptness, all the decay of the Church, all the offences of the world
come of the covetousness of Priests!'[2]

More too, had much to say of 'this blind folly of covetise—an
hard sore to cure: it is so mad'[3]—but of the clergy he wrote with

---

[1] Petrus Cocles. More to Erasmus, June 1516, Allen, ii, no. 424; Nichols,
ii, ep. 417.                [2] Lupton, *Life of John Colet*, Appendix C, pp. 295-6.
[3] More's *English Works* (1557), p. 93 (of *Covetise*).

greater moderation, probably with greater justice, than Colet.
'As for the clergy, I never said they were all faultless, nor I never
excused their faults.'[1]

'So dare I boldly say the spirituality of England is in learning and
honest living, well able to match . . . the spirituality of any nation
Christian. I wot well there be therein many very lewd and naught, and
surely wheresoever there is a multitude, it is not without miracle well
possible to be otherwise. But now, if the bishops would once take unto
the priesthood better lay men and fewer, for of us be they made, all the
matter were more than half amended. . . . Now they blame us, and we
blame them . . . If a lewd priest do a lewd deed, then we say, "Lo, see
what sample the clergy giveth us!", as though that priest were the
clergy, but then forget we to look what good men be therein, and what
good counsel they give us, and what good ensample they show us.'[2]

The reform of life preached by Colet and approved by More,
was to be brought about only by a return to the pure teaching
of the Gospels; a clearer and simpler interpretation of the sacred
scriptures; a new realization of 'the wonderful Majesty of
Christ'. It followed that the great pioneer works of Erasmus had
the warm approval of his English friends. With their cordial
encouragement he undertook his edition of the writings of St.
Jerome, and—greatest work of all—the edition of the New
Testament which has been described as the foundation of the
Reformation in England.

Erasmus, like Colet, made it his principle to go back as far as
possible to original authorities. In his *Novum Instrumentum* he
boldly set aside the Latin version of the Scriptures known as the
Vulgate, which was then universally accepted and revered, and
made a new Latin translation of the New Testament from the best
and earliest Greek manuscripts available.

'I have corrected the New Testament from the collation of
ancient Greek manuscripts', he said, 'and annotated more than a
thousand places. I have begun a commentary on the Epistles of
St. Paul. I have resolved to give up my life to Sacred Literature.'
In his prologue to the New Testament he wrote:

'The sun itself is not more common to all than the teaching of Christ.
I totally dissent from those who are unwilling that the sacred scriptures
should be read by the unlearned, translated into their own tongue, as
if Christ had taught such subtleties that they can scarcely be understood
by a few theologians, or as if the strength of the Christian religion lay in
men's ignorance of it! I wish they were translated into all languages, and

---

[1] More's *English Works* (1557), p. 868 (*Apology*, ch. X), and Bridgett, op. cit.,
p. 32.
[2] More's *English Works* (1557), p. 225 (*Dialogue*). The term 'lewd' is used
in the general sense of 'bad'.

I long that the husbandman should sing portions of them as he follows the plough, that the weaver should hum them to the tune of his shuttle, and the traveller beguile with their stories the tedium of his journey.'

The work of Erasmus was the prelude to modern Biblical criticism. This revolution in religious study, welcomed as it was by the partisans of the New Learning, was received with horror by theologians of the old school, who saw their own elaborate constructions overthrown by an appeal to the simplicity of the Gospel of Christ. In many quarters great opposition was aroused. In its most moderate form it was expressed by the friendly but anxious protest of Martin Dorp of Louvain, who wrote to Erasmus, defending the Vulgate as infallible.

At the same time Dorp deplored the publication of the *Moria*. His criticisms called forth an eager defence from More, who supported Erasmus in a long pamphlet letter addressed 'to Dorpius', full of theological and classical learning, as well as earnest and eloquent pleading. He pointed out that Erasmus, far from attacking theology, merely satirized the folly of those who prided themselves on their skill in scholastic subtleties and hair-splitting definitions of isolated texts, and whose arguments were as far removed from true theology as from common sense. More continued:

'Let us suppose that Scripture is easy and your questions difficult, yet the knowledge of the former may be far more fruitful than the guessing at the latter. To dance or to bend double like an acrobat is more difficult than to walk, and it is easier to masticate bread than to grind pot-sherds between the teeth, but who would not prefer the common processes of nature to such empty feats? Which then, is the easier, I will not ask, but I cannot hear it said that these minute questionings are more useful than the knowledge of the sacred writings to the flock for which Christ died . . . they are but kitchen-maids to the most holy Bible, the Queen of all books. . . . And to what purpose does this kind of theology serve? To convert or refute heretics? Certainly not. If these are unlearned, you might as well try to bring a Turk to the Faith by preaching a sermon in French. If they are learned, these very questions supply them with weapons.'[1]

More and Erasmus, with the Humanists, ridiculed the later development and misapplication of Scholastic philosophy, but public grievances against the priesthood were not philosophical but practical. Envy of clerical wealth, jealousy of clerical privileges, annoyance at the exactions and abuses in ecclesiastical courts—these were fruitful causes of the unpopularity of the

[1] Bridgett's translation of More's letter to Dorpius, *Life of More*, pp. 90-3.

clergy. More, however, was not concerned to defend the laity against clerical exactions. He took the part of the Bishops in the notorious case of Richard Hunne, which stirred up great bitterness of feeling in London in the winter 1514–15.

Hunne was a freeman of London, a merchant-tailor well respected for fair dealing. He had refused to pay the mortuary fee demanded by the priest for the burial of his child; he was sued for this in an ecclesiastical court, and lost the case; he thereupon brought an action for *praemunire* in the King's Bench, on the ground that the legatine court (to which he had been cited) was a foreign tribunal. He was charged with heresy and imprisoned, by order of the Bishop of London, in the Lollard's Tower. There he was found hanging from a beam in his cell early one morning; it was generally believed that Hunne was a victim of ecclesiastical revenge for his persistent opposition to clerical pretensions. The Coroner's jury brought a verdict of murder against the Bishop's Chancellor and two others, and in alarm the Bishop begged of Wolsey that the matter might be referred to the King's Council, for he said, a London jury was 'so set in favour of heretical depravity' that it would condemn any priest.[1] In the end, by the King's command, the prosecution was stayed and the prisoners released. More examined the whole case with great interest and thoroughness. He was convinced that the jury, though honest, was mistaken; he believed that Hunne committed suicide; he upheld the cause of the clerical party; in his *Supplication of Souls* he wrote an account of the inquiry held at Baynard's Castle; but all his irony, and his humorous demonstration of the futility of the witnesses, could not destroy the general belief that murder had been done with the sanction of high ecclesiastical authority.[2]

[1] *Letters and Papers*, ii, no. 2.
[2] An account of the case of Hunne and the questions involved is given in Dr. A. F. Pollard's *Wolsey* (1929), pp. 31–40. See also H. A. L. Fisher, *Political History of England*, v. 208–10.

# CHAPTER VII

# A MISSION TO FLANDERS

## 1515

IN the year 1515, More was employed for the first time in a diplomatic mission abroad.

The office of Under-Sheriff of London brought him into contact with many prominent merchants of the city, and it was at their request that he was associated with the Commissioners who were sent to Flanders in the summer of 1515, with the object of renewing free commercial intercourse between the two countries, by agreement with the government of the young prince Charles.[1] The trade in English wool and Flemish cloth was of high importance to the merchants of both countries, and great hardship was felt when political causes interrupted the export of wool from England to the Netherlands. There were, moreover, disputes to be settled between the London merchants and their rivals in the Steelyard.[2]

A commission dated the 7th of May 1515, appointed 'Cuthbert Tunstall, Richard Sampson, Sir Thomas Spynell (or Spinelly), Thomas More, and John Clifford, as ambassadors to Charles, Prince of Castile, to negotiate a continuance of the treaties of intercourse made between the late King Henry VII and Philip, late King of Castile'.[3] Sampson, afterwards successively Bishop of Chichester, Coventry, and Lichfield, was Vicar-General to Wolsey at Tournai;[4] Spinelly, a merchant of Italian birth, acted as English resident at the court in Flanders. These two were already in the Netherlands; they joined Tunstall and More at Bruges, and were met there by the representatives of Prince Charles.[5]

---

[1] Charles of Castile, already ruler of the Netherlands; grandson of the Emperor Maximilian and of Ferdinand of Spain. He succeeded to the throne of Spain and the Habsburg dominions, and was elected Emperor, as Charles V, in 1519.

[2] The Steelyard was a wharf and office on the Thames, which had been granted to merchants of the Hanseatic league, whose privileges were regarded with extreme jealousy by the English company of 'Merchant adventurers'.

[3] *Letters and Papers,* ii, no. 422. Sir Edward Poynings and William Knyght were also appointed ambassadors to Prince Charles, to renew the league of 9 Feb. 1505 (ibid. ii, no. 423). The Commission was renewed in October (ibid. ii, no 986).

[4] Henry VIII had captured Tournai in 1513, and the bishopric was conferred upon Wolsey by Pope Leo X; his tenure of the see was rendered ineffective by the opposition of a French bishop-elect.

[5] *Letters and Papers,* ii, nos. 473, 480. More described these representatives as 'all notable men, the head of whom was the Margrave of Bruges, but the chief

PLATE 4

CUTHBERT TUNSTALL. Bishop of Durham

More's mission to Flanders became known to history as the occasion on which he began to compose his famous book, *Utopia*, which will be discussed in a subsequent chapter. For the rest, the service was 'painful', for the English were unpopular, and Sampson was openly cursed in the churches of Bruges.[1] Though peace between England and France had been concluded in July 1514, French influence was adverse to the Commissioners; Prince Charles and his advisers were inclined towards an alliance with the new French king, Francis I, who was successfully invading Italy and who, in September, won the Battle of Marignano. Tunstall and his associates met with 'tauntings and checks' in the Council room, and found their foreign *vis-à-vis* 'deaf and dull to understand reason' and full of pretended surprise at their demands.[2] Autumn passed into winter before they could bring a tedious business to a fairly satisfactory conclusion.

There were, however, some compensations. In the intervals of business, More found leisure to study the handsome cities of Flanders, and to compare them with his own London, but above all, he enjoyed the opportunity of making new friendships, with his fellow commissioners first, and also with continental Humanists.

Nothing could have been happier than the association of Tunstall, Sampson, and 'young More', as they still called him. Sampson wrote to Erasmus: 'No one could surpass our friend More either in learning or in gaiety of temper. I need say nothing of his good nature and merry friendliness in everyday life and the honourable uprightness of his conversation and conduct.'

Tunstall, Bishop of London in 1522, and of Durham in 1530, was an able man, well informed in matters of state and often employed in diplomatic business; a scholar learned in Greek, Hebrew, and mathematics; an ardent collector of Greek coins and a pleasant companion for whom More felt, as his letters show, a warm admiration and friendship. Erasmus, who knew every one of note, introduced Tunstall and More to a charming young friend of his own, Peter Giles, town-clerk of Antwerp, with whom they both were delighted. Erasmus wrote to Giles: 'The two most learned men of all England are now at Bruges—Cuthbert Tunstall, the Archbishop of Canterbury's Chancellor, and Thomas More, to whom I inscribed the *Moria*—both great friends of mine. If you

speaker and the ablest of them all was George de Theimsecke, Provost of Cassel . . . a clever diplomatist of great experience' (*Utopia*, p. 1). The Netherlanders were unwilling to acknowledge the agreement which had been obtained by Henry VII from the Archduke Philip, greatly to the advantage of England, when fortune threw Philip into English hands. Henry VIII and Wolsey were anxious to confirm the agreement.

[1] *Letters and Papers*, ii, no. 679. Tunstall to Wolsey, 9 July 1515.
[2] Ibid. ii, no. 672. Sampson to Wolsey, 7 July 1515.

should have an opportunity to offer them any civility, your
services will be well bestowed.'[1] Peter Giles responded cordially
to this request, when the commissioners visited Antwerp. He
entered with appreciation into the pleasantries of More, with
whom—to quote Erasmus—he was 'simply in love', and he made
a sincere friend of Tunstall also. More wrote of Peter Giles:

'He is equally distinguished by learning and good character, for he is
most virtuous and cultured, to all most courteous, but to his friends so
open-hearted, affectionate, loyal, and sincere, that very few can be
found to compare with him as the perfect friend. . . . In conversation he
is so polished and so witty, without offence, that his delightful society
and charming discourse took away my home-sickness and made me less
conscious than before of the separation from my home, wife and children
to whom I was exceedingly anxious to get back.'[2]

Soon after his return to England, More, in lively mood, sent to
Erasmus a characteristic letter, telling him all the news of the day,
and describing his mission to Flanders; the letter is the longer and
more spontaneous for being dictated. It is easy to picture him
pacing about his panelled room, jerking up his carelessly-worn
gown as he walked—an unconscious habit so constantly practised
that it made one shoulder appear a little higher than the other—
his grey eyes alight with interest, while a stream of Latin sentences
poured forth faster than they could be written down by the eager
pen of his 'boy', John Clement.

'Since you left us, dearest Erasmus' (he says), 'I have received in all
three letters from you. If I were to say I have written to you as often,
you would probably not believe me, however solemnly I might lie, since
you know how indolent I am about letter-writing, and that I am not so
superstitious about truth as to think a white lie as bad as black murder![3]

'Our friend Pace is engaged on an embassy in your parts, though not
exactly where you are, so that he is out of my reach without being
within yours. I seem to have lost half of my second self by his absence,
and the other half by yours, and as you are set on going to Italy, you will
meet those who will not soon let you go again. I hope Pace may soon
attain a fortune worthy of him. The King's favour, the Cardinal's goodwill, and the attachment of all good men seem to point clearly to his
distinction and advancement.[4]

[1] London, 7 May 1515, Nichols, ii, p. 206. I have chosen the English
version of the name of Peter Giles, otherwise Petrus Aegidius, or Pierre Gilles.
Latinized names were used between these friends, More being known as
'Morus'.                                      [2] *Utopia*, p. 2.

[3] Strict truthfulness in social affairs was not considered of great importance
by Erasmus, and More himself was not above occasional prevarication in
minor matters, e.g. his dealings with Maruffo, and his letter to Warham saying
that *Utopia* was published without his own permission or knowledge.

[4] Richard Pace (pronounced Pacey), one of the best known diplomatists of
the time; secretary to the King, Dean of St. Paul's Cathedral. Author of the
treatise *de Fructu* and the oration *de Pace* (*D.N.B.*).

'The Archbishop of Canterbury [Warham] has at last got free from his office of Chancellor. You know how many years he sought this freedom. Having secured the privacy he has long desired, he enjoys a leisure sweetened by literature and the recollection of important affairs well administered. The King has appointed the Cardinal of York as his successor, who is conducting himself so as to surpass even the great hopes that his virtues had excited.[1]

'You will be glad to hear that our embassy was pretty successful, except that it dragged on much longer than I expected or wished. When I left home I thought I should be away for a couple of months, whereas I spent six in the legation. However, if the delay was long, the result was satisfactory; so when I saw the business for which I had come concluded, and that other affairs were likely to arise, I wrote to the Cardinal and obtained leave to return home. I managed this by the help of my friends, and especially of Pace, who had not then left England. While I was returning I met him unexpectedly at Gravelines, but he was hurrying on so fast that we had barely time to salute each other.[2] Tunstall has lately returned to England, but after scarcely ten days' interval, not spent in rest, but most tediously and anxiously, in giving a report of his mission, he is now forced upon another embassy, to his great regret, but he might not decline it.[3]

'The office of ambassador never much pleased me. It does not seem so suitable to us laymen as to you priests, who have no wives or children to leave at home—or who find them wherever you go! When *we* have been a short time away, our hearts are drawn back by the longing for our families. Besides, when a priest is sent out, he can take his whole household with him, and maintain them at the King's expense, but when *I* am away, I must provide for a double household, one at home, the other abroad. A liberal allowance was granted me by the King for the servants I took with me, but no account was taken of those whom I was obliged to leave at home. You know what a kind husband I am, what an indulgent father and considerate master, yet I have never been able to induce my family to go without food during my absence, even for a short time!

'Lastly, it is easy for princes to reward priests for their labours and expenses, by ecclesiastical promotions, without any cost to themselves. There is no such rich and easy provision for us. On my return, an annual pension was indeed appointed for me by the King, and one by no means contemptible, yet hitherto I have refused it, and I think I shall continue

[1] Wolsey was created Cardinal in Sept. 1515 and succeeded Warham as Lord Chancellor 22 Dec. 1515. He was elected Bishop of Lincoln and Archbishop of York in 1514 (*D.N.B.*).

[2] Pace was sent by Wolsey to Switzerland to counteract French influence and to hire Swiss mercenaries to oppose the army of Francis I. He passed More on 25 Oct. (Brewer, *Reign of Henry VIII*, i. 115).

[3] Tunstall had a fresh commission with Sir Edward Poynings (19 Feb. 1516) to arrange a treaty with Prince Charles. He was in London in May, and was sent to Brabant on the 19th; he urged Chièvres, Counsellor to Prince Charles, to refuse a French alliance, but failed to prevent the Treaty of Noyon between Charles, Francis, and Maximilian (Brewer, op. cit., i. 153).

to do so, because, if I accepted it, my present office in the city, which I prefer even to a better one, would either have to be resigned, or else retained not without some offence to the citizens, which I should be most loth to give. For should any question arise between them and the King about their privileges (as sometimes happens) they might have less confidence in me as a pensioner of the King.[1]

'However, in my embassy there were some things that greatly delighted me. First, the the living so long with Tunstall, who, while he is surpassed by no one in culture nor in strictness of life, is also the most delightful companion. Next, I acquired the friendship of Busleiden, who received me with a magnificence in proportion to his great riches, and a cordiality in harmony with his goodness of soul. He showed me his house so marvellously built and splendidly furnished, and so many antiquities, in which you know my curiosity and pleasure, and above all, his library so well filled, and his mind more richly stored than any library, so that he fairly astonished me.[2]

'But in all my travels there was nothing I liked better than my intercourse with your host, Peter Giles of Antwerp, a man so learned, witty, modest, and so true a friend, that I would willingly purchase his company at the cost of a great part of my fortune. I should have been glad to meet Dorpius, but not having the chance, sent my respects by a letter. I like him, not only for his learning, but for many other reasons, not least because, by taking *Moria* to task, he gave you the occasion to write the *Apology*.

'I rejoice that your *St. Jerome* and your *New Testament* are advancing so well; they are most eagerly expected by all. Linacre has the greatest esteem for you, and everywhere talks of you. This I have heard from some who were present when, at supper with the King, he spoke of you most affectionately, and the King answered in such a way that my informers were of opinion that some eminent fortune would soon be bestowed upon you. I pray God it may be so.

'Farewell, my dearest Erasmus, Salute Rhenanus and Lystrius for me. My wife salutes you, and Clement, who makes such daily progress in Latin and Greek literature that I entertain no slight hope that he will be an ornament to his country and to literature. Farewell again, and be contented with this one letter for many months, for in it I have imitated misers who rarely give entertainments, and if they do chance to give a dinner, make it a long one, so as to avoid the expense of frequent invitations.'[3]

[1] He did, however, as Councillor, accept an allowance or pension of £100 a year from the King at the end of 1517 (see p. 92, n. 3 *infra*) ; but in 1518 resigned his office of Under-Sheriff to the City of London, probably on account of the conscientious scruples mentioned in this letter.

[2] Jerome Busleiden, or Busleyden, belonged to a family of Luxembourg, and was a member of the Council of Charles V. He was a Canon of Brussels, of Cambrai, and of Mechlin. He founded the Collegium Trilingue, in the University of Louvain, for teaching Hebrew, Greek, and Latin. He died in 1517 (J. H. Lupton, *Utopia of Sir T. More*, p. xcv, note). More wrote some verses (*Epigramma*) on Busleyden's house and coins.

[3] More to Erasmus (abridged), *c.* 17 Feb. 1516, Allen, ii, no. 388; cf. Nichols,

Many passages in More's letters are concerned with the affairs of Erasmus, in which, as usual, he shows the keenest interest. He discusses the question of a canonry at Tournai, half promised to Erasmus by Wolsey, and considers the possibility of obtaining a 'fat benefice' for him, from 'my lord of York'. This perhaps explains a passage in which Ammonius says to Erasmus: 'More is returned home from his friends in Flanders, having fulfilled his Mission with great credit. He now haunts with us the smoky chambers of the Palace. No one is more punctual in carrying his morning salutation to my lord of York.'[1] Wolsey, however, was readier to offer benefits than to confer them.

The conveyance of the pension allowed by Warham was a frequent problem. Erasmus was still in need of money, and usually in need of a horse, for he was equally unsuccessful in managing the one and the other.

'Please ask the Archbishop to give you my money,' he begs: 'I have quite emptied my cash-box in clothing myself. Believe me, my dear More, I have run through more than four hundred florins, and the danger is that I shall die of hunger in my new clothes!' 'Do give Ursewick a prod'; he continues, and More thereupon goes in pursuit of the sporting Vicar of Hackney, who was a well-known judge of a horse, and who had promised to find (not for the first time) a suitably docile mount for Erasmus. The friends of Erasmus were amused by his efforts to 'turn books into horses' when he admitted: 'I have been trying to catch Ursewick by sending him a *New Testament*, in the hope that he would send me a new horse, my old one having taken his death by drinking (I mean in that Flemish plague), but as he is away for the chase, *my* chase was made in vain.'

The letters of Erasmus, written from Antwerp, Brussels, Louvain, or Basel, kept his friends in England in touch with the cause of 'good letters' on the Continent. He told them of the progress of his own work—his editions of the *New Testament* and *St. Jerome*; his *Seneca* and *Enchiridion Militis*—he could give them news of the printing-houses of Froben and of Martins, and of famous scholars of Europe—Reuchlin, William Budé, Lefèvre of Etaples,[2] Beatus Rhenanus, Ulrich von Hutten, and many others.

He sent books and pamphlets by the hand of More to Bishop Fisher, who complained that More, 'more suo', kept them back

ii, ep. 396. The letter is summarized in *Letters and Papers*, ii, no. 1552, and quoted by Bridgett, *Life of More*, p. 68–71.

[1] Ammonius to Erasmus, 17 Feb. 1516, Allen, ii, no. 389; Nichols, ii, p. 243.

[2] Lefèvre of Etaples was described by More as 'the restorer of true dialectic and philosophy; especially that founded upon Aristotle'. More to Dorpius, Bruges, 21 Oct. 1515, Nichols, ii, ep. 350, p. 223.

until he had shown them to Colet; and Colet complained that Erasmus did not send the books direct to *him*. Not that he objected to their being given to Fisher, but he did not like to be passed over when tokens of friendship were going about! The books of Reuchlin were among the treasures sent in this way.

The German scholar, Reuchlin, was researching into the older books of the Bible as thoroughly as Erasmus studied those of the New Testament. Erasmus wrote to him from Antwerp: 'The Bishop of Rochester almost adores you; to John Colet your name is sacred.' Colet, however, after reading Reuchlin's *Cabalistica*, exclaimed characteristically: 'Oh, Erasmus, of books and knowledge there is no end, but there is nothing better than that we should live a pure and holy life, which in my judgment will never be attained but by the ardent love and imitation of Jesus!'[1]

Colet, like Fisher, lamented that he had not earlier begun the study of Greek, in which More encouraged him to persevere, by lending him as a teacher, his own pupil, Clement. More suggested to Erasmus to 'send Colet a fillip from Louvain', but added with a flash of humour, 'perhaps, though, it would be better to leave him alone—you know how difficult he is to persuade, even to do the very thing to which he feels most inclined!'[2]

The resignation of the office of Lord Chancellor by Archbishop Warham is commented on with interest in More's letters to Erasmus; he intimates that the post was given up by Warham's own wish; there is no hint that Wolsey, his successor, ousted him from it. More wrote to the Archbishop:

'I do not know which to admire the most, your modesty in willingly laying down an office of such dignity and power, your unworldliness in being able to despise it, or your integrity, having no fear of resignation; but, with many other men, I give to your act my most cordial approval, as certainly most excellent and wise. Indeed I can hardly say how heartily I congratulate you on your singular good fortune and how I rejoice in it for your sake, for I see you retiring far away from the affairs of the world and the bustle of courts, raised to a rare eminence of fame, both on account of the honourable manner in which you have held your office and the honourable way in which you have resigned it. Happy in the consciousness of duty well done, you will pass your time quietly and peacefully in literature and philosophy. Whilst daily I appreciate more and more the happiness of your lot, I realize my own misery, for although I have no business worth mentioning, yet my attention is fully occupied, for poor talents find even trivial things as much as they can manage. I have so little free time that I can rarely visit you, or excuse my

---

[1] Nichols, ii, ep. 586, p. 576.
[2] 22 Sept. 1516, Allen, ii, no. 468, p. 347; cf. Nichols, ii, ep. 457, p. 393.

remissness in writing—indeed I have scarcely been able to get ready this present letter.

'Herewith I would beg your grace to accept a little book [*Utopia*] . . . relying on the ready kindness with which you welcome all works of fancy, and trusting to the favour I have always experienced from you. Thus I hope that even if the book pleases you but little, yet your good-will may extend to the author. Farewell, my Lord Archbishop.'[3]

[1] Stapleton (Hallett's ed.), pp. 82–3.

# CHAPTER VIII

# UTOPIA

## 1516

FEW books have been more widely read and discussed than More's *Utopia*; few can have received more diverse criticisms.[1] The little volume, begun in the leisure hours of his mission to Flanders in 1515, and described by himself as 'a trifle' (*meas nugas*), made his name famous throughout civilized Europe. The subtle interweaving of fiction with fact, jest with earnest, found in its pages, has caused it to be dismissed by some Catholic writers as no more than 'the best of his merry tales', while communists have hailed it in all seriousness, as a text-book for their cause. It has been accounted More's chief contribution to the European Renaissance, forming part of the general work for its advancement, together with several writings of Erasmus and More's own famous Latin letters.[2] His description of the imaginary land of Utopia was made the occasion for discussing a number of problems of intense interest in his own day, many of which are still unsolved and still the subjects of varying opinion. He gathered his material from many fields[3] and advanced a number of ideas which indicate wide reading, a keen and ironic observation, an

---

[1] See J. H. Lupton, *The Utopia of Sir Thomas More*, Introduction, xli, note 1.

[2] Joseph Delcourt, *Essai sur la langue de Sir Thomas More* (Paris 1914), pp. 18–20. More's *Letter to Dorpius*, his *Letter to a Monk* in defence of Erasmus, and his *Letter to the University of Oxford*, in defence of Greek and the New Learning; the *Encomium Moriae* and the *Enchiridion Militis* of Erasmus are included by M. Delcourt in this work.

[3] Introduction to More's *Utopia*, translated into modern English by G. C. Richards (Oxford, Basil Blackwell, 1923), xvi–xix. The principal sources of information used by More were: St. Augustine's *de Civitate Dei*; Plato's works, especially the *Republic*; Cicero, *de Finibus*; Tacitus, *Germania*; Plutarch's *Lives, Laconian Institutions*, and *On Instinct in Animals*; and *Quattuor Americi Vesputii Navigationes*, published in 1507. Possibly also an account of Japan by some mariner he met at Antwerp. Other sources were the *Laws* of Lycurgus; Lactantius, *de Falsa Religione*; Cicero, *de Natura Deorum*; More's own intimate knowledge of English Law. (References are made to the above edition of *Utopia* in the following pages.) *The Utopia of Sir Thomas More* by J. H. Lupton, B.D. (Clarendon Press, 1895), gives the Latin of the third and best edition of *Utopia*, of March 1518, and the English of the first edition of Ralph Robinson's translation, 1551. Mr. Lupton has traced many of More's veiled allusions, both to classical literature and to contemporary events and persons, which would be understood by the well-informed reader of his day. Ralph Robinson's translation—itself a classic—is found in convenient form in *The Utopia of Sir Thomas More, with Roper's life of More and some of his letters*, edited by George Sampson (introd. by A. C. Guthkelch, M.A.) in Bohn's Popular Library, Bell (1914).

open mind, and originality of thought and imagination, all displayed to advantage by his descriptive power, and enhanced by his playful wit.

He wrote in Latin for the learned world. The chief object of his book was to draw the attention of influential men to the political and social evils and injustices which oppressed his own country and others, to indicate their causes, and to suggest possible remedies. That it was by no means intended to be a confession of his own political or religious faith, is proved by many actions of his own life and by his other writings. He would have recoiled with horror from the thought that his book might become an inspiration to popular revolt. It was characteristic of More to make his propositions in a tentative and undogmatic way; he acted usually on his own principle: 'such topics should not be thrust upon people, nor such advice given, as you are sure will never be listened to.'[1] Very often it is open to doubt what was his own view of a subject under discussion.

It was ever his method to enfold a moral in a 'merry tale', and, partly from motives of prudence, partly from sheer fun, he devised the setting for his theme in a way that should mystify all but the initiated, leaving them to guess whether his story were fiction or fact. In that age of discovery it was not hard to believe in the existence of a country even so strange as Utopia; had not Amerigo Vespucci lately described, among many marvels in his book of 'voyages', the discovery of a people who held all their goods in common, and of a region where gold, pearls, and jewels were things of no account? These *Voyages*, indeed, being, as More said, 'now in print and abroad in every man's hands', gave him the actual plot for his story.

With the collusion of his friend Peter Giles, More claimed to have met one day in Antwerp a former companion of Vespucci, a Portuguese whom Peter introduced to him as Raphael Hythlodaye, a traveller lately returned from many unknown lands. The stranger was invited at once to More's lodging, and sitting on a grassy seat in the garden, in company with Peter Giles and More's 'boy', John Clement, he fell into a conversation which forms the first and introductory book of *Utopia*. The second book (which was the first to be written) gives Hythlodaye's description of a Commonwealth situated in the Island of Nowhere (*Nusquama*, or *Utopia*), which he is supposed to have discovered on his homeward journey. It is possible that More actually made the acquaintance of some Portuguese mariner who could repeat to him rumours of the still almost unknown islands of Japan, with their ancient

[1] *Utopia*, p. 33.

and polished civilization.[1]  An added air of reality was given to the
fiction by the presentation to the reader of an alphabet and
language said to be Utopian, with a verse by the imaginary poet-
laureate of the island.[2]

By this means More was enabled to advance, with disarming
simplicity and naturalness, the most revolutionary or reactionary
ideas, and to disclaim all responsibility for suggestions which,
if seriously supported, might easily have brought him to the
scaffold.

It was not without design that Hythlodaye, the 'Skilled in
Nonsense', was made the advocate of subversive propositions,
while More and Giles were represented as taking the part of
moderate and prudent conservatism.  An aspect of More's sug-
gestive work, sometimes overlooked, is the probability that it was
published in the pathetic hope of influencing the King of England.
'Guides for Sovereigns' were a fashion of the period; Erasmus had
dedicated to Charles V his *Handbook for a Christian Prince*;
Machiavelli was writing, in a different strain, his *Prince*, for the
benefit of the Medici.  From his gallant boyhood Henry VIII had
been known by More, and still he seemed to be a generous and
open-minded prince.  It did not appear fantastic to suggest to
him, as More did in *Utopia*, that 'a king should care more for the
welfare of his people than for his own'.

It might not yet be too late to persuade him 'to amend his
own self-indulgence and pride, to adjust his expenses to his
revenues, to check evil-doers, and by training his subjects aright,
to prevent, rather than to allow, that to grow up which afterwards he will have to punish'.[3]  These were bold words to speak,
even indirectly, to Henry VIII, but the King read them good-
humouredly enough, and went blandly on his way, scarcely
dreaming of any personal application.

The fundamental principle of Hythlodaye's argument in *Utopia*
was that the government of a State ought to be framed for
the benefit of the community, and not for the aggrandizement of
its rulers.  It cannot be doubted that on this point More was
deeply in earnest, nor that he saw with grave anxiety the aggressive tyranny of European monarchs and the growth of ideas which
found expression, a little later, in Machiavelli's *Prince*.

In the Utopian commonwealth imagined by More two of the
most startling principles were, the community of life and goods
and the absence of money.  Hardly second to these—at that

---

[1]  See note, p. 66.  The suggestion is made by Mr. G. C. Richards.
[2]  These were contributed by Peter Giles. Lupton, *The Utopia of Sir T. More*,
xliii.                                              [3]  Cf. *Utopia*, p. 32.

period—was the law that every man might follow what religion he chose, provided only that he refrained from violence and abuse in attempting to propagate his own opinions.[1]

Another proposition uncongenial to that age was that 'nothing is so inglorious as glory obtained in war'.[2] On these bases the people of Utopia were said to order their affairs so well, though with very few laws—and no lawyers—that 'virtue has its reward, and with equality all men have abundance of all things'.

Utopia, like other ideal States, was based on an idealized human nature; its author presupposed a small, isolated, and self-support-ing community, undisturbed by foreign intercourse or competition. Having abolished private property, and money as a medium of exchange, its citizens lived their peaceful lives untroubled by ordinary human feelings of emulation, envy, or ambition; they knew no thought of avarice or greed.

Upon these premisses, More developed his theme with the most entertaining ingenuity, drawing a picture of a nation which lived 'like a single family' and showed in all its rules and practices a feeling of brotherhood unsurpassed even in the 'truest societies of Christians'.[3] The writer himself admitted the impracticability of the dream, for, he says, 'It is impossible that all should be well, unless all men are good, which I do not expect for a great many years to come.'[4]

In More's dream-country gold and jewels were despised by the people. Vanity had no existence among them; no bright dresses, no change of fashion ever cheered their sight, nor gave relief to the dreary sameness of the coarse mud-coloured cloth in which the men and women were for ever dressed. Yet they were a cheerful and light-hearted community; they cared nothing for the pleasures of hunting, dicing, and gaming—then so popular in England—but found enjoyment, as More himself did, in literature, conversation, and music. The family was the social and political unit, but the seclusion of home-life was little sought; meals were served in public halls; the well-built houses opened on to public gardens; their folding doors, without locks, ensured a horrifying lack of privacy, and once in ten years all the families exchanged houses in a compulsory kind of 'general post'.

No one was allowed to live in idleness—there was work for all, though wages for none, in Utopia—but superfluous labour was not encouraged by the State; 'for the Constitution has this sole object, that so far as the public needs permit, as much time as

---

[1] *Utopia*, p. 107.    [2] Ibid., p. 94.
[3] An allusion to the monastic life, from which More drew many of his ideas of communism, as practised in Utopia.    [4] *Utopia*, p. 34.

possible should be withdrawn from the service of the body and
devoted to the freedom and culture of the mind, for herein do they
deem the happiness of life to consist.'[1]

Happiness was considered a legitimate aim, provided always
that no man achieve his own well-being at the expense of others,
for 'nature calls all men to help each other to a merrier life',[2] and
when nature bids you be good to others, she does not command
you to be cruel to yourself. 'To despise the grace of beauty, to
impair the strength of the body, to injure the health by fasting
and to reject the pleasant gifts of nature, they think is extreme
madness.'[3] Yet More himself practised a strict self-discipline,
finding in fasting and penance a spiritual exercise akin to prayer.
On the other hand, he never allowed these exercises to diminish
his cheerfulness, but found it a duty and a pleasure also to 'help
others to a merrier life'.

Though *Utopia* was in many remarkable ways an anticipation
of modern thought, it is equally true to say that it must be read
in the light of current events. More's own friends could find in a
hundred allusions, an acute criticism of their own century and of
the political and social conditions prevailing in Europe. The
introductory book contains an impassioned plea against the commercial revolution of the sixteenth century. Ever since his boyhood More had felt deeply concerned by the suffering of the poor
and the injustices which he saw around him.

At this period the wool trade was England's greatest source of
wealth, but while the towns were enriched by its increase, the
countryside was impoverished.

The old nobility and the great religious houses had suffered from
the civil wars; many of the estates of the nobles had been confiscated
by the Crown or had passed into the hands of newly risen men, wool
merchants and clothiers, who evicted the old agricultural tenants,
with their families, and turned cornfields into sheep-pastures for
the sake of profit. Some of the nobles and abbots, eager to acquire
wealth, followed their example, until Hythlodaye, More's prolocu-
tor in *Utopia*, could argue: 'Your sheep, which are usually so tame
and so cheaply fed, are now so greedy and wild that they devour
men, and lay waste and depopulate fields, houses and towns.'[4]

With the increase of unemployment, crime became terribly
prevalent and was punished savagely. All these things are
graphically described in More's introduction to *Utopia*; he makes
an eloquent and moving plea for the evicted labourers, driven by
want to crime.

'What do you do', he asks indignantly, 'but first make thieves of

[1] *Utopia*, p. 55.     [2] Ibid., p. 72.     [3] Ibid., p. 79.     [4] Ibid., p. 13.

them and then punish them for it?' 'You ordain terrible punishments for theft, when it would be much better to provide some means of getting a living, so that no one should be under this terrible necessity, first of stealing and then of dying for it.'

'Many tenants are compelled to leave their homes, and find no shelter to go to. . . . What remains for them but to steal and be hung—justly, forsooth, or wander about and beg, when there is no one to hire them? For one shepherd or herdsman is sufficient for land which, under cultivation, required many hands. The price of food and of wool has risen, for all has come into the hands of a few rich men, who need not sell before they wish, and do not wish, until they get the price they ask.'[1]

All these evils are traced to one source, one single monster, Pride. Pride it is, argues More, in the name of Hythlodaye, which urges men to amass wealth at no matter what cost to humbler folk. They talk of the public good, but seek nothing but their own, so that a flourishing State is no better than a conspiracy of rich people who heap up money at the expense of the labourers and the poor, the very people on whose work the State chiefly depends. It is pride which engenders the general greed for wealth, the longing to possess and to display more riches than one's fellows. The desire for money, runs the argument, is the root of evil, and when, in Utopia, the *use* of money was abolished, the desire to obtain money died away from the hearts of the people, and at once a great crop of crime and troubles vanished.[2] The whole contention is based on the assumption that an equal division of wealth would ensure an abundance for all, and that this equal division cannot be made unless private property be utterly abolished. Very often it has been asked whether these propositions represented More's own opinions, and varying replies have been given to the question. More himself answered it briefly in *Utopia*, when he objected that life would never be happy or satisfactory where all things were common: 'how can there be a sufficient supply of goods, without the motive of personal gain?' 'When a man cannot by any law keep as his own what he has gained by his labour, must there not be continual trouble from bloodshed and revolution?'

By writing *Utopia* in the form of dialogue, he was enabled to

---

[1] Cf. *Utopia*, pp. 10–16 (abridged). Under Wolsey's administration royal commissioners were appointed in 1517 and 1518 to inquire into the demolition of villages and houses, the conversion of arable into pasture and the imparking of land for sporting purposes, but the forces making for enclosure were too strong to be arrested by legislation. The average profits of enclosed pasturage were more than double the profits of open arable. In spite of repeated efforts, Wolsey was unable to stop a movement which persevered throughout the sixteenth century, and filled contemporary literature with laments (Fisher, op. cit., v. 220, 223).

[2] *Utopia*, pp. 120, 121.

debate these questions from different angles. Many passages in Hythlodaye's speeches might serve as texts for revolutionary propaganda, yet modern socialists have been forced to admit that More, while he hated tyranny, was convinced of the necessity of monarchy, and 'shuddered at every attempt to end exploitation from below'.[1] He longed to persuade the ruling classes to reform themselves; his ideal of brotherhood was not to be won by revolt, but by a change of spirit, beginning with the highest and most powerful and extending its influence to men of every rank. Wealth, he contended in his more serious writings and in his letters, should be well used for the good of others: 'It is not sin to have riches, but to love riches.'[2]

In another passage, written late in his life, he argued that the equal distribution of wealth would be worse than useless: '*For surely the rich man's substance is the well-spring of the poor man's living.*' There can be no doubt that this passage gives his considered opinion. It is to be found, as follows, in his *Dialogue of Comfort*.[3]

'Men of substance must there be, for else shall you have more beggars, pardie, than there be, and no man left able to relieve another. . . . If all the money that is in this country . . . were all egally divided among all, the best should be left little better then, than almost a beggar is now. And yet he that was a beggar before, shall not make him be much above a beggar still . . .

'Men cannot, you wot well, live here in this world, but if that some one man provide a mean living for some other many. Every man cannot have a ship of his own, nor every man be a merchant without a stock, And these things you wot well needs must be had, nor every man cannot have a plough by himself. And who might live by the tailor's craft, if no man were able to put a gown to make? Who by the masonry, or who could live a carpenter, if no man were able to build neither church nor house? Who should be the makers of any manner cloth, if there lacked men of substance to set sundry sorts a-work?

'Some man that hath not [but] two ducats in his house were better forbear them both, and leave himself not a farthing, but utterly lose all his own, than that some rich man, by whom he is weekly set a-work, should of his money lose the one half. For then were himself like to lack work.

'For surely the rich man's substance is the well-spring of the poor man's living.'

More admitted that the application of Utopian principles would subvert the whole framework of the State, and this was far from his own wish. When the forces of rebellion became clamorous in

---

[1] Karl Kautsky, *Thomas More and his Utopia*, translated by H. J. Stenning (A. & C. Black, London, 1927), pp. 125, 190.
[2] More's *English Works* (1557), p. 92.
[3] Ibid., pp. 1207–8 (slightly abridged here).

Europe, he expressed the fear that if the vices of men were to be imputed to the offices they hold, not only would the papacy fall, but also monarchy and every other kind of government. Law and order would vanish with them, and should this come to pass, it would be seen 'how much better it is for men to have bad rulers than no rulers at all'.[1]

More made Utopia a non-Christian country, partly in the interests of probability, partly because he wished to attribute to the Utopian people a freedom of thought and practice inadmissible by Catholicism, the only form of Christianity recognized by him. The account given of the principal religion of Utopia is a dignified conception of the worship of

'one unknown Divine Power, eternal, incomprehensible, inexplicable, far beyond the reach of human intellect; diffused throughout the Universe, not in bulk but in power and potency. Him they call Father, to him alone they attribute the beginnings, the growth, the progress, the changes and the ends of all things and to no other do they give divine honours . . . they think that to contemplate Nature and praise God in his works is a service acceptable to him.'[2]

It is impossible to believe that the vague, if beautiful, Deism of Utopia was at any time More's own religious ideal. There is no ground for the statement that 'at this period he was nearer to philosophic doubt than to the Roman Faith'.[3] His whole life shows that to him the truth of Christianity was incontestable, and, while he often criticized the practices of churchmen, he never failed to defend the principles of the Church itself. Yet it is equally impossible to doubt the sincerity of the remarkable plea for toleration in religion; a toleration to which the churchmen and the reformers of his day alike were bitterly opposed.

In Utopia, it was lawful for every man to follow what religion he chose; the founder of the State 'thought it both insolence and folly to require by threats and violence that all should agree with what you believe to be true'; the people were 'convinced that it is in no man's power to believe whatever he chooses'; it was thought doubtful 'whether God did not inspire different people with different views, and desire a varied and manifold worship'.[4]

Such views as these, so modern in their broad-minded tolerance, afford a startling contrast with More's later writings in his warfare against heresy. An 'inexcusable discrepancy' has been found

[1] Bridgett, *Life of More*, p. 219, quoting More's letter to Luther, published under the name of William Ross (1523).

[2] *Utopia*, p. 105.

[3] D. Nisard, *Renaissance et Réforme*, ii. 46; cf. p. 104: 'il plie un moment sous le vent de réforme et de doute.'

[4] *Utopia*, p. 107.

between his precept and practice; between his 'enlightened and vivifying theory in the study, and adherence in the workaday world to the unintelligent routine of bigotry and obscurantism'.[1]

These and other charges of inconsistency brought against More are founded chiefly on too serious an estimation of his own belief in Utopian principles. On the other hand, there is evidence that a measure of religious toleration accorded with his own inclination. Even in Utopia, however, dissidents were not allowed to attack the belief of others nor to advance their own views by violence and abuse; should any infringe this law, they were punished by exile; 'not for despising religion but for stirring up strife among the people'. It was this 'liberty of silence' that More would have accorded to the most extreme of his opponents.[2] When he engaged in religious controversy with Tyndale and other reformers, he urged them, 'if they must believe heresies, at least to be heretics alone themselves, and hold their tongues and be still'; to 'write reason and leave railing'. It was the attack upon the Church that he denounced, even more than the divergence of belief.

It must be admitted that the doctrines expounded in *Utopia* were regarded by the writer 'with almost every degree of approbation and shade of assent', while some were mere exercises in ingenuity, and a few quite palpably absurd.[3] Yet through all its imaginative pages, there runs one golden thread, his own guide through life—the Christian ideal of the brotherhood of men. This spirit of brotherhood alone was the basis of his communism; by his teaching, those who would attempt to 'have all things in common' must first be 'of one heart and of one soul'.[4]

Many subjects are discussed in *Utopia* with a breadth of view and depth of insight which have gained for More a reputation for being far in advance of his own age in social and economic thought. Very severe was his satire, when he criticized the perfidy of the powers of Europe in foreign policy and in war. Many of the questions raised are of perennial interest; the distribution of wealth; the problem of unemployment; depopulation of country districts; the equable division of labour; equality of opportunity; the position of women; education; marriage; divorce; suicide; slavery; the punishment and prevention of crime; the reformation of criminals; the prevention of war; the care of the sick;

[1] Sir Sidney Lee, *Great Englishmen of the Sixteenth Century* (1904), p. 33.
[2] An interesting discussion of this point is to be found in a lecture by Professor R. W. Chambers, 'The Saga and the Myth of Sir Thomas More" (*Proceedings of the British Academy*, xii (1926), pp. 222 seqq.).
[3] Sir James Mackintosh, *Sir Thomas More*, p. 32, in *Lives of Eminent British Statesmen*, i (1831).                                              [4] Acts iv. 32.

public health and sanitation—no subject is too great for his consideration, and none too small, from the highest problems of moral philosophy down to a proposal for the incubation of chickens.

In the press of business after his return from Flanders, More found little time for his literary work. He lamented to Erasmus: 'When you compliment me on my scholarship, I blush to think how much I am losing every day of the less than little I ever had, which cannot but be the case with one constantly engaged in legal disputations so remote from every kind of learning.' Another day he wrote: 'Maruffo's bill is, I think, much like my letter, which it will be a marvel if you can read, but you must forgive me, dearest Erasmus; I have neither time to write nor head to think, so pressed am I with constant business.'

The completion of *Utopia* was a difficult task. A letter to Peter Giles, used as a preface to the book, apologizes for his delay in preparing it for the press. This appears inexcusable, he says, since he had 'only to write out just what he had heard from Hythlodaye, without any trouble of invention or arrangement'. To illustrate his difficulties, he gives a sketch of his daily life.

'Even to carry through this simple task, my other tasks left me practically no leisure at all. While I am constantly engaged in legal business, either pleading or hearing, or giving an award in arbitration, or deciding a matter as judge; while I am paying a friendly visit to one man, or going on business to another; while I devote almost the whole day to other men's affairs and what remains of it, to my family at home, I leave to myself, that is, to writing, nothing at all.

'For when I have returned home, I must converse with my wife, chat with my children, and talk to my servants. All this I count as business, for it has to be done—and it is quite necessary unless you want to be a stranger in your own home. And one must take care to be as agreeable as possible to those whom nature has provided, or chance made, or you yourself have chosen to be companions of your life, provided you do not spoil them by kindness or through indulgence make them your masters instead of your servants.

'In these occupations that I have named, the day, the month, the year, slip away. When then can I find time to write? Nor have I yet said anything about sleep, nor even of meals, which for many take up as much time as sleep, and that takes up almost half a man's life. So I only get for myself the time I can filch from sleep and food. Slowly, therefore, because this is but little, yet at last, as it is something, I have finished *Utopia* and send it to you, dear Peter, to read, and remind me of anything that has escaped me.'[1]

In the summer of 1516, Erasmus again stayed in More's house, for he had personal affairs to discuss with him and with Ammonius,

[1] *Utopia*, pp. 123-4 (abridged).

his two most intimate friends in England.[1] At the same time he must have persuaded More to let him send *Utopia* to the famous press of Froben, his great friend at Basel. The book was written for private circulation, but Erasmus and Giles decided that it must be printed. More even went so far as to tell Archbishop Warham that this was done without his own knowledge,[2] but his letters to Erasmus prove that in fact he took great interest in its publication. His manuscript was still incomplete when Erasmus began to feel that 'More's wife had had enough of him', and left again for the Continent.

On the way, however, he stopped at Rochester to see the Bishop, and his delay gave More the chance to ride in haste after his friend to say a last farewell, and at the same time to enjoy a talk with Fisher. 'As soon as he knew I had pulled up at Rochester', says Erasmus, 'he hurried down to have another look at Erasmus, whom he seems to fear he will not soon see again!'[3] More, with his keen perception, probably saw that his wife's hospitality had been too tepid, and was eager to make amends; his friendship with Erasmus remained unimpaired, as subsequent letters show. In Fisher's draughty library they found the Bishop, avid for learning, struggling to teach himself Greek. Teachers were scarce, and they tried to persuade William Latimer to come to his aid. More soon afterwards told Erasmus:

'Your letter and mine by which we tried to persuade Latimer to stay a month or two with the Bishop of Rochester came too late, as he had determined to go to Oxford and could not be induced to put off his plan for the time. You know how philosophers of his kind treat their arrangements as immutable laws—I suppose from a love of consistency!'[4]

Latimer excused himself by saying that even More, with his quick intellect and eagerness in study, could hardly have proceeded with Greek by himself, after only a month or two of teaching, and that it would be useless to help Fisher for the short time that he could spare.

In the autumn of 1516, More was able to write to Erasmus:

'I send you our *Nowhere* (*Nusquama*), nowhere well written, and have prefixed to it a letter to my Peter. For the rest I have learned by

[1] With the help of Ammonius he obtained a pronouncement from Pope Leo X, that the doubtful legitimacy of his birth should not incapacitate him from secular orders and from acceptance of ecclesiastical preferment. He was granted a Papal dispensation from his monastic vows, so that he might give himself up wholly to literature (Leo X to Erasmus, January 1517, Nichols, ii, ep. 501).

[2] More to Warham, Stapleton (Hallett's ed.), p. 83.

[3] 22 Aug. 1516, Allen, ii, no. 455; Nichols, ii, ep. 440.

[4] 31 Oct. 1516, Nichols, ii, ep. 471.

experience that there is no need to exhort you to give it your best attention!'[1]

A little later he says:

'I sent you the *Nowhere* some time ago, and am glad to think it will come out in a handsome form, with a magnificent recommendation. . . . These matters you will arrange as you think most to my advantage, but I long to know whether you have shown it to Tunstall, or, at any rate, described it to him. I should prefer this, as it would give him double pleasure; it will appear more elegant in your narration than in my description, and you will save him the trouble of reading it!'[2]

He writes again to Erasmus:

'I am glad that my dear Peter approves of *Nusquama*. If it is liked by such persons I shall begin to like it myself. I want to know whether Busleiden approves, and your Chancellor. . . . To such men I do not believe it would be a grievance not to have under them a number of dependents and *subjects*, as kings now call the people, that is to say, worse than slaves, since it is much more honourable to rule over free men; and persons so excellent would be far removed from that jealous feeling, which makes people wish ill to others while they are well off themselves. I have some hope, therefore, that they too will like our work, and that is what I earnestly desire; but if their own good fortune has quite fixed in their minds a contrary persuasion, *your* vote alone will be abundantly sufficient for my judgment. We two are to my mind a multitude, as I think I could live happily with you in any solitude.

'Farewell, sweetest Erasmus, dearer to me than my eyes.'[3]

In December 1516 he writes:

'Your letter has excited my expectations and I now look every day for our *Utopia*, with the feelings with which a mother awaits the return of her son from foreign parts.'[4]

Though he spoke of his book with diffidence as 'a trifle', he was intensely eager to know how it appeared to the friends whose opinion he valued. With boyish delight in their praise of his work, he pictured himself as King in his own Utopia, wearing an indistinguished robe and carrying the small sheaf of corn which, in his dreamland, was the only badge of Royalty.

Erasmus again was his confidant when he wrote:

'Tunstall has lately sent me a letter full of the most friendly feeling; his judgment of our Republic, so frank, so complimentary, has given me more pleasure than an Attic talent!

[1] Ibid., ep. 450, 3 Sept. 1516; Allen, ii, no. 461. The name *Utopia* was substituted for *Nusquama*, since the latter would be more generally recognized by the uninitiated, and the fiction exposed.
[2] Oct. 1516, cf. Nichols, ii, ep. 470.
[3] 31 Oct. 1516, Allen, ii, no. 481; Nichols, ii, ep. 471.
[4] 15 Dec. 1516, Allen, ii, no. 502; Nichols, ii, ep. 489.

'You have no idea how I jump for joy, how tall I have grown, how I hold up my head, when a vision comes before my eyes, that my Utopians have made me their perpetual Sovereign! I seem already to be marching along, crowned with a diadem of wheat, conspicuous in a Greyfriars cloak and carrying for a sceptre a few ears of corn; surrounded by a noble company of Amaurotians,[1] and with this numerous attendance meeting the ambassadors and princes of other nations—poor creatures in comparison with us, inasmuch as they pride themselves on coming out laden with puerile ornaments and womanish finery, bound with chains of that hateful gold, and ridiculous with gems and other bubbly trifles.

'But I would not have either you or Tunstall form an estimate of me from the characters of others, whose behaviour changes with their fortune. . . . You shall never find me unmindful of that old familiarity which has subsisted between us while I have been in a private station, and if you take the trouble to make so small a journey as to visit me in Utopia, I will effectually provide that all the mortals who are subject to our clemency shall show you that honour which they owe to those whom they know to be dearest to their Sovereign.

'I was proceeding further with this delightful dream, when the break of day dispersed the vision, deposing poor me from my sovereignty and recalling me to prison—that is, to my legal work. Nevertheless I console myself with the reflection that real kingdoms are not much more lasting.

'Farewell, dearest Erasmus.'[2]

Erasmus was eager to have More's *Utopia* produced first by the press of Froben, with an introduction by Beatus Rhenanus, but delays occurred, and the earliest edition appeared at Louvain, from the press of Thierry Martins, about the end of 1516.

A second edition of the book was brought out rather hastily about the end of 1517, in Paris, where arrangements for printing it were made by Thomas Lupset, a young friend and protégé of Colet and Erasmus, who was acting as corrector of the press of Gilles Gourmont. This edition was introduced by a letter to Lupset from the great French scholar, Guillaume Budé. In March 1518 Froben at length presented what may be called the standard and revised edition of the now famous book, with an introduction by Erasmus; it was reprinted by Froben towards the end of the same year.[3]

---

[1] Amaurote, 'the dim, or phantom city', was the capital town of Utopia. The names chosen were all intimations of unreality, e.g. Anyder, the 'waterless river'.

[2] London, *c.* 4 Dec. 1516, Allen, ii, no. 499; Nichols, ii, ep. 486. This letter was sent to Erasmus at Brussels by the hand of Palgrave.

[3] The first edition (Louvain, 1516) was commended to the public by Jerome Busleiden (the scholar and statesman who charmed More at Mechlin); by John Paludanus, the public orator at Louvain, a friend of Erasmus; by Gerard of Nimeguen (Noviomagus), who superintended the printing of the book and promised Erasmus to 'take great care that the Utopia should appear in a handsome form'; by Cornelius Schreiber (Grapheus) and by Peter Giles. The

The publication of *Utopia* brought More into contact with many of the literary friends of Erasmus. Among these was the celebrated Budé, who was charmed with the book, and who wrote to Lupset:

'I owe you many thanks, my learned young friend, for having sent me Thomas More's *Utopia*, and so drawn my attention to what is very pleasant, and likely to be very profitable, reading. . . . I have had the book by me in the country, where my time was taken up with running about and giving directions to work-people on business connected with my country-house, and was so impressed by studying the manners and customs of the Utopians, that I almost forgot, nay, even abandoned, the management of my family affairs. For I perceived that all the theory and practice of domestic economy, all care whatever for increasing one's income, was mere waste of time.'

Budé fully agreed with the Utopian view of the general injustice of the Law, but asked pertinently, how the Utopians, who dispensed with most laws, contrived to resist greed and covetousness? He concludes:

'Greet More also for me. . . . I love and revere him in the highest degree for what he has written about this island of the New World. Our age and future ages will have this history as a precious source of noble and useful laws which each one may take and adapt to the use of his own State.'[1]

Erasmus at first had been a little doubtful of the success of the book among continental scholars; he was aware that More's Latinity, though excellent, was inclined to be laboured, in comparison with his own spontaneous and flexible language, and he was relieved and delighted by the reception of the first edition. He urged Froben to reprint the book, with More's *Lucubrationes*. 'I have always hitherto been extremely pleased with More's writings', he said, 'but on account of our close friendship, I somewhat distrusted my own judgment. But now I see that all learned men unanimously agree with me in admiring his genius—

pretence that Utopia actually existed was maintained and elaborated in the correspondence between More and Giles published with the book.

Gerard Geldenhaur of Nimeguen was a professor in philosophy at Louvain. Later he embraced the reformed faith. Some details of his career, and of that of Schreiber, are given by Lupton, op. cit., pp. 320–1.

The early editions of *Utopia* are described in detail in Mr. Lupton's introduction to *The Utopia of Sir Thomas More*, and more briefly in Mr. G. C. Richards' introduction to *More's Utopia*. The book was reprinted in Venice in 1519; Louvain 1548; Cologne 1555; Basel 1563; Louvain 1565 and 1566; Wittenburg 1591. The first English translation, by Ralph Robynson, appeared in 1551, sixteen years after the death of More.

[1] Budé's letter (Paris, 31 July 1517) is given *in extenso* in Lupton's *Utopia of Sir T. More*, introd. p. lxxx seq. It was used as preface to the second edition.

not that their affection is greater than mine, but their discernment is clearer—I applaud my own verdict and shall not hesitate in future to express my opinion.'[1]

The reception accorded to *Utopia* exceeded all that More could have hoped. It ran into four editions in two years; it was translated into French, Italian, and Flemish;[2] it was read in all civilized Europe; it was praised by all his friends. Erasmus, Budé, Tunstall, Pole, Cochlaeus, Rhenanus, Busleiden, Giles, Paludanus, Hutten, Vives, and many others joined in a chorus of commendation. A senator of Antwerp, said Erasmus, was so pleased with it that he learned it by heart.

It was taken very seriously as a literary achievement; as a bold and heartfelt denunciation of social and political evils it made a widespread appeal, but regarded as a scheme of political reconstruction it was thought, in his own day, to be merely laughable.

[1] Erasmus to Froben, prefaced to the third edition (Louvain, 25 Aug. 1517); Allen, iii, no. 635; cf. Lupton, op. cit., lxxvii.
[2] Stapleton (Hallett's ed.), p. 32.

# CHAPTER IX

# ERASMUS AND GILES

## 1517

WHILE *Utopia* was making the name of More famous in the literary world, its author was being drawn still further into the current of public life in London. In May 1517 he was involved in most un-Utopian difficulties, when popular jealousy of privileged foreign merchants in London caused the outbreak of violent riots. Aliens passing through the City streets were roughly handled by a mob of young men, and some were thrown into a canal.

A sudden rumour spread—and no man could tell how it began—that on May Day the City would rise and massacre all foreigners. Late in the evening More, as Under-Sheriff, was summoned to help the City officers to restore order, and, in a dangerous situation, but for a mischance, his gay resourceful eloquence might have persuaded the rioters to disperse. He found the City in an uproar. The picturesque language of Hall's chronicle describes how, at the dreaded cry of 'Prentices and Clubs!' men came rushing out of every door. A crowd from Cheapside and another from St. Paul's converged; they defied the Mayor and Sheriffs, who made proclamation in the King's name,

'and thus they ran aplump through Saint Nicholas' Shambles, and at Saint Martin's Gate there met with them Sir Thomas More and other, desiring them to go to their lodgings. And as they were entreating and had almost brought them to a stay, the people of Saint Martin's threw out stones and bats and hurt diverse honest persons that were persuading the riotious persons to cease, and they bade them hold their hands but still they threw out bricks and hot water. Then a Serjeant of Arms called Nicholas Downes, which was there with Master More entreating them, being sore hurt, in a fury cried "Down with them!" Then all the misruled persons ran to the doors and windows of Saint Martin and spoiled all that they found and cast it into the street and left few houses unspoiled.'

A furious search was made for foreigners; in Blanchapelton some of their houses were attacked, and 'shoes and boots thrown into the street'; rioting continued till early morning.[1]

After the riot, More was appointed to a commission of inquiry into the origin of 'that fiery conspiracy'. 'And in good faith', he reported, 'after great time taken, and much diligence used therein,

[1] Hall's Chronicle (1809), p. 589.

we perfectly tried out at last that all that business of any rising
to be made in the matter began only by the conspiracy of two
young lads that were prentices in Chepe.'[1]  It was discovered that
these two mischievous lads gained a hearing from the journeymen
first, and then from the prentices of many of the mean crafts of
the City.  They pretended that they were assured of widespread
support in a rising to drive out foreigners; by this means they
succeeded in calling out a riotous crowd, and then fled away
themselves, but some of the 'poor prentices' they had deluded,
were taken and sentenced to execution for their share in this
'Evil May Day'.

The general feeling of unrest at the time was increased by
new and severe outbreaks of the terrible epidemic known as
the 'sweating sickness' (*sudor anglicus*)—a violent inflammatory
fever which prostrated the powers at a blow, and 'with painful
oppression and lethargic stupor, suffused the whole body with a
fetid perspiration'.  This disease raged alarmingly in the summers
of 1517 and 1518 all over the country, and especially in the
crowded towns.  Business and amusements were interrupted; the
King and Court moved to one place from another to evade the
danger; no one was safe from the terror of attack.  Suddenly the
blow fell, and without warning.  'Some in one hour, many in two,
it destroyed.  As it found them, so it took them: some in sleep,
some in wake, some in mirth, some in care; some busy, some idle;
in one house sometime three, sometime five, sometime more,
sometime all, of the which, if the half in every town escaped, it
was thought great favour.'[2]

There were no known remedies for the disease: Colet died of it;
Wolsey was attacked more than once; Ammonius succumbed in
eight hours.  Insanitary conditions, open sewers, foul water,
injudicious diet, added to the danger.  No Utopian safeguards to
health were adopted by the mass of More's countrymen.  Foreigners
in London were aghast at the lack of cleanliness.  Erasmus,
lamenting the ravages of the pestilence, attributed it partly to
the general way of living.

'Englishmen', he said, 'never consider the aspect of their doors and
windows; their rooms are built so as to admit of no ventilation.  A great
part of the walls is occupied by glass casements, which admit light but
exclude the air, and yet they let in a draught. . . . The floors usually are of
white clay, and covered with rushes, occasionally removed, but so
imperfectly that the bottom layer is left undisturbed, sometimes for

[1] More's *English Works* (1557), p. 920 (*Apology*, ch. xlvii); Allen, *Selections*,
p. 109.
[2] Brewer, op. cit., i. 240.

twenty years, harbouring . . . abominations not fit to be mentioned. Whenever the weather changes a vapour is exhaled, which I consider very detrimental to health.'[1]

It appears a sufficient explanation of the mysterious disease. More himself was in the thick of the trouble. In August 1517 he wrote to Erasmus:

'We are in the greatest sorrow and danger. Multitudes are dying all round us. Almost everyone in Oxford, Cambridge and here in London has been ill lately and we have lost many of our best and most honoured friends; among them—I grieve at the grief I shall cause you in relating it—our dear Andreas Ammonius, in whose death both literature and all good men suffer a great loss. . . . In this "sweating sickness" no one dies except on the first day of attack. I myself and my wife and children are as yet untouched, and the rest of my household has recovered. I assure you there is less danger on the battle field than in this city. Now, as I hear, the plague has begun to rage in Calais, just when we are obliged to land there on our embassy—as if it were not enough to have lived in the midst of the contagion, but we must follow it also. But what would you have! We must bear our lot. I have prepared myself for any event.'[2]

During the year 1517 secret negotiations were set on foot with the government of Francis I of France, concerning the restoration of Tournai and other matters. An English mission was sent to Calais at the end of August to settle outstanding disputes between the merchants of the two kingdoms; Sir Richard Wingfield, William Knight, and Thomas More were the commissioners appointed.[3] More was by no means pleased by this compliment to his ability, but it was impossible to disobey a direct command from the King. 'More is still at Calais', wrote Erasmus to Peter Giles in November, 'utterly wearied and at great expense, and engaged in hateful negotiations. Thus it is that Kings reward their friends—this it is to be beloved by Cardinals!'

Erasmus himself terminated his last visit to England on the 1st of May in this year. His English friends had begged him to settle among them, but he was determined to preserve his independence at all costs. He dreaded 'slavery', he told More, if he stayed in England; a life at Court seemed to him 'nothing but splendid misery and counterfeit happiness'. Only complete freedom could satisfy him. He had written to Ammonius, not long before: 'I grudge those employments of yours which prevent the Muses from possessing that genius as entirely as they ought. I see More,

---

[1] Erasmus to Wolsey's physician, quoted by Brewer, op. cit., i. 239 note.
[2] London, 19 Aug. 1517, Allen, iii, no. 623; Nichols, iii, ep. 597.
[3] *Letters and Papers*, ii, no. 3634, 26 Aug. 1517. Brewer, op. cit., i. 188, 189. No reports from the commissioners are given in the *Letters and Papers*.

too, who has hitherto remained unconquered, is being snatched away by the same hurricane. For myself, always keeping my old character, "I throw away all my baggage to save my caps!"[1] Probably Erasmus was afraid, too, of the ravages of the sweating sickness, and of the riotous outbreaks against foreigners in London. He left England, never to return, and gradually the ways of the two friends diverged, though their affection did not lessen.

Erasmus was now occupied in revising and re-editing his *New Testament* in Latin and Greek. Finding Tunstall again engaged in diplomatic business in Antwerp, he secured his help in the work of collation, and announced his intention of sticking to him all the summer, wherever he might go.

More was keenly interested in this work, which was meeting with violent abuse from some of the monastic orders. He wrote, between jest and earnest:

'I do beg and beseech you to lose no time in revising and correcting the whole [of your *New Testament*] so as not to leave the smallest possible occasion for calumny, which some very shrewd persons will seize with pleasure and avidity. "Who", you will ask, "are these persons?" I am really afraid to name them, lest your spirit should be cowed by the fear of such powerful enemies! That great Franciscan theologian has made a plot with the choicest persons of the same Order and the same sort and agreed to write against your errors—if he can find any! To enable them more effectually to do this, they have conspired to divide your works between them—and having read them, to declare them incomprehensible! You see with what a serious peril you are threatened, and you must prepare your own forces. They did in fact, Erasmus, so resolve in their cups one evening, but next day, I hear, when they had slept off their flagon, they seem to have forgotten the proposal and wiped out their decree, which had been written in wine. They abandoned the attempt, and instead of reading, betook themselves again to begging, which they had found by experience to be a far more profitable trade.'[2]

It may have been a feeling of regret at parting from More, that inspired Erasmus with a happy thought. The Flemish painter, Quentin Matsys, was in Antwerp; naturally Erasmus knew him, as he knew every one of note, and he and his friend Peter Giles resolved together to have their portraits painted and to present them to More as a lasting token of friendship. A series of letters describe this pleasant incident, which illuminated for More an

---

[1] Erasmus to Ammonius, Mar. 1517, Nichols, ii, ep. 532. The allusion is not explained.
[2] 31 Oct. 1516, Allen, ii, no. 481; cf. Nichols, ii, ep. 471 (abridged).

Quentin Matsys. pinxit.                    Emery Walker Ph. sc.

*Erasmus*
aet. 50

*From the Diptych painted in May 1517 for presentation to Thomas More*
*now in the Corsini Gallery at Rome*

otherwise dreary mission in Calais. Erasmus wrote to him at the end of May:

'Peter Giles and I are being painted in one picture, which we intend to send you as a present before long. Unluckily it happened that on my return I found that Peter had been attacked by a serious illness, from which he has not even now quite recovered. I myself was fairly well, but somehow or other it occurred to my doctor to prescribe for me some anti-bilious pills, and what *he* was fool enough to prescribe, *I* was a still greater fool to take. The portrait was already begun, but when I returned to the painter after taking the physic, he said it was not the same face, so the painting has been put off for some days, until I can look more cheerful!'[1]

Erasmus said he rarely called in a physician unless he felt pretty well tired of life; however, he recovered his normal appearance sufficiently well to sit for his portrait during June. Peter's picture was finished afterwards, and in September Erasmus wrote to More:

'I send the portraits, so that we may in some way still be with you, if any chance should carry us away. Peter pays one half the cost, and I the other. Either of us would gladly have paid the whole, but we wished the gift to be from both of us. . . . I am sorry you are shut up in Calais. If nothing else can be done, write often, though it be only a few words.

'Farewell, my More, dearest of all mortals. Do, for my sake, take the best care of yourself that you can.'[2]

A week later he wrote again from Louvain:

'I am sending *Me* to you by Peter One-eye, who for this purpose is going out of his way to Calais. There is no occasion for you to pay him anything unless it be ten or twelve groats for the cost of his journey. All the rest has been settled by me. I hope you may be able without inconvenience to fly over here. We should then both begin to recover a little, for while I was trying to put Peter Giles on his legs again, I caught a most horrible cold, which worries me so much that I am almost dead with it. Do, my More, take care to keep your health, and then we shall be well too.

'I have received a commission on the part of the Emperor about some matters of importance, but shall do anything rather than become entangled in that kind of business, and how glad I should be if *you* were clear of it!'[3]

More replied to this:

'I quite approve of your resolve not to meddle with the laborious triflings of princes, and you show your love for me by wishing that I may

[1] Antwerp, 30 May 1517, Allen, ii, no. 584; cf. Nichols, ii, ep. 563.
[2] Antwerp, 8 Sept. 1517, Allen, iii, no. 654; cf. Nichols, iii, ep. 624.
[3] Louvain, 16 Sept. 1517, Allen, iii, no. 669; cf. Nichols, iii, ep. 639.

extricate myself from them. You can scarcely believe how unwillingly I am engaged in them. Nothing could be more hateful to me than this mission. I am relegated to this little sea-side town, with disagreeable surroundings and climate. I have the greatest abhorrence of litigation, even at home where it brings me gain; how vexatious then must it be here, where it brings only loss! My lord kindly promises that the King shall re-pay me the whole; when I receive it I will let you know!'[1]

The two portraits by Quentin Matsys formed the panels of a diptych. Erasmus is shown surrounded by books, in the act of beginning his paraphrase of St. Paul's Epistle to the Romans. Peter Giles is seen holding a letter directed to him in More's hand-writing, which is so closely imitated by the painter that More observed with amusement:

'Our friend Quentin, dearest Peter, has not only marvellously well copied all the objects he has depicted, but has also shown his ability to be a most skilful forger, if he chose; he has copied the address of my letter to you so well that I could not write it so like again myself! If the letter is not wanted, please send it back to me; if it is put beside the picture it will seem still more marvellous.'

At the same time, after anxious inquiries about Peter's health, he says: 'I have written for you a few verses on the picture, though they are as unskilful as that is skilful. If you think them worth it, show them to Erasmus; if not, throw them in the fire.'[2]

To Erasmus he wrote with extravagant, though sincere, delight and compliment:

'Peter One-eye has at last, my dearest Erasmus, brought me the long awaited portraits of you and Peter Giles. How delighted I am with them it would be easier to imagine than to say. Who could either explain in words, or fail to understand in thought, how enchanted I am when the features of my friends are brought before me, delineated and expressed with such skill! They appear more like sculpture than painting, so distinctly do they stand out in relief in the true proportions of the human form!

'You cannot believe, my most *erasmic* Erasmus,[3] how this eagerness of yours to bind me still more closely to you has heightened my love for you, though I thought nothing could have been added to it. . . . It may seem presumptuous, but certainly I deem your gift to mean that you wish my remembrance of you to be renewed, not only every day, but every hour. You know me so well that I need not labour to prove to you that, with all my faults, I am not conceited, yet, to tell the truth, there is *one* craving for fame that I cannot shake off, and I feel wonder-fully elated when the thought occurs to me that I shall be commended to the most distant ages by the friendship of Erasmus. . . . I have given

---

[1] Calais, 25 Oct. 1517, Allen, iii, no. 683. 'My lord' is Cardinal Wolsey.
[2] Calais, 6 Oct. 1517, Allen, iii, no. 684; cf. Nichols, iii, ep. 654.
[3] *Erasme mi ἐρασμιότατε*, 'most beloved'.

Quentin Matsys, pinxit.

Emery Walker Ph. sc.

*Peter Gilles*
aet. c. 30

*From the Diptych painted in May 1517 for presentation to Thomas More*
*Now at Longford Castle*

Peter a noble, which for bringing *that* picture was very poor payment, but he appeared satisfied!'[1]

In his comments on the portraits More shows that he had observed the realism which distinguishes the work of Matsys from the flat paintings of an earlier school, and the exquisite finish, especially in minor details, for which it is noted. He speaks also of another characteristic of the painter—the admirable colour which gives life to the pictures, portraying so vividly the expressive, intellectual features of Erasmus, and the frank and engaging countenance of Peter Giles.[2]

His verses on the portraits are full of compliment to painter and subject. They conclude with a lament that 'fragile wood' should hold so precious a legacy for posterity.

> For if a distant age have any care
> For art or letters, nor Minerva's light
> Be quenched by hateful Mars, at what a cost
> Posterity this panel may redeem!

There was an amusing sequel to these verses. More had compared the two friends, Erasmus and Giles, to Castor and Pollux; a critical friar (unnamed) objected that Castor and Pollux were *not* friends, but brothers. Theseus and Pirithous, or Pylades and Orestes, would, he thought, provide a more apt comparison. More said to Erasmus: 'I could not bear this friar, though there is some truth in what he says, so I followed up his good suggestion with a bad epigram.'

The epigram is as follows:

> Duos amicos versibus paucis modo
> Magnos volens ostendere,
> Tantos amicos dixeram quanti olim erant
> Castor Polluxque invicem.
> 'Fratres amicis' ait 'inepte comparas'
> Ineptiens fraterculus.
> 'Quidni?' inquam, 'An alteri esse quisquam amicior
> Quam frater est fratri potest?'
> Irrisit ille inscitiam tantam meam
> Qui rem tam apertam nesciam.
> 'Est ampla nobis' inquit 'ac frequens domus
> Plus quam ducentis fratribus,
> Sed ex ducentis pereo si reperis duos
> Fratres amicos invicem.'[3]

[1] Calais, 7 Oct. 1517, Allen iii, no. 683; cf. Nichols, iii, ep. 655 (abridged).

[2] I have not discovered what became of these portraits after More's death. That of Erasmus is now in the Corsini Gallery, Rome. That of Peter Giles is in possession of Lord Radnor at Longford Castle. I am grateful for the permission to reproduce them.—E. R.

[3] Allen, iii, no. 706; cf. Nichols, iii, ep. 676.

This has been paraphrased neatly by Father Bridgett:

> All brothers are not friends, you truly say,
> For friars are brothers, yet what friends are they ?[1]

A letter written by Erasmus to Peter Giles, though not strictly belonging to the story of More's life, is interesting from the light it throws on the character of his two friends.

'Most of our diseases proceed from the mind and you will be less upset by the labours of study, if you regulate your studies by reason.

'Arrange your library, and all your letters and papers, in certain settled places. Do not allow yourself to be attracted now to one author and now to another, but take one of the best in hand, with no intention of letting him go until you have come to the last page, noting as you go on, whatever seems worth remembering.

'Lay down for yourself a definite scheme of life, determining what you want to do and at what hours; do not crowd one thing upon another without finishing what you begin first; in this way you will lengthen your day which is now almost totally lost. And whereas you find fault with your memory, you will do well, in my opinion, to make a diary for each year—it is no great trouble to do so—and note down daily, in a word or two, if anything has taken place that you wish not to forget. . . .

'Above all things I beg and entreat you in the conduct of life to be guided by judgment and not by impulse. If you have made any mistake, consider at once whether you can set it right in any way, or diminish the evil; this you will do better if you do it quietly, than in an excited state. . . .

'If you can keep your fortune without loss of health, do so by all means; if not, you lose more than you gain, when you preserve your fortune by risking your health or quiet. . . .

'Do not take too much pains about trifling matters. Life is fleeting, health is brittle, and not to be casually squandered. Some things must be disregarded, and the mind raised to what is great.'[2]

In another letter of good advice, Erasmus warned his young friend not to give way to an irritable temper, for this was very detrimental to his health—words of wisdom derived presumably from the personal experience of the writer.

---

[1] Bridgett, *Life of More*, p. 110.

[2] Erasmus to Peter Giles, Brussels, 6 Oct. 1516, Allen, ii, no. 476; cf. Nichols, ii, ep. 462. Peter Giles, born at Antwerp about 1486, died in November 1533. No correspondence between him and More after the publication of *Utopia* appears to have been preserved.

# CHAPTER X

## THE KING'S SERVICE

### 1517–1518

NOT long after the publication of *Utopia*, More found himself permanently engaged in the royal service. At this period of his reign, King Henry VIII delighted to surround himself with men of note and learning; Humanist scholars found a cordial welcome from him and from the Queen. Colet was their chosen preacher, Linacre, the royal physician, Tunstall, Master of the Rolls. Mountjoy was head of the Queen's Household; one of the King's secretaries was Richard Pace 'with a character akin to that of More'. Only More, it seemed, was missing from the circle— More 'the supreme delight of the Muses, of Pleasantry and the Graces'.[1] His wide learning, his shrewd common sense, his ability in public speaking, his interest in astronomy, his love of music— all these qualities commended him to the King, and not least, his quickness of wit, his amiability and his fund of amusing anec- dotes. Besides all this, his popularity with the London merchants —a wealthy and powerful class of men—lent him some impor- tance in political circles, and his legal knowledge and experience were desirable in the King's Council. His missions to Flanders in 1515 and Calais in 1517 gave him a name for 'wise and discreet dealing' and his reputation was enhanced by his able advocacy in the Star Chamber, when he won a case on behalf of the Papal Legate, against the Crown.[2]

The King was determined to attach so brilliant a man to his Court, and would not be gainsaid. 'He could not rest until he had dragged More to his Court—*dragged* is the word', said Erasmus, 'for no one ever tried more strenuously to gain admission to Court, than he did to escape from it.' Wolsey, eager to please the King, used all the arts of his 'filed tongue and elegant eloquence' to overcome More's resistance, promising that his income should not be diminished by his acceptance of the King's offers. The time came when More could no longer contrive to excuse himself, though a life at Court did not attract him; for its luxury and display he felt nothing but contempt. 'He hates despotism and likes equality,' wrote Erasmus, 'he is fond of liberty and leisure, though no one is more ready and industrious when duty requires

[1] Erasmus to Paulus Bombasius, Basel, 26 July 1518, Allen, iii, no. 855; cf. Nichols, iii, ep. 805. Pace, however, for all his ability, was not the equal of More in discretion or good temper. Cf. Brewer, op. cit., ii. 12, 13.

[2] Roper, p. 11.

it. He was much averse from spending his time at Court, though
one could not wish to serve a kinder or more unexacting prince.'
To Tunstall, Erasmus remarked: 'I should deplore the fortune of
More in being enticed into a Court, if it were not that under such
a King and with so many learned men for companions and col-
leagues, it may seem, not a Court, but a Temple of the Muses.
But meanwhile, nothing is brought us from Utopia to amuse us,
and he, I am quite sure, would rather have his laugh, than be
borne aloft on a curule chair.'[1] To another friend he observed:
'More is now absorbed by the Court, and always attending on the
King, in whose inmost counsels he is. Pace is openly triumphant.'[2]
And to More himself he lamented 'there is no doubt that you will
be carried away from us and from Literature'.[3]

It has been asked very often what motive could have induced
More to follow a course which he disliked, and which has been
decried as a betrayal of his Utopian principles. Yet, with all his
idealism, there was a practical side to his character. He proved,
later on, that he was willing to sacrifice his head to save his
conscience, but we have his own word for it that he was by no
means anxious to lose it for any lesser cause. He knew that, in
Tudor England, to incur the anger of the King might have a
fatal consequence; his only alternative to compliance would lie in
escape to the Continent, where many friends would welcome him
to the hearth of 'Good Letters'. This course, however, would entail
the loss of his legal practice and the greater part of his income,
and what then would become of his own family? He loved his
home and his country; he was fond of his wife and devoted to
his children; his duty to them was one of his first considerations.

There is no doubt that the influence of his own relatives supported that of Wolsey and Pace. His father was not likely to
advise the rejection of promised fortune and fame; his wife was
an ambitious woman who urged him to accept it. Probably to this
period may be attributed a little scene depicted with vivid
humour in a page of More's *English Works*. He speaks of the
ambition of worldly men to obtain posts of authority; their
desire to control others and to live uncontrolled themselves. He
had little esteem for such a position, he said until 'his wife once
in a great anger taught it him'.[4]

---

[1] (i.e. to be chaired like a Roman praetor or consul) Erasmus to Tunstall,
24 Apr. 1518, Allen, iii, no. 832; Nichols, iii, ep. 790.
[2] To W. Nesen, 17 Apr. 1518, Allen, iii, no. 816; cf. Nichols, iii, ep. 774.
[3] To More, *c.* 23 Apr. 1518, Allen, iii, no. 829; Nichols, iii, ep. 794.
[4] *English Works* (1557), p. 1224 (*Dialogue of Comfort*). This anecdote, he
says, 'a good friend of ours merrily told me once', but it is usually accepted as
a piece of autobiography, thinly disguised in his usual manner.

'For when her husband had no list [liking] to grow greatly upward in the world, nor neither would labour for office of authority, and over that forsook a right worshipful room [place, post] when it was offered him, she fell in hand with him and . . . . all to rated him, and asked him: "What will you do, that you list not to put forth yourself as other folk do? Will you sit by the fire and make goslings in the ashes with a stick, as children do? Would God I were a man, and look what I would do;" "Why wife," quoth her husband, "what would you do?" "What? by God, go forward with the best. For as my mother was wont to say, God have mercy on her soul, 'it is ever better to rule than to be ruled.' And therefore, by God, I would not I warrant you, be so foolish to be ruled, where I might rule."

' "By my troth, wife", quoth her husband, "in this I dare say you say truth. For I never found you willing to be ruled yet."'

To the end of his life More expressed the same mockery of the empty pleasures of authority and the ceremonies of a court. In his last years he wrote:

'I wist once a great officer of the king's say (and in good faith I ween he said but as he thought) that twenty men standing bare head before him, kepte not his head half so warm as to keep on his own cap. Nor he never took so much ease with their being bare head before him, as he caught once grief with a cough that came upon him, by standing bare head long before the king . . . nor twenty mens courtesies do him not so much pleasure as his own once kneeling doth him pain, if his knee hap to be sore!'[1]

He was, then, by no means dazzled by the prospect before him when he yielded to persuasion and decided to enter the service of the State. Stronger even than the interests of his family were the reasons of patriotism urged upon him by his friends, though he felt doubtful of his own ability to be of use. His perplexity was expressed in his introduction to *Utopia* where, in a closely reasoned discussion, his own mental conflict may be traced. He feared that it would be futile to offer good advice to princes and courtiers or to advocate a policy of peace and moderation, 'for they care more to acquire new kingdoms than to administer well those they possess already'. By such means it would be more than possible to accomplish nothing, but to 'share the madness of others while I attempted to cure their lunacy'. His doubts were combated, probably by Pace or Tunstall, as well as by Wolsey, who spoke on behalf of the King, with such arguments as the following:

'You will do what is worthy of your generous and philosophic spirit, if you so order your life as to apply your talent and industry to the

---

[1] *English Works* (1557), p. 1224 (*A Dialogue of Comfort*).

public interest, even if it involve some disadvantage to yourself. This
you can never do with as great profit as if you are counsellor to a great
prince, and make him follow, as I am sure you will, straightforward and
honourable courses. For from the prince, as from a never-failing spring,
flows a stream of all that is good or evil over the whole nation. Now you
possess such complete learning that even had you no great experience of
affairs, and so great experience of affairs that even had you no learning,
you would make an excellent member of any king's council.'[1]

The final answer to his problem may be found in the following
passage in *Utopia*:

'Suppose wrong opinions cannot be plucked up by the root, and you
cannot cure, as you would wish, vices of long standing, yet you must not
on that account abandon the ship of state and desert it in a storm,
because you cannot control the winds. But neither must you impress
upon them [the King and his council] new and strange language, which
you know will carry no weight with those of opposite conviction; but
by indirect approach and covert suggestion you must endeavour and
strive to the best of your power to handle all well, and what you cannot
turn to good, you must make as little bad as you can. For it is impossible
that all should be well, unless all men are good.'[2]

In the end, loyalty and patriotism overcame More's reluctance.
An invitation to join the King's Council seemed to promise the
best opportunity he could look for, to use his influence for the
welfare of his country, and so, with a sigh and a smile, he turned
from the service of 'Good Letters' to that of Henry VIII.
When More returned from Calais in October 1517, he was
appointed one of the King's councillors, and a Judge in the Court
of Requests, or, as it was then called, the 'Poor Men's Court', or
'Court of Poor Men's Causes'. The title 'Master of Requests' did
not come into use until some time after More held the office. He
does not appear to have taken up regular duties at Court before
the spring of 1518.[3]

---

[1] *Utopia*, p. 7.                              [2] Ibid., p. 34.
[3] Roper (p. 11) said the King 'made him Master of the Requests and within
a month after, Knight, and one of his privy council'. The title, 'Master of
Requests' would be familiar to Roper, when he wrote his biography; More
was not knighted, however, before 1521. Mr. I. S. Leadam says: 'I first find
the name "Court of Requests" in 1529' (*Select Cases in the Court of Requests*,
introd., p. xiv). For 'Masters of Requests', ibid., pp. xvi, xix, and xxxi.
Roper's recollection of the sequence of events is sometimes at fault. The date
of More's admission to the King's Council (which was not yet known as the
privy council) was for some time in doubt. Erasmus wrote on 17 Apr. 1518,
*Morus totus est aulicus, regi semper assistens* (Allen, iii, no. 816). In July 1518
he alluded to More as 'one of the council' (ibid., no. 855), and in September,
Giustiniani spoke of his being 'newly-made councillor' (*Letters and Papers*, ii,
no. 4438). An annuity of £100 was granted to More by the King himself, 21 June
1518, to date from Michaelmas 1517. This latter date apparently gives the

The Court of Requests was one of the extensions of the King's Council, and was regarded less as a court of law than as a committee of the council acting for the King, especially for the remedy of the grievances of poor petitioners. The judges or masters of requests were members of the council who also frequently sat in the Star Chamber. This court, in the early years of the reign of Henry VIII, attended the royal progresses and sat at Greenwich, Woodstock, or wherever the King might be; later in the reign it became a stationary court, fixed by Wolsey in the White Hall at Westminster; it was connected with the Star Chamber and the Court of Chancery, and supplemented and assisted both.[1]

To the judges of the Court of Requests, in attendance on the sovereign, naturally fell the duty of examining petitions to the Crown; the post, therefore, was well chosen to attract More to

approximate time of More's appointment to the Council (Public Record Office, C 66, no. 637, m. 12 (patent roll); E 405, no. 202). The annuity or fee, either word being used in the Treasury accounts, which was charged on the petty customs of the Port of London, was to be paid quarterly, the first payment being reckoned as due at Christmas 1517. More received payment of the three quarters thus due on St. John the Baptist's day, 1518, and afterwards received the annuity fairly regularly. The payments for the last years of his life were as follows:

For the year ending 29 Sept. 1532, the four quarterly payments were made (E 405, no. 102).

For the year ending 29 Sept. 1533, only the payment due at the quarter of Michaelmas 1532 was paid (E 405, no. 103).

For the year ending 29 Sept. 1534, five payments, due at Christmas 1532, Easter, St. John the Baptist's Day, Michaelmas, and Christmas 1533, were made at Christmas 1533.

The last payment was made at Easter 1534 (E. 405, no. 104 and no. 202).

The researches made by Miss C. Jamison in the P.R.O. show that too early a date (i.e. 1516) is assigned to the granting of More's fee as Councillor, in *Letters and Papers*, ii, no. 2736 (p. 875). Cf. *Letters and Papers*, ii, no. 4247, 21 June 1518.

[1] Authorities for the above passage are Leadam, op. cit., introduction xi–xxi; Holdsworth, *History of English Law* (1922), i. 413–14; Pollard, *Wolsey*, pp. 82, 83, 87. A summons for appearance at the Court was usually issued by writ under Privy Seal. The Court did not restrict itself in jurisdictional area, but sometimes remitted cases to local tribunals. It was constantly in collision with the Courts of Common Law. Its injunctions to 'stay the sutes at Common Lawe' were numerous. All the Courts were comprised in the injunctions laid upon defendants not to arrest, sue, or implead the plaintiff during the dependence of his suit in this Court, or after judgement given by it. On the other hand, the judges of the Court at times, like the Chancellor, consulted the judges of the Common Law (Leadam, op. cit. xxii). Cases tried by the Court of Requests included questions of title to, and possession of, land, executorships, wardships, marriage settlements, contracts and covenants generally; forfeitures to the King, damages claimed for injuries, &c. (ibid. lxxxix). The Court was popular, for its process 'was summary, simple, honest and cheap, as contrasted with a Common Law procedure which was dilatory, complex, frequently corrupt, and consequently expensive' (ibid. lv). Wolsey is thought to have developed the Court in his struggle with the aristocracy. As its position developed from a committee of the Privy Council into a Court of equity, the professional lawyers on the council gradually assumed more importance, as Judges in the Court.

the King's side, for it brought him into contact with poor and unfortunate people and gave him an opportunity of helping them in the most practical way.[1]

The King's Council at this time was becoming the centre of national affairs; it was through the Council, acting as an executive and a judicial body, that the Tudor sovereigns built up a strong and competent government. 'As the Tudor rule became more and more firmly established, the king's government was regarded as a kind of administrative providence, set to guide, to regulate and to instruct the manifold energies of the nation. Every description of local and municipal difficulty came to be referred to the King's Council.'[2]

The duty of the councillors was to advise the King in matters of State—but only when their advice was required. The King alone appointed them to office. Some of them were members of the old nobility, and from time to time commoners were promoted for their ability; to the work of such men as Wolsey, Pace, and More, was largely due the efficiency of the council, but they were literally the servants of the King. To Wolsey alone did he allow any independence of action.[3]

When More joined the government, he quickly found that everything of importance must be referred to Wolsey, whose

[1] When orders were given for the remodelling of the royal household, in January 1526, More was retained as one of the examiners of petitions presented to the King as he moved from place to place (*Letters and Papers*, iv, no. 1939).

[2] H. A. L. Fisher, *Political History of England*, v. 220.

[3] An illuminating account of the Council is given by Dr. A. F. Pollard: 'The early Tudor council still defies historical definition. One misconception can however be removed; the council was not an administrative but an advisory body . . . in Wolsey's time there was no distinction, in form or in meaning, between the words counsel and council—the king's council consisted of king's counsel, of whom there were more than a hundred . . . some of them learned in various kinds of law, some of them expert in finance, diplomacy, languages, or arms. Out of this body of counsel, were formed from time to time, groups to sit in the star-chamber, in the court of requests, or with the king wherever he might be. . . . Out of the numerous counsel, kings were in the habit of selecting from time to time a few for more private and regular consultation on matters of state, i.e. affecting the king's estate (Pollard, *Wolsey*, pp. 105–6). 'As the Tudor scheme of government through the council developed . . . two lines of cleavage gradually grew up within the council. The first was a distinction between the council with the King and the Council at Westminster; the second was a distinction between the full members of the Privy Council and the ordinary members of council. . . . The one following the King, known as the Council at Court, became the King's Privy Council which considered all questions of domestic and foreign policy. The other was the King's Council in the Star Chamber, which transacted administrative and judicial business at Westminster. . . . Helped by the Council, the Tudor kings mastered the lawlessness of the preceding period, successfully piloted the state through the difficult transition from mediaeval to modern, and reformed the Church on lines which harmonised with the form which the modern English state was assuming' (Holdsworth, *History of English Law* (1922), i. 492, 495, 496).

'prudent counsel and politic advice' was sought by the King on every point. He was already Archbishop of York and Cardinal, and soon to be Papal legate *a latere*; he had succeeded Warham as Chancellor in 1515, and was the chief of the executive committee of the council, having as coadjutors the old Duke of Norfolk as Treasurer—jealous of Wolsey but unable to withstand him—and Ruthall, Bishop of Durham, his own faithful supporter, as Lord Privy Seal, who 'sang treble to Wolsey's bass'.

Though More did not always approve Wolsey's foreign policy, he felt a genuine respect for his capable administration of law and order at home, and sympathized with his projected reforms, devised to secure justice for the poor. Usually he showed no resentment towards Wolsey's assumption of authority, and frequently served him by interpreting his wishes with acceptable tact and intelligence. On one occasion, however, according to Stapleton, he criticized Wolsey's arbitrary conduct in the council, and opposed him with success. The story is that Wolsey proposed the creation of a Supreme Constable to represent the King in the whole kingdom; doubtless hoping to be himself appointed to the new office. No one dared to raise any objection, until More, who spoke last, as the latest member, opposed the suggestion with such powerful arguments that the council began to waver. Wolsey, angry at the check, said sharply to More that, by differing from all the others, who were noble and prudent men, he showed himself to be a stupid and foolish councillor; whereupon More cheerfully replied: 'God be thanked that the King has but *one* fool in his Council!' He said no more, but the plan was postponed, and finally rejected.[1]

It was only to be expected that More's friends, seeing him so greatly favoured by the Sovereign, should overrate his power at Court. In legal questions, indeed, his opinion must have carried weight, and in individual cases his kindly counsels no doubt influenced the King, but he had no illusions as to his own power in general policy. He replied to the congratulations of Bishop Fisher:

'It was with the greatest unwillingness that I came to Court, as everyone knows, and as the King himself in joke often throws up in my face. I am as uncomfortable there as a bad rider is in the saddle. I am far from enjoying the special favour of the King, but he is so courteous and kindly to all, that everyone who is in any way hopeful finds a ground for imagining that he is in the King's good graces; like the London wives,

---

[1] Stapleton (Hallett's ed.), pp. 136–7. The story may be true, but Stapleton, like other Catholics of his time, was prejudiced against Wolsey on account of his supposed support of Henry VIII's divorce, which contributed to the breach with Rome.

who, as they pray before the image of the Virgin Mother of God, which
stands near the Tower, gaze upon it so fixedly that they imagine it smiles
upon them! I am not so happy as to perceive signs of favour, or so
hopeful as to imagine them. But the King has virtue and learning, and
makes great progress in both with daily renewed zeal, so that the more
I see his Majesty advance in all the qualities that befit so good a monarch,
the less burdensome do I feel this life of the Court.'[1]

Within certain limits, however, More was enabled to obtain
many benefits for those who sought his aid. For instance, Fisher
begged his commendation for a young scholar of Cambridge 'well
versed in theology and a zealous preacher to the people':

'Please now give your help to this young man', he wrote; 'we have
very few friends at Court who have the will and the power to commend
our interests to the King's Majesty, and among them we reckon you the
chief.' More replied: 'Whatever influence I have with the King—it is
very little, but such as it is—is as freely at your disposal, for yourself or
your scholar, as a house is to its owner. I owe your students constant
gratitude for the heartfelt affection of which their letters to me are the
token.'[2]

Erasmus had the testimony of intimate friends when he
described More's activities in his new position.

'Whatever influence he has acquired by his dignity, whatever favour
he enjoys with his powerful Sovereign, he uses for the good of the State
and for the assistance of his friends. He was ever desirous of conferring
benefits and wonderfully prone to compassion. This disposition has
grown with his power of indulging it. Some he assists with money,
others he protects by his authority, others he advances by his recommendation. If he can help in no other way, he does it by his counsels; he
sends no one away dejected. You would say that he had been appointed
the public guardian of all those in need.

'He counts it a great gain to himself, if he has relieved some oppressed
person. . . . No man more readily confers a benefit, no man expects less
in return—and, successful as he is in many ways, I have never seen any
mortal more free from self-conceit.

'In serious matters no man's advice is more prized, while, if the king
wishes to recreate himself, no man's conversation is gayer. Often there
are deep and intricate matters that demand a grave and prudent judge.
More unravels them in such a way that he satisfies both sides. No one
however, has ever prevailed on him to receive a gift for his decision.
His elevation has brought with it no pride. Amidst all the weight of
State affairs he remembers the humble friends of old, and from time to
time returns to his beloved literature.'[3]

It is true that for a time, at least, More was not quite 'carried
away from the service of literature'. It happened that in 1518 he

[1] Stapleton (Hallett's ed), p. 77.                          [2] Ibid., p. 48.
[3] Erasmus to Hutten, Allen, iv, pp. 20-1; cf. Nichols, iii, p. 397.

accompanied the Court to Abingdon, in its flight from the epidemic raging in London. From there he was sent to Oxford, where he superintended the measures taken to mitigate the spread of contagion in the University.[1] It was at this time that he composed the famous address in which he defended with all his force the New Learning of the Humanists, with special reference to the teaching of Erasmus.

For some years the University had been divided into two camps, calling themselves 'Trojans' and 'Greeks'. With increasing violence the Trojans opposed the 'new' learning of the classics; one of their preachers condemned all studies save that of the old-style theology. With the approval of the King, More made his defence in the form of a *Letter to the Fathers and Proctors of the University of Oxford.*[2] He wrote:

'I heard lately that either in some fool's frolic, or from your dislike of the study of Greek, a clique had been formed among you, calling themselves Trojans, and that the object was to throw ridicule on the Greek language and literature. This action of yours is foolish in itself and gives an unpleasing impression of your general intelligence. I was sorry to hear that men of learning were making so poor a use of their leisure, but I had concluded that in a large number there would always be some block-heads, and that it was only a passing absurdity.

'I have been informed, however, on coming to this town of Abingdon, that folly has grown into madness, and that one of these Trojans, who thinks himself a genius, has been preaching a course of sermons during Lent, denouncing not Greek classics only, but Latin classics too, and all liberal education. A fool's speech comes out of a fool's head. . . . But for a scholar in gown and hood, in the midst of an academy which exists only for the sake of learning, so to rail at it is malicious ignorance. What right has he to denounce Latin, of which he knows little; Science, of which he knows less, or Greek, of which he knows nothing? He had better have confined himself to the seven deadly sins, with which perhaps he has closer acquaintance. Of course we know that a man can be saved without securing learning. Children learn from their mothers the essential truths of Christianity. But students are sent to Oxford to receive general instruction. They do not go there merely to learn theology. Some go to learn law, some to learn human nature from poets and orators and historians—forms of knowledge useful even to preachers, if their congregations are not to think them fools. Others again go to Universities to study natural science and philosophy and art: and this wonderful gentleman is to condemn the whole of it under one general sentence. He says that nothing is of importance except theology. How can he know theology if he is ignorant of Hebrew and Greek and Latin?

[1] *Letters and Papers,* ii, no. 4125, John Clerk to Wolsey, 28 Apr. 1518.
[2] Translated in Froude's *Life and Letters of Erasmus* (from Jortin, ii, Appendix viii), pp. 131–4. The translation is abridged here.

He thinks, I presume, that it can all be found in the scholastic conundrums. These, I admit, can be learned with no particular effort. But Theology, that august Queen of Heaven, demands an ampler scope. The knowledge of God can be gathered only out of Scripture—Scripture and the early Catholic Fathers. That was where for a thousand years the searchers after truth looked for it and found it, before these modern paradoxes were heard of; and if he fancies that Scripture and the Fathers can be understood without a knowledge of the languages in which the Fathers wrote, he will not find many to agree with him.

'He will pretend perhaps that he was not censuring learning itself, he was censuring only an excessive devotion to it. I do not see so great a disposition to sin in this direction that it needs to be checked by a sermon. He calls those who study Greek, heretics. The teachers of Greek, he says, are full-grown devils, the learners of Greek are little devils and he was aiming at a certain person whom I think the devil would be sorry to see in a pulpit. He did not name him, but everyone knew to whom he alluded.[1]

'It is not for me, illustrious masters, to defend Greek. You know yourselves that it needs no defence. The finest writings on all subjects, theology included, are in Greek. The Romans had no philosophers save Cicero and Seneca. The New Testament was written in Greek. Your wisdoms will acknowledge that not all Greek scholars are fools, and you will not allow the study of it to be put down by sermons or private cabals. Make these gentlemen understand that, unless they promptly cease from such factious doings, we outside will have a word to say about it. Every man who has been educated at your University has as much interest in its welfare as you who are now at its head. Your Primate and Chancellor[2] will not permit these studies to be meddled with, nor allow fools and sluggards to ridicule them from the pulpit. The Cardinal of York[3] will not endure it. The King's Majesty our Sovereign has himself more learning than any English monarch ever possessed before him. Think you that he, prudent and pious as he is, will look on passively when worthless blockheads are interrupting the course of sound instruction in the oldest University in the realm—a university which has produced men who have done honour to their country and the Church? With its colleges and its endowments there is nowhere in the world a place of education so richly furnished as Oxford; and the object of these foundations is to support students in the acquirement of knowledge. Your wisdoms therefore will find means to silence these foolish contentions. Useful learning, of whatever kind it be, shall be protected from ridicule and shall receive due honour and esteem. Be you diligent in so doing. Improve the quality of your own lectures and so deserve the thanks of your Prince, your Primate and the Cardinal.

'I have written thus out of the regard I feel for you. My own services you know that you can command if you need them. God keep you all in safety and increase you daily in learning and godliness of life.'

[1] Obviously Erasmus.       [2] William Warham, Archbishop of Canterbury.
[3] Thomas Wolsey, Archbishop of York.

This address, distinguished as it is by the force of its logic and its irony, has been accounted the finest example of More's composition in Latin prose. It may be that the eloquence of his defence of classical learning was heightened by a feeling of regret that his own path in life was leading him to desert the service of the mistress whose cause he yet earnestly upheld.

The attacks made on Erasmus with increasing venom by monks who resented his work on the New Testament and dreaded his criticisms of their own orders, were answered by More in another celebrated Latin epistle, his *Letter to a Monk*, which has been already cited. Indignantly he repudiated the calumnies aimed at his friend; eloquently he defended his work on behalf of Christian learning.

'You adjure me to beware of Erasmus!' he exclaimed. 'I am in danger, forsooth, because I consider Erasmus to have given a better rendering of passages in the New Testament than I find in the received translation. Where is the danger? May I not find pleasure in a work which the learned and pious admire, and which the Pope himself has twice approved? . . . You charge Erasmus with having said that Jerome, Ambrose, Augustine and other Fathers made occasional mistakes. Since the Fathers admit it themselves, why do you blame Erasmus? When Augustine translates one way, and Jerome another; they cannot both be right. . . . You complain of the study of Greek and Hebrew. You say it leads to the neglect of Latin. Was not the New Testament written in Greek? Did not the early Fathers write in Greek? Is truth only to be found in Gothic Latin? You will have no novelties; you say "the old is better". Of course it is; the wisdom of the Fathers is better than the babbling of you moderns. . . . As for the Vulgate, it was the best version or the first which the Church could get. When once in use it could not easily be changed, but to use it is not to approve of it as perfect.'

The letter goes on with scathing irony to rebuke those monks who trusted too much in ceremonies and observances.

'When Erasmus ridicules your ceremonies', More explains, 'he ridicules only the superstitious use of them. Do not your orders quarrel and abuse each other over the cut and colour of their gowns? Yet the same men who think the Devil will have them if they change the shape of their frocks, are not afraid to intrigue and lie. They strain at a gnat and swallow an entire elephant. They fancy themselves the holiest of men and yet commit the most abominable crimes. Flattery makes friends and truth makes enemies. Erasmus has written the truth and you abuse him. You call him a vagabond because he has moved from place to place to carry on his work. A saint, I suppose, must remain fixed like a sponge on an oyster! You forget your own mendicants. They wander wide enough, and you think them the holiest of mankind.'

In another passage of the letter, More urged the young monk to whom he wrote, to place his hopes rather in the Christian faith than in his own.

'Trust not in those things which you can do alone—such as fasting, vigil and prayer—but in those things which you cannot achieve without God. For Christian faith, which Christ Jesus said truly to be in spirit; Christian hope, which, despairing of its own merits, confides only in the mercy of God; Christian charity, which is not made angry, and does not seek its own glory; none can attain these except by the grace and favour of God alone. Trust then in those virtues, rather than in private ceremonies, and God will esteem you a faithful servant, when you count youself good for nothing.'[1]

More had to defend Erasmus and his work not only against the prejudices of the monastic orders, but even against his own friends. As he had written in amicable expostulation to Martin Dorp, so he engaged in the defence of Erasmus against the criticisms of Edward Lee, Dean of Colchester and afterwards Archbishop of York. It was inevitable that the reforms advocated by Erasmus should be confused with the vehement attack made by Luther against ecclesiastical abuses, though the moderation of the one and the violence of the other precluded any union between them. Erasmus was accused of 'laying the egg which Luther hatched', and Lee, who had given some attention to Biblical study, published some unfavourable comments on the *Annotations on the New Testament* by Erasmus, even going so far as to denounce him for a heretic. Erasmus was deeply hurt by the attack, and More had great difficulty in composing the differences between his two friends, and in persuading them for a time to sheathe their hostile pens. He lamented that his influence with both combatants was only great enough to persuade them to make a truce, but not to maintain peace. He urged Erasmus not to retaliate against the ill-founded criticisms of Lee, but in a Christ-like spirit to render blessings for curses.[2] He remonstrated with Lee, saying: 'If the Pope should withdraw his approval of the *New Testament* of Erasmus, Luther's attacks on the Holy See would be piety itself compared with such an act!'[3]

Some pamphlets by Lee directed against Erasmus were published in Paris, and the writer feared that he might lose thereby the favour of More, his old and valued friend, but More, while deploring the controversy, replied:

'You ask me, my dear Lee, not to lessen my affection for you in any

[1] More's *Letter to a Monk* (abridged). The letter is translated in Froude's *Life and Letters of Erasmus*, pp. 135–9, and a considerable part of it in Bridgett's *Life of More*, pp. 94–8.
[2] More to Erasmus, Apr. 1520, Allen, iv, no. 1090.
[3] *Letters and Papers*, iii, no. 640, Feb. 1520.

way. Trust me, good Lee, I shall not. Although in this case my sympathies are with the party which you are attacking, yet I trust that you
will withdraw your troops from the siege with perfect safety. I shall ever
love you and I am proud to find that my love is so highly valued by you.'[1]

While More was endeavouring to compose the differences
between Erasmus and Lee, Erasmus was engaged upon an
attempt to check a vigorous literary quarrel waged by More with
the French poet Germain de Brie.

De Brie, or Brixius, had celebrated in verse the exploits of a
French ship, the *Cordelière* (Chordigera), in the war of 1512,
making some disparaging allusions to the English. More, in
patriotic mood, composed some Latin *Epigramma* in reply, and
drew the fire of Brixius upon himself, in the form of a sarcastic
poem called *Antimorus*. With less than his usual equanimity,
More showed himself to be sorely piqued by the criticisms it
contained. He addressed to Erasmus a long and tedious com-
plaint, in which he accused Brixius of 'pouring out abuse such as
a drunken old woman might have babbled'. After writing thirty
pages in his own defence—an unexpected example of literary
vanity—he excused himself by observing that he would not have
thought such insane writings as those of Brixius worthy of reply,
had not his friends advised him to defend himself against these
absurd accusations.[2] Erasmus, who esteemed de Brie, as he said,
'on account of the attitude he exhibits in his writings both towards
sound learning and towards myself', deplored the tragic quarrel
between two followers of his beloved learning. 'I do not see how
this can survive', he lamented, 'unless the body of scholars, their
ranks joined shield to shield, defends it against the stubborn
attacks of the barbarians. . . . I am moved in this desire, not so
much on account of Brixius whom I do esteem highly, but rather
for your sake my More, whom I value still more highly.' He
urged More not to injure his own reputation by making a reply
unworthy of his dignity and learning, and answering insult with
insult, 'a thing so difficult to avoid when the pen grows hot'.
'Not the least part of your reputation', he continued, 'is due to
the gentleness of your character and the sweetness of your
manners, and I would wish nothing of it to be lost. I beg you to
make allowances, and not to make ill-tempered and provocative
accusations, but to fight with reason, not bitterness. Nevertheless I would much prefer you to keep silence, so that the whole
affair may be forgotten.'[3] To Brixius, Erasmus wrote in the same

[1] Stapleton (Hallett's ed.), p. 47.
[2] Greenwich, Mar.–Apr. 1520, Allen, iv, no. 1087.
[3] Erasmus to More (abridged), Antwerp, 26 Apr. 1520, Allen, iv, no. 1093.
The reference is to Juvenal, ii.

strain, but far more strongly, impressing upon him the futility of attacking so distinguished a writer as More, who was unlikely to be injured by his insults.[1] He enlisted the help of other friends also, in calming the unedifying quarrel, which gradually died away.

[1] Antwerp, 25 June 1520, Allen, iv, no. 1117.

# CHAPTER XI

## LIFE AT COURT

### 1518–1521

EVEN in the 'splendid misery of a Court', life held much happiness for More. He had a great capacity for enjoyment, he was surrounded by some of his closest friends, the ablest men of their age. He took pleasure in the society of foreign diplomatists, and for their part, they found him both likeable and learned. His gifts as an orator were brought into use in many a Latin speech of welcome on the arrival of distinguished foreign visitors and envoys; he was one of the 'noble, sage, and wise personages' whom the King specially desired to have about him, 'to receive strangers that should chance to come'.[1]

He expressed himself as 'quite charmed' with the Venetian ambassador, Sebastien Giustiniani, who described More as 'most sage and virtuous and the most linked with me in friendship of any in this kingdom'. The ambassador's secretary, Sagudino, was devoted to More, whose wit and eloquence, he declared, were remarkable.[2]

The claims of public service naturally were detrimental to More's private practice at the Bar; he found it necessary to accept, as councillor, a grant from the Crown of one hundred pounds a year,[3] which he had previously declined, and in the summer of 1518—not without regret—he resigned the post of Under-Sheriff of London, lest his duty to the King should conflict with his obligations to the City.

It is difficult to know how far he was made acquainted with the secrets of foreign policy. As time went on, it seems that his discretion was relied upon to a great extent, though, by the King's command, the intricate details of Wolsey's diplomacy were withheld from the knowledge of the council.[4] The Cardinal sometimes knew more of foreign negotiations than the King himself; foreign ambassadors arriving at Court greeted him before the King, so great was his authority.[5]

Wolsey used the utmost skill to prevent too close a union between the great powers of the Continent. After the passing of the old sovereigns—Ferdinand of Spain, Louis XII, and the

---

[1] *Letters and Papers*, iii, no. 2317, Sampson to Wolsey, 4 June 1522.
[2] *Four years at the Court of Henry VIII*. A selection of the dispatches of Giustiniani, edited by Rawdon Brown (1854), ii, p. 162. Cf. also Allen, ii, no. 461.
[3] See note, p. 92 *supra*.          [4] Brewer, op. cit., i. 195.
[5] *Cal. of State Papers*, Venetian, iv, no. 694.

Emperor Maximilian—the hegemony of Europe was shared by three young monarchs: Henry VIII of England, Francis I of France, and Charles of Spain, who was elected Emperor as Charles V in 1519. All were jealous and suspicious of one another, and from this time onwards 'the political history of Europe is little more than the combinations of these monarchs to prevent any one of their number from rising to a dangerous superiority'.[1]

It was owing to Wolsey's genius for diplomacy, his marvellous command of detail, and his exclusive devotion to the King, that Henry was enabled to play so important a part in continental politics.

In Wolsey's hands were gathered all the threads of an enormous correspondence with the chief powers of Europe—the Papal See, the Emperor, the Lady Margaret, Regent in the Netherlands, the King of France, the Republic of Venice, the Queen of Scots. Many of the letters passed through the hands of More, but the control of all the intricate negotiations was reserved for the Cardinal and the King.

Pace, the ablest of the royal secretaries, was frequently sent as ambassador abroad, and in his absence More acted in his place. Wolsey would 'command' More to his house at eight in the morning to receive instructions, with dispatches from abroad, to convey to the Court. It was one of his duties to read aloud to the King letters from the Cardinal, and to explain, *viva voce*, Wolsey's views. The King would indicate the substance of the replies, which were then drafted by More, and were 'read and reformed' by the King himself before being dispatched.[2]

In this way More must have become acquainted with many matters of State and of diplomacy; with scrupulous fidelity he fulfilled the duties of a highly trusted secretary. It was evident that he stood high in the King's favour, but it does not appear that his advice was either sought or given in any question of national policy. When once, after several years of service, he ventured to offer an opinion on a problem of maintaining commerce with the Flemings—a matter well within his knowledge— the King checked him impatiently, and More reported to Wolsey: 'When I was about to have showed his Highness somewhat of my poor mind in the matter, he said this gear could not be done so suddenly, but that his Grace and yours shall speak together first.'[3]

There seems to be little ground for the supposition that More's

---

[1] Brewer, op. cit., i. 151.

[2] *State Papers, Henry VIII*, i, part i, no. LXXV (1523), p. 140; also given by Ellis, *Original letters* (2nd ed. 1825), i. 195 note, and i. 253 (More to Wolsey).

[3] *State Papers, Henry VIII*, i, part i, no. CXL (1528), p. 286; and Sir Henry Ellis, *Original Letters*, i. 302, letter xcviii.

advice was specially responsible for Wolsey's efforts to enforce the Statutes against unauthorized enclosures of land;[1] he had indeed, in *Utopia*, made a most eloquent arraignment of the agrarian revolution, but he was not alone in his plea on behalf of the poor labourers; the problem was acknowledged to be one of national importance, but many interests were involved, and the movement was too strong to be arrested by legislation.

There is equally slight reason for the surmise that the rendition of Tournai to the French was due to More's influence, which had little effect in checking Henry's ambitious policy. A superior argument was supplied by the offer of half a million crowns from the French government.

On the other hand, his indirect influence was not inconsiderable in tempering royal severity. It is recorded, for example, that when he was told to devise a sharp letter to the Earl of Arundel, characteristically, he 'thought it better to send him a loving letter first'.[2]

An echo of Utopian teaching may be heard in Henry's words to Giustiniani, concerning the aggressions of Francis I.

'I am King of this Island and I am perfectly satisfied. Yet it seems to me I do not do my duty thoroughly nor govern my subjects well, and if I could have greater dominion—nay, upon my oath, if I could be lord of the world I would not, as I know I could not do my duty, and that for my omissions, God will call me into judgment.'[3]

But these exemplary reflections did not preclude from Henry's mind the ambition to reconquer the kingdom of France.

In 1518, however, Wolsey's thoughts were directed towards an alliance with France. French commissioners were sent to England in the summer; the King entrusted everything to Wolsey and negotiations were kept profoundly secret from every one besides. The project of a betrothal between the infant Dauphin and Henry's daughter Mary—a child two years old—was, however, suspected. The Venetian ambassador, bewildered by inconsistent statements, and anxious to discover the truth, rode over to Eltham one day in September, but failed to elicit any information from the King. He then contrived a conference with Thomas More, 'newly made councillor and attending on the King as one of his secretaries'. He reported to his government:

'I adroitly turned the conversation to those negotiations concerning peace and marriage, but More did not open, and pretended not to know in what the difficulties consisted, declaring that the Cardinal of York

---

[1] Bridgett (*Life of More*), p. 179, says, however, 'There is no doubt these measures were taken at his suggestion'.
[2] *Letters and Papers*, iii, no. 2636, Oct. 1522.        [3] Brewer, op. cit., i. 193.

most solely transacted this matter with the French ambassador, and
when he has concluded, he then calls the counsellors, so that the King
himself scarcely knows in what state matters are.'[1]

Triumph crowned the diplomacy of Wolsey, 'the arbiter of
Europe'. Early in October a treaty of 'Universal Peace' was
signed in London, followed by treaties arranging for the cession of
Tournai, the settlement of maritime disputes, and the marriage
of the Princess Mary to the Dauphin. The betrothal ceremonies
were celebrated at Greenwich with the most extravagant festivi-
ties, though a few months later, Henry offered to bestow his
daughter's hand on Charles of Spain, with a cool disregard of
the French engagement.

More was frequently employed in drafting treaties on behalf
of the English government. With Ruthall, Tunstall, and Pace,
he drew up the articles of an agreement between Henry VIII and
Charles—now elected Emperor—concluded in London on the
11th of April 1520, and ratified on the 8th of May, by which an
interview between the two monarchs was arranged.[2] Later in
May, More was at Canterbury with the King when the Emperor
arrived on his promised visit to England, and he noted the delight
with which Charles was welcomed by the English court and by the
people.[3] It was an indication of the unpopularity of alliance with
France; yet at that very time Henry was on his way to meet the
French king, Francis I, with protestations of undying friendship,
amidst the gorgeous pageantry of the 'Field of the Cloth of Gold'.[4]

More crossed the Channel in the King's train, but in those
brilliant scenes of insincerity he had no special part. While the
kings of France and England rivalled each other in splendid display and unscrupulous intrigue, More was appointed to his usual
prosaic task of bargaining with foreign merchants on questions
concerning trade.

On the 10th of June, with others, he was commissioned to settle
disputes with envoys from the Teutonic Hanse.[5] Their work continued at Bruges, while Henry again met the Emperor Charles at
Gravelines and Calais in order to settle the terms of a defensive
alliance to the disadvantage of France.[6] 'From the Field of the

[1] *Letters and Papers*, ii, no. 4438, Giustiniani to the Doge, 18 Sept. 1518;
and *Cal. of State Papers*, Venetian, ii, no. 1072.

[2] *Letters and Papers*, iii, no. 798.

[3] Ibid., no. 838, More to Erasmus, 26 May 1520.

[4] Ibid., no. 869, 11 June 1520. An account of proceedings at the 'Field of
the Cloth of Gold'.

[5] Ibid., no. 868, Calais, 10 June 1520; a commission given to Will: Knight,
John Husee [Hussey], Thomas More, and John Hewster, Governor of the
Company of English Merchants.

[6] Ibid., nos. 903, 906, 914; Brewer, op. cit., i. 356 (July 1520).

Cloth of Gold', writes Dr. Brewer, 'where he and his French ally had met as brothers in arms, and to all outward appearance brothers in affection, Henry retired to meet the Emperor at Calais, to betray and sacrifice to a new alliance the monarch whose hospitality he had accepted and returned.'[1]

More's former colleague, Richard Sampson, joined the commissioners at Bruges, where they were still engaged in September, and, as usual in these missions, were running short of money.[2] The business appears to have been conducted to the satisfaction of Wolsey and the King, and it afforded to More the long-looked-for opportunity of a meeting with Erasmus.

More continued to advance in the royal favour. On the 2nd of May 1521, without any request of his own, he was given the post of Under-Treasurer, with the usual large salary of £173 6s. 8d. per annum, in succession to Sir John Cutte, who died on the 4th of April 1521.[3] The Under-Treasurer was customarily a knight, and the date of More's knighthood, which has been the subject of some discussion, may no doubt be assigned to this time.

His new office has been described as a post corresponding in

[1] Brewer, op. cit., i. 415.　　[2] *Letters and Papers*, iii, no. 979, 15 Sept. 1520.
[3] Chancery inquisition post-mortem, c. 142, vol. 36, P.R.O. Roper (p. 13) says: 'Then died one Master Weston, treasurer of the Exchequer, whose office, after his death, the king of his own offer, without any asking, freely gave unto Sir Thomas More.' Researches lately made in the Public Record Office by Miss C. Jamison, prove conclusively, however, that More followed Sir John Cutte in this office a month after Cutte's death. She has discovered in the records of the Treasury of Receipt a rough entry book of daily receipts by the Tellers (E 405, no. 480), with the following note against an entry of the payment, on 26 October 13 Hen. VIII (1521), by the collectors of the subsidy in the Port of London, of £71 14. 6:
'For Sir Thomas More, Knight, Sub-Treasurer of England, of a certain payment, a year, *pro rata* for the time, at £173. 6. 8. per annum owed from 2nd May, 13th year, until the feast of Michaelmas next following for 151 days by the hands of Thomas Elrington' (translated).
This fixes the date of More's appointment as Sub-Treasurer, though he does not appear to have taken up his duties at the Treasury until Michaelmas. Sir John Cutte held the office from very early in the reign until his death on 4 Apr. 1521. Miss Jamison suggests that More may have succeeded Sir Richard Weston in the Court of Requests in 1518, and that Roper confused the two appointments. The names of councillors sitting in the Court are not given in the *Decrees and Orders* after Mich. term 7. Hen. VIII (1515). Weston, however, may have left the Court, as he was a much occupied man, and also went abroad in 1519.
The Declaration of the State of the Treasury, Mich. 1520 to Mich. 1521, was made in the name of Sir John Cutte (E 405, no. 192, P.R.O.). The Declaration for the year Mich. 1521 to Mich. 1522 is missing. The Declaration for the year Mich. 1522 to Mich. 1523 is accounted for by Sir Thomas More (E 405, no. 193). The last payment of his fee as Sub-Treasurer was made up to 24 Jan. 1525/6, when Sir William Compton assumed office. Sir Richard Weston succeeded Compton in 1528.
More's salary as Sub-Treasurer and as Councillor was charged on the Customs, the safest of the King's revenues, being paid directly into the Treasury of Receipt.

some respects with that of Chancellor of the Exchequer. The exchequer officials had to deal with the receipt and issue of the royal revenues, which were regarded as the King's personal property.[1] They had the custody of the records, the treasure, and the Great Seal, which were kept in the Royal Treasury at Westminster.[2] The duties of the Under-Treasurer (originally a clerk) were delegated to him by the Lord High Treasurer, an office at this time held by the Duke of Norfolk.[3] More was frequently engaged at the Exchequer, in financial business, or in making research among the records kept there, which included accounts, diplomatic treaties, and State Papers dealing with Ireland, Scotland, and France.[4]

It was the duty of the Under-Treasurer to make to the King each year a Declaration of the State of the Office of Treasurer, giving an account of the receipts of the customs and similar sources of income; receipts from farmers of lands in the hands of the King; allowances made to customs officials and sheriffs for expenses incurred, &c., and the payment of annuities and fees to various court officials. Besides this, the Under-Treasurer was responsible for the arrangements for council meetings, and for receiving recurring payments for the expenses of the lords and other magnates attending the council. Wolsey one day apologized to the King because 'Sir Thomas More could not be spared from the Exchequer for four or five days in consequence of great matters at the knitting up of this term'.[5]

More's promotion, Erasmus thought, might have been more rapid still had he cared to press his claims and to spend less time in his own home. Unmarried men were more readily advanced, but More was 'so mixed up with marriage that nothing could disentangle him from its delights'.[6]

The King valued him even more as an agreeable companion than as a painstaking official; Roper relates that:

'The King used upon Holy Days, when he had done his own devotions, to send for him into his traverse, and there sometimes in matters of astronomy, geometry, divinity and such other faculties, and sometimes of his worldly affairs, to sit and confer with him. And other whiles

[1] Cf. A. F. Pollard, 'The Council Under the Tudors' (*Eng. Hist. Review*, xxxvii (1922).

[2] Hubert Hall, F.S.A., *Antiquities of the Exchequer* (Camden Library, 1891).

[3] Norfolk resigned the office in Dec. 1522, when it was conferred upon his son, Thomas, Earl of Surrey, who succeeded to the dukedom in May 1524.

[4] H. Hall, op. cit., pp. 35, 60, 61. *Letters and Papers*, iii, nos. 1709, 1774; iv, no. 345.

[5] Ibid., iii, no. 3563, and *State Papers, Henry VIII*, i, pt. i, p. 146, 26 Nov. 1523.

[6] Erasmus to Budé, 1 Sept. 1521, Allen, iv, no. 1233.

would he in the night have him up into his leads [on the roof] there to
consider with him the diversities, courses, motions and other operations
of the stars and planets. And because he was of a pleasant disposition,
it pleased the King and Queen, after the council had supped, at the time
of their supper, for their pleasure commonly to call for him to be merry
with them. Whom when he perceived so much in his talk to delight,
that he could not once in a month get leave to go home to his wife and
children, whose company he most desired, and to be absent from the
Court two days together but that he should be thither sent for again:
he much misliking this distraint of liberty, began thereupon somewhat
to dissemble his nature, and so little by little, from his accustomed
mirth to disuse himself, that he was of them from thenceforth at such
seasons no more so ordinarily sent for.'[1]

It is a pleasant picture of More, struggling to be stolid and dull,
while the expectant Sovereigns sit at supper waiting to be amused!

Nothing is more difficult to transcribe than the flashes of wit
or humour that pass in talk, and owe as much to the manner as
to the substance of their saying. More, with a perfectly serious
face, could keep an audience in continual laughter with his ready
repartee and amusing tales, but the irresistible drollery which, on
ample testimony, gave them added point, can be better imagined
than described.

The incidents best remembered by his hearers were related to
a play upon his own name. On one occasion a member of the
Manners family said to him rather truculently: '*Honores mutant
Mores*.' More instantly replied, 'after his merry fashion': 'True
indeed, my lord, but *Mores* in English is not *More*, but *Manners*.'
On another occasion, More having requested a debtor to repay
what he owed, the man reminded him that he should die, 'God
knoweth how soon, and then he would have little use for money';
adding 'Memento morieris!' 'Of course you mean', replied More,
'Memento Mori aeris—remember More's money—to remind yourself of your obligation to me!'[2]

There were critics who objected that 'he was too much given to
mocking, which was to his gravity a great blemish'.[3] It should be
said, however, that there was nearly always a moral to his 'merry
tales'. If excuse be needed, it may be found in his own words in
his *Dialogue of Comfort*. He confesses that the habit of jesting
is a fault, and says:

'of truth, myself am of nature even half a gigglot and more. I would
I could as easily mend my fault as I well know it, but scant can I refrain
it as old a fool as I am: howbeit, so partial will I not be to my fault

[1] Roper, p. 12.
[2] Cresacre More, op. cit., pp. 190–1.
[3] Hall's *Chronicle* (1809), p. 761.

as to praise it. But for that you require my mind in the matter, whether men in tribulation may not lawfully seek recreation and comfort themself with some honest mirth, first agreed that our chief comfort must be in God, and that with him we must begin and with him continue and with him end also. A man to take now and then some honest worldly mirth, I dare not be so sore as utterly to forbid it, sith good men and well learned, have in some case allowed it, specially for the diversity of divers mens minds . . . he that cannot long endure to hold up his head and hear talking of heaven, except he be now and then between (as though heaven were heaviness) refreshed with a merry foolish tale, there is none other remedy but you must let him have it: better would I wish it but I cannot help it.'[1]

The passage is illustrated by an anecdote from Cassianus, of a preacher who, while discoursing of heavenly things, perceived that his audience was peacefully falling asleep. Suddenly he said: 'I will tell you a merry tale'. Thereupon the whole congregation sat up and began to listen; 'they lift up their heads and hearkened unto that, and after the sleep therewith broken, heard him tell on of heaven again'.

[1] More's *English Works* (1557), p. 1171. (*Second book of Comfort Against Tribulation.*)

# CHAPTER XII

# DIPLOMACY

## 1521–1523

IN spite of his desire to remain at home, More was unable to evade another mission to Bruges in July 1521, to attend a conference on mercantile disputes.[1] After his arrival he was directed to join Wolsey, who landed again at Calais on the 2nd of August.

Pace, writing from Windsor, said to Wolsey just before his departure:

'The King signifieth your Grace that whereas old men do now decay greatly within this his realm, his mind is to acquaint other, young men, with his great affairs, and therefore he desireth your Grace to make Sir William Sandys and Sir Thomas More privy to all such matters as your Grace shall treat at Calais.'[2]

Wolsey's ostensible business in France on this occasion was to compose the differences between Charles V and Francis I; his real object—quite contrary to this pretence—was to prevent a union between them. The two monarchs had accepted his mediation, though they could hardly have credited the sincerity of the mediator, for no one was more experienced than they in the uses of deceit in diplomacy. Wolsey's whole thought was directed to the delicate adjustment of England's relations with the French and Imperial powers. To balance one against the other, to prevent the predominance of either over the Papal power in Italy, to keep them from too close a union with each other, and from their differences to obtain the advantage of Henry VIII and the security of England—these were the objects to which he devoted a mind of exceptional ability and a remarkable capacity for intrigue. He took with him commissions empowering him to settle the differences between Francis I and Charles V; to conclude a marriage treaty between Charles and Princess Mary, and to arrange a secret league between Henry VIII and Charles with the object of carrying war into France and 'recovering the King's dominions'.

By another set of commissions, he was authorized to treat of a closer amity with Francis, and if need be, to make a general confederation of all the great powers of Christendom.[3]

---

[1] *Letters and Papers*, iii, no. 1775; his allowance was 20s. a day.
[2] Ibid., no. iii. 1437 and *State Papers, Henry VIII*, i, pt. i, p. 20, 24 July 1521.
[3] *Letters and Papers*, iii, nos. 1340, 1383, 1443. Cf. Fisher, op. cit., pp. 231–2,

The Imperial and French ambassadors, the Papal nuncios, the Venetian envoys to London and to the Imperial court, all gathered at Calais, eagerly awaiting the pleasure of the Cardinal. From Calais Wolsey rode to Bruges to meet the Emperor Charles, followed by a crowd of anxious diplomatists. For an hour and a half he kept the Emperor with his whole court waiting outside the gates of Bruges: when they met, he remained seated on his mule, receiving him as an equal.

Rumours flew about concerning the negotiations between Cardinal and Emperor; the Papal nuncios and the Venetians knocked in vain at Wolsey's door and failed to gain an audience. Very different was their experience with More, whose charming courtesy won their liking, though his unalterable discretion gave them no information of the Cardinal's proceedings. The Venetian envoy, Contarini, reported to the Signory:

'On coming away from the Mass, I invited an English gentleman, by name Master Thomas More, a very learned man, to dine with me. He had accompanied Wolsey to Bruges. During dinner we discussed the business negotiated with the Emperor, but More did not drop the slightest hint of any other treaty than that of peace between the King of France and his Imperial Majesty.'[1]

Wolsey was the King's representative, and his arrogance was calculated to impress upon foreigners the magnificence of his master; More, in a humbler position, exercised his usual unaffected friendliness. He was not ignorant of ceremonious usages, but found them tedious and trivial, and dispensed with them when he could do so without giving offence. Continental diplomatists sometimes would have preferred to treat with More, but it was observed that Wolsey 'chose to do everything himself'.[2]

Negotiations were prolonged through the autumn, until an agreement was signed by the Cardinal and the Emperor on the 24th of November. Before this, Wolsey had allowed More to return home with a confidential verbal report and a commendatory letter to the King. On the 14th of October he wrote that he was sending

'urgent causes and considerations, too long and tedious for your Grace to read if they were committed to writing, which I have declared by word of mouth to your right trusty councillors Sir Thomas More and Sir William Fitzwilliam; to the which your councillors it may like your Grace not only to give firm credence in, but also to give unto them your

and Brewer, op. cit., i. 419. Dr. A. F. Pollard's *Wolsey* throws a new light on Wolsey's foreign policy.

[1] *Cal. of State Papers*, Venetian, iii, no. 302. Contarini's report, 19 Aug. 1521.
[2] Ibid., iii, no. 899. Contarini to the Signory, 1 Dec. 1524.

gracious thanks for such their laudable acquittal and diligent attendance
as they have done and taken in this journey for the advancement of
your honour and contentation of your pleasure.'[1]

Wolsey returned to receive the hearty thanks of the King for
his diplomatic success, and More was rewarded a few months later
by a grant of the Manor of South in Kent, .which came into the
King's hands by the attainder and execution of the Duke of
Buckingham.[2]

In May 1522 the Emperor again visited the English Court to
cement the alliance, and More was among the officials appointed
to attend the King when he rode to meet his guest at Canterbury.
When Charles V was welcomed to the City of London on the 6th of
June, More made the oration to the Emperor and the King, 'in
praise of the two princes and of the peace and love between them,
and what comfort it was to their subjects to see them in such
amity'.

Many 'pageants' were devised for the Emperor's diversion,
and More's imaginative brother-in-law, John Rastell, surpassed
himself in designing a remarkable show near his printing-house by
Paul's Gate, where he built 'a place like Heaven, curiously
painted with clouds, orbs, stars and the hierarchies of angels'.
In the top of the pageant 'suddenly issued out of a cloud a fair
lady richly appareled, and then all the minstrels which were in
the pageant played and the angels sang, and suddenly again she
was assumpted into the cloud which was very curiously done, and
about this pageant stood the Apostles'.[3]

The alliance with the Emperor led to the declaration of war by
Henry against France; the King hinted to More that he aspired
to be the 'Governor' of France, 'if room were made for him as it
was made for his father by King Richard'. More heard him with
silent misgiving, but only ventured to say to Wolsey: 'I pray
God, if it be good for his Grace and for this realm, that then it
may prove so, and else in the stead thereof I pray God send his
Grace an honourable and profitable peace.'[4]

Though his missions abroad were not much to his liking, More
found compensation, as usual, in his friendships. More than once
he had the valued companionship of Tunstall, and the happiness
—eagerly look for by both friends—of a meeting with Erasmus,
who delighted in the opportunity of drawing him once again into
the scholarly circle to which in spirit he belonged.

[1] *State Papers, Henry VIII*, i, pt. i, no. xliv. Sir William Fitzwilliam was
ambassador to France; created Earl of Southampton 1537; died 1542 (*D.N.B.*).
[2] *Letters and Papers*, iii, no. 2239, 8 May 1522.
[3] Hall's *Chronicle* (1809), pp. 637–40. For Rastell, cf. Reed, *Early Tudor
Drama*, p. 17.            [4] *Letters and Papers*, iii, no. 2555, 21 Sept. 1522.

After the publication of *Utopia*, a friendly correspondence had passed between More and Guillaume Budé, one of the greatest and most broad-minded scholars of his age, whose works on philosophy, philology, and jurisprudence displayed extensive learning. More had praised Budé's great work on ancient coinage, and had sent him complimentary presents in return for his preface to *Utopia*. Budé expressed himself delighted with More's praise, and wished for another of his witty letters. In a Greek play upon words he declared that More should have been called *Oxymorus*, on account of his pointed wit.[1] He was deeply interested in *Utopia* and announced his intention of following More's example by cultivating an Utopian intimacy with his own wife and children. Though he wrote in denunciation of private property, he by no means practised Utopian simplicity in his own life, for the Spanish scholar Vives—another friend of More—was 'dazzled' by the magnificence of his establishment in Paris. Budé was summoned to attend the French King at the Field of the Cloth of Gold in June 1520, and here he met More for the first time, when the usual lavish compliments were exchanged between them. More wrote afterwards:

'I doubt, my dear Budé, whether it is advisable ever to possess what we dearly love unless we can retain possession of it. For I used to think that I would be perfectly happy if it should once be my lot to see Budé face to face, of whom by reading I had created a beautiful image in my mind. When at last my wish was fulfilled, I was happier than happiness itself. But, alas! our duties prevented our meeting often enough to satisfy my desire of conversing with you, and within a few days, as our kings were obliged by affairs of state to separate, our intercourse was broken off when it had scarce begun; and as each of us had to follow his own prince, we were torn apart, perhaps never to see each other again. My sorrow at having to leave you can only be compared to my joy at meeting you. . . .'[2]

More bestowed unstinted though not indiscriminating praise upon Budé's *De Asse et Partibus ejus*, to which he gave very special attention. He wrote to Budé:

'If anyone will turn his eyes to what you have written and give it careful and continued attention, he will find that the light you have thrown upon your subject brings the dead past to life again. Whilst he ponders your words, he will live in imagination through all the past ages, and will be able to gaze upon, to count, and almost to take into his hands, the hoarded wealth of all kings, all tyrants and all nations, which is more than any misers have been able to do.'[3]

---

[1] *Letters and Papers*, ii, no. 4421; iii, no. 413.
[2] Stapleton (Hallett's ed.), pp. 51–2.
[3] Ibid., p. 52 (both letters abridged).

Later on, there was a suggestion of the publication of some of More's letters in a volume of Budé's correspondence, after the fashion of the day, but, on thinking over the matter, he wrote to Budé:

'It would be safer if you would wait awhile, at least until I revise my letters. It is not only that I fear there may be passages where the Latin is faulty, but also in my remarks upon peace and war, upon morality, marriage, the clergy, the people, &c., perhaps what I have written has not always been so cautious and guarded that it would be wise to expose it to captious critics.'[1]

The author of *Utopia* was learning to be prudent as a minister of State.

Some of More's letters were published with those of another friend, Francis Cranefeld, a Councillor of the Emperor, who expressed the warmest gratitude to Erasmus for giving him an introduction to More.

'I cannot refrain from thanking you', wrote Cranefeld to Erasmus, 'for the benefit you have lately conferred upon me, which I value so highly that I would not exchange it for all the wealth of Croesus. "What benefit?" you ask. For introducing me to More, your most dear friend, or, as I may now call him, our friend. At his invitation, I visited him often after your departure, not so much to enjoy his more than Sybaritic banquets, as his learning, his urbanity and his generosity. . . . More has sent for my wife a gold ring on which is written in English "Good will gives value to all things". To me he has given ancient coins, one of gold and one of silver, the one having the effigy of Tiberius, the other of Augustus. I wanted to tell you this, for I will ever acknowledge that to you also I owe gratitude for all these benefits.'[2]

More's friendship with Cranefeld continued by correspondence after his return to England. He wrote in thanks for several letters:

'My dear Cranefeld, I realize and acknowledge my debt to you. You continue to do what is to me more pleasant than anything else, i.e. writing to me of your affairs and your friends. . . . As often as I read what you have written, I seem to myself to be conversing with you face to face. Thus my greatest grief is that your letters are not longer, although even for this I have found some sort of a remedy. For I read them very often and very slowly, so that rapid reading may not too soon deprive me of my pleasure.

'As to what you write about our friend Vives—I refer to the discussion about ill-tempered wives—I am so far of your opinion that I do not think it possible to live, even with the best of wives, without some discomfort. "If anyone is married he will not be free from care", says

---

[1] Ibid., p. 86.  [2] Ibid., p. 58 (slightly abridged).

Metellus Numidicus, and rightly, in my opinion. This I would say with all the more confidence were it not that generally we make our wives worse by our own fault. But Vives is of such wit and prudence, and has such an excellent wife, that he can not only escape all the troubles of married life as far as that is possible, but can even find great enjoyment therein.

'But the minds of all are so fully occupied with public affairs, now that war begins everywhere to rage so fiercely, that no one has leisure to attend to domestic cares. If hitherto a man has had family troubles, they are now quite forgotten in the general calamity. But enough of this.

'My thoughts come back to you, for as often as I call to mind your courtesy and love towards me, as I do very often, all my griefs vanish. I thank you for the pamphlet which you sent me. I offer you my hearty congratulations on the increase in your family, not only for your own sake, but also for the sake of your country, to which it is a matter of the greatest concern that parents, by large families, should increase the population. None but children of highest excellence can spring from such a father as you. Farewell, and give to your good wife my affectionate regards. Tell her I offer my heartfelt prayers for her health and prosperity. My wife and children send you their best wishes, for, from what I have told them, they have become as well acquainted with you and as fond of you as I am myself. Once more, good bye.'[1]

Jean Luis Vives of Valencia, who is spoken of in the foregoing letter, came to England with the encouragement of Wolsey in 1523, and spent some time at the royal Court.[2] He was appointed tutor to the Princess Mary, and also became a lecturer at Oxford. One of the foremost educationists of the day, he had many interests in common with More, who, long before knowing him personally, had been an admirer of his books. When he first read the works of Vives, More wrote to Erasmus:

'It makes me ashamed, my dear Erasmus, of the output of myself and others like me, who have published one or two little books—often of little value—when I realize that Vives, still so young, has published so many, of such length, of such elegance of style and of such abstruse reading. It is a great thing to be proficient in one or other language; he proves himself expert in both. It is an even greater and more profitable thing to be trained in many branches of learning, and who has shown himself to be learned in more and better ones than Vives? And it is the greatest thing of all so to have absorbed the liberal arts of learning, that you can teach them to others; and who can teach more clearly, pleasantly and successfully than he?. . .

'He presents the events of past ages so vividly that he seems to have drawn what he declaims, not from books, but almost to have been present at the events. . . . Even if he excelled so greatly in one part only, he would

[1] London, 10 Aug. 1524, Stapleton (Hallett's ed.), pp. 60–1.
[2] Cf. *Vives and the Renascence Education of Women*, edited by Foster Watson, D.Lit. (London, 1912), in Arnold's *Educational Classics*.

still be worthy of admiration, but he proves himself so great in both that you might think he changed colour like a chameleon against the background!'[1]

More was particularly delighted with the writings of Vives against the 'stupid subtleties' of scholasticism, and in his *Pseudialectiones* recognized arguments which he himself had put forward independently. In 1522 Vives edited St. Augustine's *de Civitate Dei*—the subject of More's early studies—which he dedicated to Henry VIII. He was favoured by Queen Catherine, whose compatriot he was, and dedicated to her his treatise *de Institutione Foeminae Christianae*. When he came to the English Court he 'often experienced the fruits of More's benevolence', and became interested in the educational work carried on in More's home. It was Richard Hyrde, a young tutor to More's children, who translated into English this treatise of Vives, under the title of *The Instruction of a Christian Woman*. More had been requested by the Queen to undertake this translation himself, but being too much occupied he relinquished the task to Hyrde, who said that, having made the translation, he

'shewed it unto my singular good master and bringer up, Sir Thomas More, to whose judgment and correction I use to submit whatsoever I do or go about that I set any store by. . . . I besought him to take the labour to read it over and correct it, which he right gladly did . . . if anything be well in this translation, thanks be to the labour of my good master.'[2]

It would make too long a list to enumerate here all the foreigners with whom More is known to have had relations, chiefly through the agency of Erasmus. The capacity of both for making and keeping friends seems to have been unlimited, and Erasmus possessed the rare faculty of causing his friends to become friends of each other. He wrote to More on this subject:

'This disposition of yours I commend most highly, that nothing gives you greater pleasure than to become rich in faithful and sincere friends; in this you find the chief pleasure of this life. While others take the greatest care not to be deceived by false gems, you despise that kind of wealth, but feel yourself rich if you can add to your possessions a friend in no wise counterfeit. Games of chance, hunting, or music give no more pleasure to others, than does free intercourse with a learned and sincere friend, to you. Although you are extremely rich in this kind of wealth, yet, as I know that a greedy man never has enough, I will introduce to you one more to whom you can give your whole-hearted affection; Conrad Goclenius, a Westphalian by race. . . . I hope that when you

[1] More to Erasmus, 26 May 1520, Allen, iv, no. 1106 (abridged).
[2] Foster Watson, op. cit., p. 31.

know him better, I shall have thanks from both of you, as happened formerly in the case of Francis Cranefeld, who has won you so completely that I am almost jealous of him.'[1]

After a few years of life at Court More seems to have felt himself in danger of becoming absorbed in worldly affairs, and, probably somewhere about 1522, he began a treatise, which he never had time to finish, on the most serious of subjects.

In an endeavour to fix his mind upon the text: 'Remember the last things and thou shalt never sin', he composed the first part of his reflections upon death.[2] The remaining three essays on judgement, hell, and heaven, were never written, or at any rate not prepared for the press. His daughter Margaret undertook a dissertation of her own on the same words, on her father's advice; this he declared was in no way inferior to his own; but her essay has not survived.

More begins by inquiring 'For what would a man give for a sure medicine that were of such strength, that it should all his life keep him from sickness?' In his text he finds a prescription for a remedy against spiritual ills: 'no strange thing therein, nothing costly to buy, nothing far to fetch, but to be gathered all times of the year in the garden of thine own soul'. His moralizing was often harsh in tone and sometimes morbid. He draws a strange picture of the divine Creator as a jailer, tormenting his human prisoners on earth with divers ills. The treatise contains horrifying pictures of the pains and terrors of death, with some remarkable passages of very grim humour, interspersed with sound practical advice. He speaks of the folly of a man who makes provision for his own fine funeral.

'So many torches, so many tapers, so many black gowns, so many merry mourners laughing under black hoods, and a gay hearse, with the delight of goodly and honourable funerals, in which the foolish sick man is sometime occupied as though he thought he should stand in a window and see how worshipfully he shall be brought to church.'

On 'Silence', he writes:

'I would have folk in their silence take good heed, that their minds be occupied with good thoughts for unoccupied be they never. For if ever the mind were empty, it would be empty when the body sleepeth. But if it were then all empty, we should have no dreams. . . . Whensoever the communication is naught and ungodly, it is better to hold thy tongue and think on some better thing the while, than to give ear thereto and

[1] Anderlecht, 5 July (?) 1521, Allen, iv, no. 1220.
[2] *A Treatise (unfinished) upon these words . . . Memorare novissima et in eternum non peccabis.* More's *English Works* (1557), p. 72 seq.; cf. Campbell's ed. i. 459 seq.

underpin the tale. And yet better were it than holding of thy tongue, properly to speak and with some good grace and pleasant fashion to break into some better matter: . . . Howbeit if thou can find no proper mean to break the tale . . . better were it for the while to let one wanton word pass uncontrolled, than give occasion of twain. But if the communication be good, then is it better, . . . your thought [go] not wandering forty mile thence and while your body was there. As it oft happeth that the very face sheweth the mind walking a pilgrimage in such wise that other folk suddenly say to them: a penny for your thought. . . . Which manner of wandering mind in company . . . is never taken for wisdom nor good manner.'

More explains his own asceticism and continued use of self-discipline, contrary though it were to his Utopian teaching, by describing the 'delight and pleasure' to be found in such 'spiritual exercises as labour and pain taken in prayer, alms-deeds, pilgrimage, fasting, discipline, tribulation, affliction'. 'The best souls, and they that have best travailed in spiritual business, find most comfort therein.'

He speaks vehemently against the 'cursed root of pride'—a favourite theme—denouncing the spiritual vices of pride, wrath, and envy, as far worse than carnal sins.

Attention has been drawn lately to the influence of the devotional prose literature of the fourteenth and fifteenth centuries upon More's writing.

'His prose style is like nothing that preceded it so much as the natural, lucid and easy prose of the school of Hilton. Nor is this surprising if we remember that More spent three or four years of his early manhood in the Charterhouse of London, where, and apparently when, Hilton's works were being copied. May we not say with some assurance that he knew the works of Hilton, and look for the marks of their influence on his own direct and intimate prose?'[1]

More's work on this unfinished moral treatise may have been interrupted by a summons from the King in 1523 to enter into controversy with Luther. During the years in which More was engaged officially in furthering Wolsey's diplomacy, his anxiety was aroused by the growing strength of the Protestant reformers in Europe.

In 1517 Martin Luther had denounced the sale of indulgences, or pardons for sin, by the Papacy; and had fastened his famous theses to the Church door at Wittenburg. In June 1521 appeared the Papal Bull declaring Luther a heretic. A month earlier More probably heard a sermon preached against him by Fisher, at St. Paul's, in the presence of Wolsey, Warham, and Tunstall, and

[1] Professor R. W. Chambers, *On the Continuity of English Prose*, p. cxxx, quoting Professor A. W. Reed.

saw the blaze of Lutheran books publicly burnt in St. Paul's Churchyard.

In England, the spirit of Wycliffe and the Lollards still lived, in spite of stern suppression. Not only in the Universities, but in the diocese of London and other places, there were many who were ready to welcome the works of the German reformer. The clergy were widely unpopular and the English bishops had cause to fear the spread of subversive teaching.

More had sympathized most deeply with the hopes of those who urged reform within the Church, but he was a consistent opponent of heresy.[1] He did not realize that it would be useless to expect the Papacy to initiate reforms which would destroy the sources of its own wealth and temporal power. His own criticisms were inspired by his intense loyalty to the Church itself, and he was filled with horror by the violence of Luther's attack on beliefs and practices accepted by the larger part of Christendom. Averse though he might be naturally from disputes about religion, it was inevitable that he should be drawn into discussion of the problems which were forced upon every thinking mind. He was constantly with the King, who interested himself greatly in theological questions and delighted to discuss them with More, who was reputed to be so proficient in sacred learning that he could hold his own among great theologians. He had studied deeply the works of the early Fathers; he could illustrate and enforce a point by apt quotations from Augustine, Jerome, Chrysostom, Cyril, Hilary, Bernard, or Gerson; he was familiar also with the arguments of scholastic writers, and Stapleton, himself a practised theologian, was astonished by his knowledge and almost professional accuracy in theological subjects.[2]

It was, then, only to be expected that when Henry produced his book against Luther in 1521 he should seek the advice of More.[3] More, however, expressly denied that he had any part in the composition of the book, which won for the King the title *Fidei Defensor* and the high commendation of the Pope, whose authority was vindicated in it.

'After it was finished', More explained, 'I was only a sorter out and placer of the principal matters therein contained.' Thirteen years later, when Henry wished to repudiate the Papal authority,

[1] The term 'heresy' is used to denote 'the holding of opinions opposed to established or usually received doctrine, tending to division or party' and 'heretic' one who held such opinions.

[2] Cf. Stapleton (Hallett's ed.), pp. 37, 38. Dean Hutton (*Sir Thomas More*, p. 210), however, gives a comparatively low estimate of More's theological knowledge, and considers that his most important controversial work, the *Dialogue*, owes all to its skill, nothing to its learning.

[3] *Assertio septem sacramentorum adversum Martinum Lutherum.*

More was accused, with monstrous injustice, of provoking the King, by 'subtle sinister sleights', to write his book, and thereby causing him 'To put a sword in the Pope's hand to fight against himself'.

The true story of his connexion with the King's book is told by Roper, in More's own words:

'When I found the Pope's authority highly advanced and with strong arguments mightily defended, I said unto his Grace: "I must put your highness in remembrance of one thing, and that is this. The Pope, as your Grace knoweth, is a prince as you are, and in league with all other Christian princes. It may hereafter so fall out that your Grace and he may vary upon some points of the league, whereupon may grow breach of amity and war between you both. I think it best therefore, that the place be amended and his authority more slenderly touched." "Nay," quoth his Grace, "that shall it not, we are so much bounden to the See of Rome that we cannot do too much honour to it."'[1]

More, with his usual common sense, reminded the King, though without avail, of the limitations to the Papal power in England which the statutes called *Praemunire* had been devised to secure.

When, in 1522, Luther launched a reply to the King's book, full of abuse of the most coarsely offensive kind, Henry was debarred by his royal dignity from responding, and More, much against his own wish, was persuaded to enter the controversy in his stead.

Under the name of 'William Ross', he composed a rejoinder in a tone and temper as bitter as Luther's own.[2] He wrote unwillingly, but in writing 'the pen grew hot' indeed. In commenting on this rejoinder, Dr. Brewer wrote: 'I should be glad to believe that More was not the author of this work. That a nature so pure and gentle, so adverse to coarse abuse, and hitherto not unfavourable to the cause of religious reform, should soil its better self with vulgar and offensive raillery, shocks and pains, like the misconduct of a dear friend.'[3] But More was writing to command, in defence of the King as well as of the Church. He was alienated by Luther's excessive violence and became convinced that the weapon of abuse was a fitting means of reply to such an opponent. He apologized to his readers for using language which must cause them shame to read. 'Nothing', he said, 'could have been more painful to me than to be forced to speak foul words to pure ears. But there was no help for it, unless I left Luther's scurrilous book utterly untouched, which is a thing I most earnestly desired.'

[1] Roper, p. 66.
[2] *Vindicatio Henrici VIII a calumniis Lutheri* (Gulielmus Rosseus), *Latin Works* (1565).                    [3] Brewer, op. cit. i. 609.

# CHAPTER XIII

## MORE AND EDUCATION

IT was one of the penalties of More's official life that it entailed a frequent absence from home. He accompanied the Court to Greenwich, Hampton Court, Woodstock, Abingdon, Eltham, Windsor, or Guildford, for the King moved restlessly from one place to another, either for sport, or to evade the sweating-sickness, or to view the palaces which he built or restored with extraordinary lavishness.

While he travelled on the King's business, More's thoughts were never far from his own family, to whom he returned on every possible occasion. To these enforced absences, either abroad or in England, we owe the letters to his children, which display one of the most delightful aspects of his character. 'I assure you', he told his young daughters, 'that I have no greater solace in all the vexatious business in which I am immersed, than to read your letters.'

Plodding on a tired horse through the muddy lanes of Flanders, he turned loving thoughts to the little party awaiting him at home, and forgot his discomfort in expressing his affection in a letter of Latin verse—a letter of praise and encouragement to his 'sweetest children, Margaret, Elizabeth, Cecily, and John'. 'The man does not merit the name of father', he says, 'who does not weep at the tears of his children.' He reminds them that he always brings them from his journeys some little present—cakes or fruit or a piece of silk—many kisses he has given them—if he has beaten them ever, it was with a peacock's feather! Let them still progress in goodness and learning and he will love them even more—so much that his present great love for them will seem as nothing!

He wrote to his eldest daughter:

'I was delighted to receive your letter, dearest Margaret, and should have been more delighted still if you had told me of the studies you and your brother are engaged in, of your daily reading, your pleasant discussions, your essays; of the swift passage of the days made joyous by literary pursuits. For although everything you write gives me pleasure, yet the most exquisite delight of all comes from reading what none but you and your brother could have written.'

The letter concludes:

'I beg you, Margaret, to tell me about the progress you are all making in your studies. For I assure you that, rather than allow my children to be idle, I would make a sacrifice of wealth and bid adieu to other

PLATE 7

MARGARET ROPER.  Eldest daughter of Sir Thomas More
*By* HOLBEIN

cares and business, to attend to my family, amongst whom none is more dear to me than yourself, my beloved daughter.'[1]

In another letter to Margaret, he says:

'You ask, dear Margaret, for money, with too much shyness, from a father who is eager to give, when you have written me such a letter that I would not only repay each line of it with a gold Philippine (as Alexander did the verses of Cherilos) but, if my power equalled my wish, I would reward each *syllable* with two gold pieces! As it is, I send what you have asked; I would have sent more, but that, as I enjoy giving, so do I like to be asked and coaxed by my daughter, especially by *you*, whom virtue and learning have made so dear to my heart. So, the sooner you spend this money well (as you are wont to do), and the sooner you hasten to me for more, the more you will be sure of pleasing your father. Farewell, my dearest child.'[2]

More's deep interest in the new learning found practical expression in the education of his children. He not only chose for them the best available teachers in divinity, classics, astronomy, and music, but himself supervised and shared their studies, using for their benefit his inimitable gift for turning the driest subjects into a delightful pastime. 'It surely must have been More's children', says Mr. Seebohm, 'of whom Erasmus speaks, as learning the Greek alphabet by shooting with their bows and arrows at the letters.'[3] One seems to hear an echo of discussions in More's house, in the words of Sir Thomas Elyot, who wished that children should be 'not enforced by violence to learn, but according to the counsel of Quintilian, to be sweetly allured thereto with praises and such pretty gifts as children delight in, and their first letters to be painted or limned in a pleasant manner, wherein children of gentle courage have much delectation'.[4]

The new methods of teaching were introduced at Court; More was consulted about the education of the King's illegitimate son, the Duke of Richmond, whom Henry wished to make his heir to the Crown. The boy was brought up in royal state; his tutors were Richard Croke, the famous Greek scholar, and John Palsgrave, author of the first French grammar in the English tongue. Palsgrave, who was commanded by the King to bring up his 'jewel' in virtue and learning, told More that he never allowed his pupil to continue in a course of study till he was wearied, but

[1] Stapleton, *Tres Thomae* (1588), p. 233 (abridged); cf. Hallett's ed., p. 108.
[2] Stapleton, *Tres Thomae* (1588), p. 236; cf. Hallett's ed., p. 111.
[3] Seebohm, *The Oxford Reformers* (1887), p. 500 (from *Erasmi Opera*, i, p. 511 E).
[4] Sir Thomas Elyot, *The Book named the Governour* (H. S. Croft's ed., 1880), i. 32.

tried to make his lessons pleasant (after More's own fashion), so
that onlookers sometimes wondered whether he were engaged in
teaching the young duke or in playing with him.[1]

More was greatly interested in natural history, and delighted to
study with his children the forms and habits of different creatures;
in his house and garden he kept a numerous and strange collection of animals and birds.  Fortunately his wife shared his liking
for them, for the pets included not only dogs and rabbits, but also
foxes, ferrets, weasels, and a monkey, whose mischievous tricks
furnished him with many an illustration for moral lessons to his
children.  In teaching them 'to withstand the devil and his
temptations valiantly', he would tell them that they would 'find
him much like to an ape' which must be constantly watched.
'Like as an ape, not well looked unto, will be busy and bold to do
shrewd turns, and contrarywise being spied, will suddenly leap
back and adventure no further', so was the devil, and they must
therefore never relax their vigilance.

Even his frequent absence from home was turned to account in
his plan of education, and Latin composition was practised and
improved by correspondence.  His letters to his family, composed
in careful Latin, were full of good advice, and never without some
amusing pleasantry.  They were eagerly read, and read again, till
they almost fell to pieces.  He demanded replies from each one
of the children, and these were closely criticized, but always with
loving appreciation and encouragement.  In one letter he speaks
of their practice in logic, their composition of themes and verses.
A young scholar who is returning home with him, hopes to find
them not too far advanced for him to join in the witty and acute
discussions of which he has heard.  'I have a great hope,' adds
More, 'knowing how persevering you are, that soon you will be
able to overcome your tutor himself, if not by force of argument,
at any rate by never confessing yourselves beaten.'

The following letter is given by Stapleton:

'Thomas More to his dearest children, and to Margaret Gigs, whom
he numbers among his own:

'The Bristol merchant brought me your letters the day after he left
you, with which I was extremely delighted. Nothing can come from
your workshop, however rough and unfinished, that will not give me
more pleasure than the most accurate thing any one else can write. So

---

[1] *Letters and Papers*, iv, no. 5806; Brewer, op. cit. ii. 105.  In June 1525 Henry
conferred upon this boy, a child of six years, the title which had been borne by
the King's father, Henry VII.  More was commanded to read aloud the Patent of
Nobility, amid a scene of pomp and splendour very displeasing to Queen
Catherine. The boy showed great promise, but died in 1536.

much does my affection for you recommend whatever you write to me. Indeed, without any recommendation, your letters are capable of pleasing by their own merits, their wit and pure Latinity.

'There was not one of your letters that did not please me extremely; but to confess frankly what I feel, the letter of my son John pleased me most, both because it was longer than the others, and because he seems to have given to it more labour and study. For he not only put out his matter prettily, and composed in fairly polished language, but he plays with me both pleasantly and cleverly, and turns my own jokes on myself wittily enough. And this he does not only merrily, but with due moderation, showing that he does not forget that he is joking with his father, and that he is careful not to give offence at the same time that he is eager to give delight.

'Now I expect from each of you a letter almost every day. I will not admit excuses—John makes none—such as want of time, the sudden departure of the letter-carrier, or want of something to write about. No one hinders you from writing, but on the contrary, all are urging you to do it. And that you may not keep the letter-carrier waiting, why not anticipate his coming, and have your letters written and sealed, ready for anyone to take? How can a subject be wanting when you write to me, since I am glad to hear of your studies or of your games, and you will please me most if, when there is nothing to write about, you write about that nothing at great length! This must be easy for you, especially for the girls, who, to be sure, are born chatterboxes, and who have always a world to say about Nothing!

'One thing however I admonish you; whether you write serious matters or the merest trifles, it is my wish that you write everything diligently and thoughtfully. It will be no harm if you first write the whole in English, for then you will not have much trouble in turning it into Latin; not having to look for the matter, your mind will be intent only on the language. That, however, I leave to your own choice, whereas I strictly enjoin you, that whatever you have composed, you carefully examine before writing it out clean, and in this examination first scrutinise the whole sentence, and then each part of it. Thus, if any solecisms have escaped you, you will easily detect them. Correct these, write out the whole letter again, and even then examine it once more, for sometimes, in re-writing, faults slip in again that one had expunged. By this diligence your little trifles will become serious matters, for while there is nothing so neat and witty that may not be made insipid by silly and inconsiderate chatter, so also there is nothing in itself so insipid, that you cannot season it with grace and wit if you give a little thought to it.

'Farewell, my dear children.

'From the Court, the 3rd September.'[1]

As time went on, More gathered round him so large a group of

---

[1] Stapleton, *Tres Thomae* (1588), p. 231; cf. Hallett's ed., p. 106.

young people that he referred to them playfully as his 'School'.
He wrote one day from Court:

'Thomas More to his Whole School.

'See what a compendious salutation I have found, to save both time
and paper, which would otherwise have been wasted in reciting the
names of each one of you, and my labour would have been to no purpose
since no one is dearer to me by any title than each of you by that of
scholar. Your zeal for knowledge binds me to you almost more closely
than the ties of blood. I rejoice that Mr. Drew has returned safely, for
I was anxious, as you know, about him. If I did not love you so much I
should be really envious of your happiness in having so many and such
excellent tutors. But I think you can have no longer any need of Mr.
Nicholas, since you have learnt *all* that he knows about astronomy!
I hear you are so far advanced in that science that you can not only
point out the polar-star, or the dog-star, or any of the constellations,
but also—and this requires a skilful and profound astronomer—among all
those heavenly bodies, you can even distinguish the sun from the moon!

'Go forward then in that new and admirable science by which you
ascend to the stars. But while you gaze on them assiduously, consider
that this holy time of Lent warns you, and that beautiful and holy
poem of Boëtius keeps ringing in your ears, to raise your mind also to
heaven, lest the soul look downward to the earth, after the manner of
brutes, while the body looks upward.

'Farewell, my dearest ones.

'From the Court, the 23rd March.'[1]

Sir Thomas Elyot, deeply interested in the theory of education,
criticized the general practice of sending young boys to the house
of a nobleman who would allow them to live in idleness, 'banished
from all virtuous study or exercise of that which they before
learned'. Elyot's charming young wife sometimes joined in the
studies of More's daughters, and probably he had in mind the
excellent teachers chosen for them, when he noted by contrast
the example of those gentlemen who, he observed sarcastically,
would take far more trouble to engage a good cook for themselves
than a good tutor for their children.[2]

Among the older-fashioned gentry of the time, hunting, dicing,
and card-playing were the favourite pastimes; education was
despised among them. The Duke of Norfolk was not alone in his
opinion that 'England was merry England, before all this New
Learning came in'! More's friend and 'other self', Richard Pace,
related to Colet that one day when the subject of schools was
being discussed, a gentleman in the company—'one of those who

---

[1] Stapleton, *Tres Thomae* (1588), pp. 229–30; cf. Hallett's ed., p. 105.
[2] Elyot, op. cit. i. 113, 115.

always wear a horn hanging on the shoulder, as if he were ready to rush from the dinner-table to the chase'—abused learning because it led to poverty, giving Erasmus as an instance, and exclaimed with an oath: 'I would sooner have my son hanged than a book-worm. It is a gentleman's calling to be able to blow the horn, to hunt and hawk. He should leave learning to the clodhoppers.'[1] Much more would this sportsman and his fellows have considered learning unnecessary and even harmful to girls and women.

It was a fortunate occurrence for More's countrywomen that his three elder children were daughters, and girls of a high level of intelligence. In his own household Utopian principles of equal instruction for the sexes were put into practice, and in this way More did as much to advance the education of girls in England as Colet did for boys at his school of St. Paul's.

One has only to read letters of the period—letters of Erasmus, Budé, and others—to realize how rare a thing it was for a man of learning to find or even to seek mental companionship among the women of his family. A few royal ladies, indeed, were well educated. The Lady Margaret,[2] grandmother of Henry VIII, was a scholar of considerable attainment; her grandchildren, sisters of the King, were by her wish well instructed. The Queen, Catherine of Aragon, was a patroness of scholars; herself intelligent and accomplished, she desired the best teachers for her daughter, Princess Mary—but it was left to Thomas More to set the fashion among his own social equals.

'More does not adorn letters merely by his own learning or his partiality for learned men,' wrote Erasmus to Budé, 'for he has brought up his whole family in excellent studies—a new example, but one which is likely to be much imitated, unless I am much mistaken, so successful has it been. . . . A short time ago, love of literature was held to be useless either for practical or ornamental purposes, now, there is scarcely a nobleman who considers his children worthy of his ancestors, unless they are educated in good letters. . . . Almost everyone thinks learning useless to the reputation and good name of women, but More repudiates this idea and considers idleness a greater snare to them than literature.'

In the same letter, speaking of More's children, Erasmus says:

'A year ago it occurred to More to send me a specimen of their progress in study. He bade them all write to me, each one without any help, neither the subject being suggested nor the language corrected, for when they had offered their papers to their father for correction, he affected to be displeased with the bad writing, and made them copy out their letters

[1] *Letters and Papers*, ii, no. 3765.
[2] Lady Margaret Beaufort, Countess of Richmond and Derby. Foundress of Christ's College and St. John's College, Cambridge. Died 1509.

more neatly and accurately. When they had done so, he closed the letters and sent them to me without changing a syllable. Believe me, dear Budé, I was never more surprised; there was nothing whatever either silly or girlish in what was said, and the style was such that you could feel they were making daily progress. . . . They can read such authors [as Titus Livius] without a translation, unless there occurs some such word as would perhaps perplex myself. His wife, who excels in good sense and experience rather than in learning, directs the whole company with wonderful skill, assigning to each a task and requiring its performance, allowing no one to be idle, or occupied in trifles.'[1]

More's ideas on education are so well expressed in a letter to William Gunnell,[2] tutor to his children, that it is worth quoting at some length, so clearly does it show his principle that the chief aim of education should be, not a mere accumulation of knowledge, in order to make an effect, but the development of a sincere and modest character.

'I have received your letters, my dear Gunnell, elegant as your letters always are, and full of affection.

'From your letters I perceive your love for my children, and their diligence I see in their own. Every one of their letters delighted me, but I was particularly pleased to observe that Elizabeth shows as much gentleness and self-command in her mother's absence, as would be possible were she present. Let her understand that this pleases me more than all possible letters from anyone!

'Though I esteem learning joined to virtue more than all the treasures of kings, yet renown for learning, when it is not united with a good life, is no more than distinguished infamy. This would be especially the case in a woman; since learning in women is a new thing and a reproach to the slothfulness of men, many will be ready to attack it, and will impute to learning what is really the fault of nature, thinking that the vices of the learned will allow their own ignorance to be esteemed as virtue. . . . Among all the benefits bestowed by learning, I count this first, that we are taught by the study of books to value that study, not for the sake of gaining praise, but for its own true usefulness.

'I have said the more, dear Gunnell, on this matter, because of the opinion you express, that the lofty quality of my Margaret's mind should not be depressed.

'I do agree with you in this judgment, but it seems to me, and no doubt to you also, that he who accustoms a generous mind to admire what is vain and low, depresses it, and on the other hand, he who rises to virtue and true good, elevates it.'[3]

---

[1] Erasmus to Budé, *c.* Sept. 1521, Allen, iv, no. 1233, p. 577; cf. Bridgett, *Life of More*, p. 114.

[2] Gunnell, or Gonell, was a friend of Erasmus at Cambridge. Rector of Conington, 1517. At an earlier date his home was at Landbeach, about five miles from Cambridge. He kept a school, assisted by his brother, before he became tutor to More's children (Nichols, ii. 91 note; and *D.N.B.*).

[3] 'In Margareta mea altam illam et excelsam animi indolem non esse

'I have often begged you, and not only you, my dearest Gunnell, who would do it of your own accord out of affection for my children, and my wife, who is sufficiently urged to it by her motherly love for them, which has been proved to me in so many ways—but also all my friends, to warn my children to avoid the precipices of pride and to walk in the pleasant meadows of modesty; not to be dazzled by the sight of gold, not to sigh for those things which they mistakenly admire in others; not to think more of themselves for the possession of gaudy trappings, nor less for the want of them; not to spoil by neglect the beauty that nature has given them, nor to heighten it by artifice. Let them put virtue in the first place, learning in the second, and esteem most in their studies whatever teaches them piety towards God, charity to all, and Christian humility in themselves. So will they receive from God the reward of an innocent life, and in this expectation, they will not dread death. . . . The harvest will not be affected, whether it be a man or a woman who sows the seed. Both are reasonable beings, distinguished in this from the beasts; both therefore are suited equally for those studies by which reason is cultivated, and like a ploughed field, becomes fruitful when the seed of good precepts is sown.

'If it be true that the soil of a woman's brain is naturally poor, and "more apt to bear bracken than corn"—(a saying by which many keep women from study) then so much the more, for that reason, should a woman's mind be diligently cultivated, so that the defect of nature may be redressed by industry. This was the opinion of the ancients, of those who were the wisest and most holy. . . .

'Do you then, my most learned Gunnell, of your goodness make it your care that my girls learn well the works of those holy men. . . .

'I fancy I hear you object that these precepts, though true, are beyond the capacity of my young children, since you will scarcely find a man, however old and advanced, who is not stirred sometimes with the desire of glory. But, dear Gunnell, the more I see the difficulty of getting rid of this pest of pride, the more do I see the necessity of getting to work at it from childhood. For I find no other reason why this evil clings to our hearts so closely, than because almost as soon as we are born, it is sown in the tender minds of children by their nurses, it is cultivated by their teachers and brought to its full growth by their parents, no one teaching what is good, without at the same time awakening the expectation of praise as of the proper reward of virtue.

'That this plague of vain glory be banished far from my children, I do desire that you, dear Gunnell, and their mother and all their friends, would sing this song to them, and repeat it and knock it into their heads, that vain glory is a despicable thing, and that there is nothing more sublime than the humble modesty so often praised by Christ. This your prudent love will so enforce as to teach virtue rather than reprove vice, and make them love good advice instead of hating it. To this purpose

dejiciendam . . . sed is mihi . . . dejicere videtur animi generosam indolem, quisquis assuescit vana atque inferna suspicere; erigere contra quisquis in virtutem ac vera bona consurgit.' Stapleton, *Tres Thomae* (1588), pp. 225–6.

nothing will more conduce than to read to them the lessons of the ancient
.Fathers . . . in addition to their lesson in Sallust (to Margaret and Elizabeth, who are more advanced than Cecily and John). If you will do this,
you will bind me and them still more to you.'[1]

No one ever praised his children more freely than Thomas
More, and yet constantly exhorted them to beware of pride and
vanity.

'How delectable is that dainty damsel to the devil', he said, 'that
taketh herself for fair, weening herself well liked for her broad forehead,
while the young man that beholdeth her, marketh more her crooked
nose! How proud be many men of these glistening stones, of which the
very brightness, though he cost thee twenty pounds, shall never shine
half so bright nor show thee half so much light, as shall a poor halfpenny
candle! How proud is many a man over his neighbour, because the wool
of his gown is finer! And yet as fine as it is, a poor sheep ware it on her
back before it came upon his, and though it be his, is yet not so verily
his as it was verily hers! All that ever we have, of God we have received;
riches, royalty, lordship, beauty, strength, learning, wit, body, soul and
all. And almost all these things hath he but lent us. For all these must
we depart from, every whit again, except our soul alone. And yet that
must we give God again also.'[2]

In later years More's children remembered the quaint and
homely sayings with which he was wont to encourage them on the
Heavenward road.

'He would sometime use these words unto them', wrote William Roper.
"It is now no mastery[3] for you children to go to heaven, for everybody
giveth you good counsel; everybody giveth you good example. You
see virtue rewarded and vice punished, so that you are carried up to
heaven even by the chins. But if you live in the time that no man will
give you good counsel, no man will give you good example, when you
shall see virtue punished and vice rewarded, if you will then stand fast
and firmly stick to God, upon pain of life, though you be but half
good, God will allow you for whole good." If his wife or any of his
children had been diseased or troubled, he would say unto them: "We
may not look at our pleasures to go to heaven in feather-beds; it is not
the way; for our Lord himself went thither with great pain and by many
tribulations. . . . The servant may not look to be in better case than his
master." '[4]

More's own three daughters responded eagerly to his teaching;
his son, John, was a quiet thoughtful boy, a little overshadowed
by his more brilliant sisters, but diligent and studious. Margaret
Giggs, the adopted daughter, became a learned student of medi-

---

[1] More to William Gunnell, Stapleton, *Tres Thomae* (1588), pp. 224–8; cf.
Hallett's ed., pp. 101–4.
[2] More's *English Works* (1557), p. 1272 (abridged); Allen, *Selections*, pp. 152–3.
[3] i.e. no great achievement.                                    [4] Roper, p. 26.

PLATE 8

The Lady Barkley.

ELIZABETH DAUNCE. Second daughter of Sir Thomas More
*By* HOLBEIN

cine and a competent Greek scholar, under the guidance of John Clement, More's favourite pupil. In their common studies, mutual sympathy developed, and later, a happy marriage was arranged between these two, best beloved by More after his own children.[1]

Margaret More, his eldest daughter, was considered to be the most like her father 'as well in wit learning and virtue as also in merry and pleasant talk, and in feature of body'. Many friends sought her advice, 'and', says one of More's biographers, 'she would give very sound counsel, which is a rare thing in woman'.[2]

Between Margaret and her father there grew a beautiful and confident friendship, which increased from earliest years until the last unforgettable scene of their final parting.

There is no more striking testimony to the training of character in More's school, than the example of the two Margarets, one his daughter by birth, the other by adoption—both, in spite of their great abilities, ordinarily extremely unassuming and retiring, and both, in the face of emergency, if report be true, utterly forgetful of themselves and full of a devoted courage which shrank from no difficulty or danger.

More arranged marriages for all his children at a very early age, although in *Utopia*, eighteen was the lowest marriageable age for a woman, and twenty-two for a man. Margaret More was scarcely sixteen when she became, in 1521, the wife of William Roper—the 'son Roper', who learnt, from his association with More, the art of prose narrative and the reconstruction of dialogue which resulted in his well-known biography of his father-in-law, the source of many charming pictures of a delightful family life.

William Roper was a clerk of the Pleas, or Protonotary of the Court of King's Bench, an office held also by his father. He was the eldest son of John Roper[3] and of his wife Jane, daughter of Sir John Fineux, Chief Justice of the King's Bench; he inherited the larger part of the family property, including estates at Eltham, Kent, and in the parish of St. Dunstan's, Canterbury. His up-

[1] Their daughter Winifred married William Rastell, More's nephew, and editor of his *English Works* (*D.N.B.*).

[2] Anonymous *Life of More* in *Ecclesiastical Biography* (ed. Christopher Wordsworth, M.A.), ii. 141; cf. Nicholas Harpsfield, *The Life and Death of Sir Thomas More*, ed. by Dr. E. V. Hitchcock and Prof. R. W. Chambers for the E.E.T.S. (1932), p. 78.

[3] John Roper may possibly have been the 'Mr. Rooper' appointed by Wolsey, with other councillors, to hear 'poor men's causes' depending in the Star Chamber (*P.R.O. Court of Requests*, i, no. 4). The order (undated) is assigned by Mr. Leadam to 1516 or 1517 (*Select Cases in Court of Requests*, lxxxiii, note 8). It could not refer to William Roper, as he was born in 1496, and would have been too young at that time.

right character commended him to his father-in-law, and he regarded More with the most respectful affection.

The Ropers after their marriage lived on happily in More's house. Margaret, as daughter, sister, wife, and mother, was greatly beloved by all. 'She was so debonair and gentle a wife that Master Roper thought himself a happy man that ever he happened on such a treasure', and she deemed herself equally fortunate, for he 'was so sober to her, so sweet, so modest and so loving a husband'.[1] Margaret's education proceeded after her marriage, when she and her husband worked industriously together in More's 'school'.

More wrote to his daughter concerning these studies:

'You tell me that Nicholas, who is fond of you, and so learned in astronomy, has begun again with you the system of the heavenly bodies. I am grateful to *him*, and I congratulate *you* on your good fortune, for in the space of one month, with only a slight labour, you will thus learn these sublime wonders of the Eternal Workman, which so many men of illustrious and almost superhuman intellect have only discovered with hot toil and study—or rather, with cold shiverings and nightly vigils in the open air!—in the course of many ages.

'I am delighted that you have made up your mind to give yourself diligently to philosophy, and to make up by your earnestness in future for what you have lost in the past by neglect. My darling Margaret, indeed I have never found you idling, and your unusual learning in almost every kind of literature shows that you have been making active progress. But if you mean that you will give yourself so earnestly to study, that your past industry will seem like indolence by comparison, nothing could be more delightful to me, or more fortunate, my sweetest daughter, for you.

'Though I earnestly hope that you will devote the rest of your life to medical science and sacred literature, so that you may be well furnished for the whole scope of human life, which is to have a healthy soul in a healthy body, yet I am of opinion that you may with great advantage give some years of your yet flourishing youth to humane letters and liberal studies. And this both because youth is more fitted for a struggle with difficulties, and because it is uncertain whether in future you will ever have the benefit of so sedulous, affectionate and learned a teacher. I need not say that by such studies a good judgment is formed or perfected.

'It would be a delight, dear Margaret, to me to converse long with you on these matters, but I have just been interrupted and called away by the servants who have brought in supper. I must have regard to others, else to sup is not so sweet as to talk with you. Farewell, my dearest child, and salute for me my most gentle son, your husband. I am extremely glad that he is following the same course of study as yourself. I am wont to persuade you to yield in everything to your husband; now,

---

[1] *Life of More* in *Eccles. Biog.* ii. 142; cf. Harpsfield, *Life of More* (1932), p. 80.

on the contrary, I give you full leave to strive to get before him in the knowledge of the celestial system! Farewell again.

'Salute your whole company, but especially your tutor.'[1]

Margaret Roper's learning was considered remarkable; she wrote excellent prose and verse both in Greek and Latin 'in style elegant and graceful, while in treatment they hardly yielded to her father's compositions'. Stapleton, who read some of her essays which are now lost, spoke highly of her eloquence and wit, and her clever use of oratorical devices, and praised her apt emendation of a corrupt passage from St. Cyprian, which had puzzled other scholars.[2]

Her father took an irrepressible delight in the surprise of his friends when they found that 'in literature and other branches of study she had attained a degree of excellence that would scarcely be believed in a woman'. He could not refrain from telling her of his own intense pleasure when he received her 'most charming letter' while he was in the company of Reginald Pole, the future Cardinal, who thought it 'almost miraculous' that Margaret should compose a well-expressed letter in correct Latin, without assistance from a master, and could scarcely believe it to be true.

'But I told him', said More to his daughter, with loving pride, 'that one could hardly find a man whom *you* would not be able to help in composing letters, rather than that you should need *his* assistance! . . . I once said in joke, and I realize how true it was, that you would never win the praise you so richly deserve, because men would never believe, when they read what you had written, that you had not availed yourself of another's help, whereas of all writers you least deserve to be thus suspected. Even as a tiny child you could never endure to be decked out in another's finery.'[3]

More was delighted with the praise of Pole, whom he described as a young man of noblest rank and widest attainments in literature, conspicuous for piety as for learning. On another occasion, one of Margaret's letters was read by John Vesey, Bishop of Exeter, who was so charmed with it and with a declamation and some verses written by her, that 'his words were all too poor to express what he felt'. More continues:

'He took out at once from his pocket a portague which you will find enclosed in this letter.[4] I tried in every possible way to decline it, but was unable to refuse to take it to send to you as a pledge and token of his goodwill. This hindered me from showing him the letters of your sisters,

---

[1] More to Margaret Roper, Stapleton, *Tres Thomae* (1588), pp. 244-5; cf. Hallett's ed., pp. 117-19.

[2] Stapleton, *Tres Thomae* (1588), pp. 237-8; cf. Hallett's ed., p. 113.

[3] Stapleton, *Tres Thomae* (1588), pp. 61, 244-5; cf. Hallett's ed., pp. 46, 115.

[4] A *portague* = a Portuguese gold coin.

lest it should seem that I showed them to obtain for the others too, a gift which it annoyed me to have to accept for you. But, as I have said, he is so good that it is a happiness to be able to please him. Write to thank him with the greatest care and delicacy. You will one day be glad to have given pleasure to such a man.

'Farewell.

'(From the Court, just before midnight, September 11th.)'[1]

Margaret's genuine modesty was proof even against her father's extravagant praise, and she sought no audience beyond him and her husband. The fame of More's daughters, however, reached the Court, and on one occasion, no doubt by royal command, they 'disputed in philosophy afore the King's grace'.[2] Learned 'disputations' or debates were constantly practised in More's school, after the fashion made familiar to him at the universities; he shared with Erasmus and Vives a great appreciation of the art of declamation,[3] and he encouraged his daughters to compose set speeches on philosophical subjects, and also to exercise their skill and readiness in *ex tempore* discussions. It was his own practice, whenever he visited Oxford or Cambridge, or any foreign University, to take part in such debates as he found in progress.

One of Margaret Roper's works was a translation into English of a treatise by Erasmus on the Lord's Prayer.[4] An introduction to her translation was written by Richard Hyrde, 'a young man learned in physic, Greek and Latin, who once dwelled with Sir Thomas More, and resorted much there to Stephen Gardiner'.[5]

This introduction has been described as 'the first Renascence document in English on the education of women'.[6] It is a vindication of the study by women of the classics and humanities, advancing in this beyond the medieval tradition which limited them to the educational ideals of the convent. Hyrde's essay might well have been composed by More himself, and is evidently inspired by his teaching. He begins:

'I have heard many men put great doubt whether it should be expedient and requisite or not, a woman to have learning in books of Latin and Greek. And some utterly affirm that it is not only nother necessary nor profitable, but also very noisome and jeopardous.'

[1] Stapleton, *Tres Thomae* (1588), pp. 241–2; cf. Hallett's ed., p. 116.
[2] *Letters and Papers*, iv, no. 5806.
[3] More to Erasmus, Allen, iv, no. 1106.
[4] *Precatio dominica in septem portiones distributa*, printed by Froben at Basel, 1523.
[5] *Letters and Papers*, iv, no. 4090. Hyrde (Hart, Hirtius, or Herde) accompanied Gardiner and Foxe to Italy in 1528. He died there in the same year.
[6] Foster Watson, D.Lit., op. cit., p. 159.

The writer goes on to defend this dangerous experiment,

'for he that had leaver have his wife a fool than a wise woman, I hold him worse than twice frantic'. He argues that 'reading and studying of books so occupieth the mind that it can have no leisure to muse or delight in other fantasies, wherein all handiworks that men say be more meet for a woman, the body may be busy in one place, and the mind walking in another: and while they sit sewing and spinning with their fingers, may cast and compass many peevish fancies in their minds, which must needs be occupied with good or bad, as long as they be waking.'

He adds that the 'young virtuous well-learned gentlewoman of nineteen years of age' who translated the treatise, and her 'virtuous worshipful wise and well-learned husband', had 'by the occasion of her learning, and his delight therein, such especial comfort, pleasure and pastime as were not well possible for one unlearned couple either to take together, or to conceive in their minds, what pleasure is therein'.[1]

The New Learning made its appeal in many forms; the work of Erasmus prepared the way for innovations, and by 1521 the doctrines called 'Lutheran' were being widely though secretly circulated in England. William Roper was among those who were attracted by the doctrine of 'justification by faith alone', and it is related that for a time he became 'a marvellous zealous protestant and so fervent and withal so properly liked of himself and his divine learning that . . . neither was he contented to whisper it in hugger-mugger, but thirsted very sore to publish his new doctrine and divulge it, and thought himself very able to do so an it were even at Paul's Cross'. More, however, gently dissuaded him from taking this step, asking him with a smile, if it were not enough that his friends should know him to be a fool, but that he would have his folly proclaimed to the world? The laws and penalties against heresy were severe, and Roper was putting himself into serious danger. With some others he was 'convented of heresy' before Cardinal Wolsey, 'but for love borne by the Cardinal to Sir Thomas More, his father-in-law, was, with a friendly warning, discharged'. More said to his daughter:

'Meg, I have borne a long time with thy husband. I have reasoned and argued with him in those points of religion and still given him my poor fatherly counsel, but I perceive none of all this can call him home again. And therefore Meg, I will no longer argue or dispute with him, but will clean give him over and get me another while to God and pray for him.'

[1] Ibid., pp. 162, 166-8.

The influence in More's house was strong, and before long Roper 'turned him again to the Catholic faith'.[1] He relates the following conversation with his father-in-law.

'It fortuned,' writes Roper, 'when I in talk with Sir Thomas More, of a certain joy commended unto him the happy state of this realm that had so Catholic a prince that no heretic durst show his face; so virtuous and learned a clergy, so grave and sound a nobility, and so loving and obedient subjects, all in one faith agreeing together.

' "Truth it is indeed, son Roper", quoth he—and went far beyond me in commending all degrees and estates of the same: "and yet, son Roper, I pray God", said he, "that some of us, as high as we seem to sit upon the mountains treading heretics under our feet like ants, live not the day that we gladly would wish to be at league and composition with them, to let them have their churches quietly to themselves, so that they would be contented to let us have ours quietly to ourselves."

'After that I had told him many considerations why he had no cause so to say; "Well," said he, "I pray God, son Roper, some of us live not till that day";—showing me no reason why I should put any doubt therein. To whom I said: "By my troth, Sir, it is very desperately spoken." That vile term, I cry God mercy, did I give him. Who by these words perceiving me in a fume, said merrily unto me: "Well, well, son Roper, it shall not be so, it shall not be so." Whom in sixteen years and more, being in his house conversant with him, I could never perceive as much as once in a fume.'[2]

More's younger daughters are known rather as members of a brilliant group than as individuals. Elizabeth married William Daunce, the son and heir of Sir John Daunce, who was frequently employed in financial matters by Henry VIII and whom More must have met often at Court.[3] Cecily, the youngest daughter, became the wife of Giles Heron, a ward of Sir Thomas More, and son and heir of Sir John Heron,[4] who had been treasurer of the King's Chamber between 1515 and 1517. Cecily Heron's married life ended in tragedy in 1540, when her husband was executed at Tyburn on a charge of treason.[5]

[1] The story is given by Harpsfield, with whom Roper was personally acquainted (Life and Death of Sir Thomas More, Harleian MS. 6253 (Brit. Mus.), f. 42); and Hitchcock and Chambers ed. (1932), pp. 84–8. It is repeated in the anonymous Life of More in Eccles. Biography ii. 149, and by Cresacre More, op. cit., p. 134.

[2] Roper, pp. 34, 35.

[3] Sir John Daunce (or Dauncey) was receiver-general of the lands of minors, 1509–18; in 1511 he was collector of the Petty Customs in the Port of London, and one of the general surveyors of Crown Lands. He was present at the Field of the Cloth of Gold in 1520, and sat in the Parliament of 1529 as Knight of the Shire for Oxfordshire (Sir John Daunce's account of moneys received from the Treasurer of the King's Chamber, by Charles Trice Martin; Archaeologia, xlvii, part 2, p. 295).          [4] Letters and Papers, iv, no. 314, 8 May 1524.

[5] Reed, Introduction to More's English Works, Campbell's ed., i. 7.

PLATE 9

CECILY HERON.  Youngest daughter of Sir Thomas More
*By* HOLBEIN

The report which once gained credence, that More's only son John was deficient in intellect, appears to have rested on an unexplained joke of his father's, who once remarked that the boy 'would remain a boy as long as he lived'. In reality, though not exceptionally clever, he was 'a young man deeply versed in Greek and in philosophy'. Erasmus dedicated to him his Greek edition of Aristotle; Simon Grynaeus, who, with the support of More, brought out an edition of Plato's works in Greek, with some Greek commentaries of Proclus, inscribed his books to John More in the hope, as he said, 'that they may be of considerable use to you, conversant as I know you to be with all these serious questions. ... Enthusiasm for learning has carried you and your sisters —a prodigy in our age—to such heights of proficiency that no difficult question of science or philosophy is now beyond you. To minds so appreciative of all that is beautiful, what can be more suited than this author?'[1]

In 1533, young John More translated from the Latin an account of the court and life in Abyssinia, contained in the report on the Church and Commonwealth of Prester John, addressed by Damyan Goes, a Portuguese, to the Bishop of Upsala.[2] The choice of subject was probably due to the influence of More's *Utopia*. John More married a young gentlewoman and heiress, Anne Cresacre, of Yorkshire, a ward of the Crown, whom Sir Thomas More 'bought of the King'; though by some mistake he was not given the lady he expected.[3] Pretty Anne, at fifteen, must have felt a little out of her element among More's learned daughters, she 'not being much sensible of spiritual exercises, being carried away in her youth with the bravery of the world'.[4] She could not repress a laugh when she chanced to discover one day that her father-in-law wore a hair shirt—a fact he tried to keep from all but his daughter Margaret. She had a liking for finery, and asked Sir Thomas to give her a 'billiment of pearls'. At last he solemnly presented her with a box, which she opened in joyful expectation, only to find an ornament set with white peas, instead of pearls. The poor girl nearly cried with disappointment, but 'never after had any great desire to wear any new toy'.[5] More spoke of her later as his 'loving daughter'.

---

[1] Stapleton (Hallett's ed.), pp, 63, 82, 110.
[2] Reed, *Early Tudor Drama*, pp. 79–80.
[3] Cresacre More, *Life of Sir Thomas More* (1828), p. 41 and Preface xlii. More had apparently chosen for his son's wife a lady who was heiress to the other moiety of Barnborough, Yorks.
[4] Ibid., pp. 24–5.
[5] *Life of More* in *Eccles. Biography*, ii. 136. A somewhat similar story, told in the *Moria* of Erasmus, seems to refer to More's first wife (Allen, iv, p. 18 note).

The family group often included Sir John More, Judge of the King's Bench, who no longer showed the asperity of former years, but, mellowed by age and prosperity, was glad to bask in the reflected fame of his distinguished son, who treated him always with the utmost deference. Sir John had a reputation for jocose sayings, and is credited with the remark that 'matrimony is like to a man who puts his hand into a bag containing twenty snakes and one eel. It is twenty to one that he catches the eel.' For all that, the gay old gentleman had the courage to make four dips into the matrimonial lucky bag, and met with very fair success.

Thomas More, who possessed the rare and convenient ability to bestow his liking where duty called it, contrived to give to all his stepmothers in turn the affection due from a son, and said they were excellent women.[1]

Even when he became Lord Chancellor, More continued to treat his father with the extreme deference usually shown only by young children to their parents, yet naturally and without any affectation. When he passed through Westminster Hall to the Chancery, he would enter the Court of King's Bench if Sir John were sitting there, 'and there reverently kneeling down in the sight of them all, duly ask his father's blessing'.

When, in 1530, Sir John More lay on his death-bed, his son 'oftentimes with comfortable words most kindly came to visit him, and also at his departure out of the world, with tears taking him about the neck, most lovingly kissed and embraced him, commending him into the merciful hands of Almighty God'.[2]

[1] Erasmus to Hutton, Allen, iv, p. 19.          [2] Roper, p 42.

PLATE 10

John More S⸌ Thomas Mores Son.

JOHN MORE. Son of Sir Thomas More. *By* HOLBEIN

# CHAPTER XIV

## HOME AND HOUSEHOLD

AS the years passed, More's household increased in number and he felt the need to leave the crowded city for a quieter and more spacious home. When his children married, he could not bear to part from them, or they from him, and his house was designed to find room for the younger families who made their home with him. His movements between 1514 and 1524 are uncertain; in 1523 he bought the lease of Crosby Hall in Bishopsgate Street, the historic house with its fine hall, once lived in by Richard III.[1] It may be that the Mores lived for a few years in this house when they left Bucklersbury, before they moved to the pleasant country village of 'Chelsey'. There, on the banks of the Thames, More bought land in 1520 and again in 1524, and there he built a large and comfortable house, surrounded by a spacious garden, with fields and farm buildings close at hand.[2] He filled his house with interesting and beautiful things; he had a collection of ancient coins, and a large number of valuable books; when he met with anything strange or curious the temptation to buy it was quite irresistible to him. He cared more for beauty of workmanship than for the intrinsic worth of his treasures, and valued them the more for the pleasure he felt in showing them to his children and his visitors. Among these treasures was a heart of amber, in which a fly was imprisoned— the gift of Tunstall—an emblem of friendship, said More, which could not fly away nor perish.

His garden was described as a place of marvellous beauty, full of lovely flowers and blossoming fruit-trees, with a beautiful view of the Thames, and with green meadows and wooded hills on every side.[3] It is said that the rosemary which grows to this day in many a garden about Chelsea was introduced there by Sir Thomas More, who liked to 'let it run alle over his garden walks, not onlie because his bees loved it, but because 'tis the herb sacred to Remembrance and therefore to Friendship'.

A portion of this garden was entrusted to the care of each of the

---

[1] Charles W. F. Goss, *Crosby Hall* (London 1908), pp. 43, 47. The date of purchase is given as 1516 in *Footsteps of Sir Thomas More*, by A. B. Teetgen, p. 71. It is thought that More may have lived in Crosby Hall as a tenant, before his purchase of the lease, which he sold again, to Antonio Bonvisi, in January 1524.

[2] He may have lived also in another house in Chelsea, before his own house was built.

[3] Ellis Heywood, *Il Moro* (1556).

many servants whom his position obliged him to maintain. He
would have no idle retainers in his service; dicing and cards were
strictly forbidden, and those whose duty it was to attend him as
Chancellor were expected to occupy their leisure with gardening,
music, or books.

Near the house, but apart from it, he built also a library, a
gallery, and a private chapel.[1] To this he would come every
morning with his children for prayer, and in the evening he
assembled all his household to say with them in the chapel
'certain psalms and collects'. To this building he would often
resort for a period of quiet reading, meditation, and prayer; on
Fridays he would spend the whole day there, when he could
escape from his duties at Court. Turning his steps away from
his busy, cheerful house, in solitude he would pour out his heart
to God.

He described his own practice when he wrote:

'Let him use often to resort to confession and . . . let him also choose
himself some secret solitary place in his own house, as far from noise and
company as he conveniently can, and thither let him some time secretly
resort alone. . . . There let him open his heart to God, and confess his
faults such as he can call to mind, and pray God of forgiveness. Let him
call to remembrance the benefits that God hath given him . . . and give
him humble hearty thanks therefore. There let him declare unto God,
the temptations of the devil, the suggestions of the flesh, the occasions
of the world, and of his worldly friends, much worse many times in drawing a man from God, than are his most mortal enemies . . . and so dwelling
in the faithful trust of God's help, he shall well use his prosperity.'[2]

Sadly and anxiously one day he came to his 'New Building',
for his dearly loved daughter Margaret, attacked by the dreaded
'sweating sickness', lay at death's door, so that, as her husband
wrote afterwards, 'both physicians and all other there despaired
of her recovery and gave her over'. Then her father, 'there in his
chapel upon his knees with tears most devoutly besought Almighty
God that it would like his goodness . . . to vouchsafe graciously to
hear his humble petition'. While he prayed, there came into his
mind a possible remedy for his daughter's illness; he suggested it
to the physicians, who tried the experiment with success, and

[1] I am indebted to Reginald Blunt, Esq., Hon. Sec. to the Chelsea Society,
for the following notes. 'No trace remains of More's chapel and library. It
seems probable that it was where Danvers House afterwards stood (across the
present Danvers Street). Crosby Hall is re-erected on the river front on the
east side of Beaufort Street. Beaufort House (which was More's) stood across
what is now Beaufort Street, about half-way between Cheyne Walk and the
King's Road, and at least 100 yards north of Crosby Hall (1930).' It was
pulled down c. 1740, by Sir Hans Sloane.
[2] English Works (1557), p. 1201 (Second Book of Comfort against Tribulation).

PLATE 11

SIR JOHN MORE. *By* HOLBEIN

'she, contrary to all their expectations, was, as it was thought, by her father's most fervent prayers miraculously recovered, and at length again to perfect health restored. Whom if it had pleased God at that time to have taken to his mercy, her father said he would never have meddled with worldly matters more.'[1]

All through his life he looked familiarly at death; he talked with his friends about a future life in such a way as to make them feel that he believed what he said, and did not speak without the brightest hope. A vivid conception of the next life put before his mind the alternatives of a material fiery hell, and a cheerful heaven in which he would chat as merrily with his friends as he did in his Chelsea garden.

On Sundays, when at home, he attended regularly his parish church with all his household, and allowed no one to be late for the service; he rebuilt a chapel, still known by his name, in the church of All Saints at Chelsea,[2] where the Rev. John Larke was vicar, and he gave many gifts to the Church, saying, 'let good folks give apace, for there will be found too many that will take away as fast!'

Even when he became Lord Chancellor, he would take his place among the choristers. Erasmus, indeed, said that More could not sing, but, it has been observed, the two things are not incompatible. However, he had an ear for music. Roper relates that the Duke of Norfolk

'coming on a time to Chelsea to dine with him, fortuned to find him at the Church, in the choir, with a surplice on his back, singing. To whom, after service, as they went homeward together arm in arm, the Duke said, "Godsbody, Godsbody! My Lord Chancellor a parish clerk—*a parish clerk!* You do dishonour the King and his office."

' "Nay", quoth Sir Thomas More, smiling on the Duke: "Your grace may not think that the King, your master and mine, will with me for serving of God his master be offended, or thereby account his office dishonoured." '[3]

More's charitable deeds were continual; he would seek out the needy in obscure lanes and courts and give substantial aid to his poor neighbours. Margaret Clement often acted as his almoner, and Margaret Roper took especial charge of a house in Chelsea in which he provided for a number of old or infirm people,

---

[1] Roper, p. 29. This was probably in 1528. Harpsfield, *Life of More* (1932), p. 333 note.

[2] In 1819 an Act was passed for the building of the present parish church of St. Luke, Chelsea; the old church then became the parish chapel of the parish of St. Luke, Chelsea (Rev. W. H. Stewart, M.A., *Chelsea Old Church*).

[3] Roper, pp. 49–50.

most of them dependents who were past work in his own household.

Besides More's own children, a number of others were confided to his care. John Colt of Essex, father of More's first wife, by his will drawn up in 1521—ten years after the death of Jane More —bequeathed to his 'son More', his 'best *colt*' and ten marks 'to the finding of my young son Thomas Colt, till he come to the age of twenty years, and he to order him and bring him up in learning as he thinketh best'.

Erasmus sent home to More his own pupil and servant, honest John Smith, who was stolid and English, useful enough, but not sufficiently intelligent to please so exacting a scholar. 'He makes no real progress in good letters,' Erasmus complained, 'and his mamma does not think him safe out of England'; so honest John came home again and found a place in More's generously hospitable house.

The group of young people gathered together in the famous house at Chelsea were devoted to More and deeply influenced by his teaching. Their literary and dramatic talents presented an interesting aspect of Renaissance culture in England. Among the more intimate members of the group were the Rastells, Heywoods, and Clements, some of whom were dispersed into exile after the death of More, when the shadow of religious strife darkened the English scene. Many of their writings in consequence were lost, yet their contribution to the literature of their age was one of no little value.

A notable member of More's 'school' was John Clement, who entered his service after leaving St. Paul's school, and who held the post of his 'boy' for some years. Attached to such men of learning as Erasmus, Colet, and More, there might usually be found a young man who was at the same time, servant, pupil, secretary, and companion. He attended his master on journeys, and was prepared to see to his comfort, to care for his horses, to carry his messages, to listen to his conversation, to write letters from dictation, to copy manuscripts, and to pick up a knowledge of the world and a more or less substantial acquaintance with 'good letters'. Many references to Clement are made by More, who wrote of him: 'he is so proficient in Latin and Greek that I have great hopes of his becoming an ornament to his country and to literature.' Clement was behind the scenes when the Utopian fiction was concocted by More with Peter Giles. He lived for some years in More's house, and acted as tutor to his children. He became equally renowned as a classical scholar and a Doctor of Medicine. In 1519 he was appointed Wolsey's reader in rhetoric at Oxford, and he also lectured there on Greek literature. More wrote to Erasmus:

'My Clement lectures at Oxford to an audience larger than has ever gathered to any other lecturer. It is astonishing how universal is the approbation and love he gains. Even those to whom classical literature was almost anathema attend his lectures and gradually modify their opposition. Linacre, who, as you know, never praises any one very much, admires him greatly, so that if I did not love Clement so much, I should be almost tempted to envy the praise he wins.'[1]

Clement's wife Margaret, formerly one of his pupils, became so proficient a scholar that she helped her husband to get the exact force of the Greek idiom in the more difficult passages of his translations; she was also deeply read in the science of medicine, to which Clement devoted himself when he resigned his Oxford readership to Lupset in 1520. He was admitted a member of the London College of Physicians in 1528 and became its President in 1544. For some time he lived in More's old house at Walbrook.

Another of 'More's young men' who rose to distinction in later life was his nephew William Rastell, who carefully collected and preserved all the writings of More that he could obtain, and who wrote a biography of his uncle, of which only fragments remain.[2]

William Rastell was associated with his father's printing-house, but at the age of twenty-one, he set up his own printing-press in St. Bride's Churchyard, and he published many of More's controversial writings between 1529 and 1533. After the arrest and imprisonment of More, Rastell gave up his press, and took seriously to his profession of the law, being called to the Bar in 1539 and to the Bench in 1546.[3] He had industry and ability and distinguished himself in both his professions. Although his father adopted the tenets of the Reformers, William Rastell remained devoted to the teaching of More. With his wife and her parents, the Clements, he left England during the reign of Edward VI, and again in the reign of Elizabeth, for religious reasons. In exile he prepared for the press the works of More which were printed in 1557, but his own papers and his *Life of More* disappeared after his death in 1565.[4]

William Rastell's sister, Joan, married John Heywood, the dramatist and epigrammatist, one of the closest of More's

[1] Stapleton, *Tres Thomae* (1588), pp. 221–2; cf. Hallett's ed., pp. 98–9.
[2] Published with Harpsfield's *Life of More*, edited by Dr. Hitchcock and Prof. Chambers (1932), pp. 221–52.
[3] *Black Books of Lincoln's Inn*, i, pp. 254, 274.
[4] Reed, *Early Tudor Drama*, pp. 87, 88; cf. also Reed, Introduction to More's *English Works* (Campbell's ed.), i. 7, and Harpsfield's *Life of More* (1932), p. 91.

younger friends. 'Merry John Heywood', singer and player on the
virginals, is said to have been introduced at Court by Thomas
More, whom he had met at Gobions, John More's country house
at North Mimms. Heywood trained a company of boy-players
and performed with them an interlude in the presence of Princess
Mary, whose approval was won by his 'dancing and wit, music,
mimicry and frankness'.[1] When the Renaissance spirit in England was quenched by religious strife, John Heywood and his
wife were among the younger members of More's circle who fled
to Flanders. It is told of him that, like More, he died with a jest
on his lips; a priest who came to console his last hours could only
murmur ineffectively 'the flesh is weak, the flesh is weak'. John
Heywood at last roused himself to respond, 'But you shouldn't
blame the Almighty for not making me a fish!' and so saying
died.[2]

His brother, Richard Heywood, who was present as a law clerk
at More's trial, was a close friend and lifelong associate of William
Roper. The two young men were legal partners in the office of
Protonotary of the King's Bench, and shared quarters in Lincoln's
Inn.

One of More's personal servants, Walter Smyth, was the writer
of a humorous poem called *The XII mery gestys of one called
Edyth, the lyeing widow whyche still lyveth*; printed by John
Rastell in 1525. It has been ascertained that this extraordinary
tale was a narrative of facts.[3] It relates the adventures of an
impostor, the daughter of a yeoman of Exeter, who travelled
from place to place, obtaining money under false pretences, by
many an ingenious tale, usually pretending that she was a woman
of great wealth. In Smyth's verses,

> She walked to a thorp called Batersay
> And on the next day after, she took a Whery
> And over Thames she was rowed ful mery. . . .
> At Chelsay was her arivall
> Where she had best cheare of all
> In the house of Syr Thomas More.

Here, after her usual custom, she began to tell of her great
possessions, until three young men in the house, tempted by the
prize set before them, 'all woed her a good pace', paying her

---

[1] The 'interludes' or short dramatic pieces composed by Heywood form a
link between the old morality plays (in which moral qualities were personified)
and the modern drama. He introduced the novelty of making his characters
represent classes, e.g. *The Play called the four P's, a new and very merry interlude
of a Palmer, a Pardoner, a Poticary, and a Pedlar.*
[2] Cf. Reed, *Early Tudor Drama*, p. 49.
[3] Ibid., pp. 156–8.

every attention. One of them 'in her chamber the candels did light, and tymbred her fyres in the chymney', bringing her 'good Malmsey' at bedtime. The widow proved good company,

> And in her chamber, the next night folowing,
> There was the revell and the gossuping,
> The general bumming, as Marget Giggs sayde.
> Everybody laughed and was well apayde.

The next day, however, the adventuress was exposed, found to be 'not worth the sleeve-lace of a gowne', and ignominiously dismissed from the house. Undeterred by three weeks imprisonment for fraud, she continued her adventurous career, obtaining money from rich and poor by her specious tales.[1]

Walter Smyth remained in More's service from 1520 to 1529, when his master obtained for him the post of sword-bearer to the Lord Mayor. He bequeathed to young John More his copies of Chaucer's *Tales* and Boccaccio.

Clement was succeeded as More's secretary by John Harris, described by Stapleton, who knew him well, as a man of great industry, well versed in literature, and a first-rate Patristic scholar. After More's death he married Dorothy Colley, a maid and friend of Margaret Roper. His duties ranged from reading the Lessons in Chapel, to remonstrating with the Chancellor for going out in a most disreputable pair of old boots. More was careless in dress, and would continue to wear the same clothes until reminded by a servant, whom he called his 'tutor', who was appointed to buy for him what was necessary. His official gold chain he regarded as a veritable badge of servitude.[2] His indifference to finery was noticeable at a time when courtiers were magnificent in velvets and satins, furs and jewels, and ten or twelve fine gowns were insufficient for a gentleman of fashion. The clergy emulated the nobles in splendour; Wolsey usually appeared 'in fine crimson satten engrained, his pillion of fine scarlet, with a neck set in the inner side with black velvet, and a tippet of sables about his neck'.

John Harris was deputed by More to act as guide to a distinguished foreigner who visited him in 1531, with an introduction from Erasmus. This was Simon Grynaeus, the German scholar and theologian, who had been Professor of Greek and of Latin at the University of Heidelberg. Grynaeus was the friend of

---

[1] *Shakespeare Jest-Books*, vol. iii, edited by W. Carew Hazlitt, 1864. Her three suitors in More's house were Walter (or 'Water') Smyth, More's man; Thomas Arthur, servant to William Roper; and Thomas Croxton, servant to 'Master Alington' (Sir Giles Alington, the second husband of More's step-daughter, Alice), ibid., p. 76.

[2] His portrait shows him wearing the beautiful collar of S.S.

Melancthon and Oecolampadius, and an adherent of the reformed Churches. More carried on an argument with him on religious topics, but gave him a friendly warning not to speak to any one else in England on the subject.[1] Grynaeus wrote gratefully of the kindness shown to him.

'For the love of learning,' he said to young John More, 'in the midst of public and private business he found time to converse much with me; he, the Chancellor of the Kingdom, made me sit at his table; going to and from the Court he took me with him and kept me ever at his side. He had no difficulty in seeing that my religious opinions were on many points different from his own, but his goodness and courtesy were unchanged. Though he differed so much from my views, yet he helped me in word and in deed and carried through my business at his own expense. He gave me a young man, of considerable literary attainments, John Harris, to accompany me on my journey, and to the authorities of the University of Oxford he sent a letter couched in such terms that at once, not only were the libraries of all the Colleges thrown open to me, but the students, as if they had been touched by the rod of Mercury, showed me the greatest favour. Accordingly I searched all the libraries of the University, some twenty in number. They are all richly stocked with very ancient books, and with the permission of the authorities I took away several books of the commentaries of Proclus.[2] I returned to my country overjoyed at the treasures I had discovered, laden with your father's generous gifts and almost overwhelmed by his kindness.'

Another distinguished visitor to More's house, also introduced by Erasmus, was the painter, Hans Holbein the younger, of whom More wrote: 'Your painter, dearest Erasmus, is a wonderful craftsman, but I fear that he may not find England so fruitful and fertile as he hoped. Whatever is possible, I will do to prevent him finding it wholly sterile.'[3]

He was as good as his word, and gave more than one commission and many introductions to the painter, whose art was a revelation to most Englishmen of the possibilities of portraiture. To the generosity of More and the genius of Holbein are due many life-like Tudor portraits which enrich the galleries of England. One of the finest of these is the portrait of More, painted probably

---

[1] Grynaeus was a representative of the Swiss reformed churches at the conference at Worms in 1540. Stapleton expresses the opinion that, under colour of courtesy, More kept Grynaeus under constant observation and guard, John Harris acting as private detective, lest his visitor should attempt to disseminate heretical opinions (*Tres Thomae* (1588), pp. 81-2; cf. Hallett's ed., p. 64).

[2] Stapleton, *Tres Thomae* (1588), p. 82; cf. Hallett's ed., p. 63. These were given him in order that he might have them printed on the Continent. There was an idea at the time that manuscripts were of no value after copies of them had been printed; many valuable manuscripts were lost in this way (cf. P. S. Allen, *The Age of Erasmus*).

[3] *Letters and Papers*, iv, no. 1826, 18 Dec. [1526]. Allen, vi, no. 1770.

PLATE 12

SIR THOMAS MORE AND HIS FAMILY FROM A PENCIL STUDY BY HOLBEIN

Names, from left to right: ELIZABETH DAUNCE, MARGARET GIGGS, SIR JOHN MORE, ANNE MORE, SIR THOMAS MORE, JOHN MORE, JNR., HENRY PATTISON, CECILY HERON, MARGARET ROPER, DAME ALICE MORE

in 1527 and shown by Mr. Edward Huth in the Tudor exhibition of 1890.[1] A number of sketches by Holbein of More and his family are now in the royal collection at Windsor Castle. Holbein painted also a large portrait-group of More and his family; the original painting is lost, though copies survive. The original sketch for this picture is in the Museum at Basel.[2]

The group includes More and his wife, his father, his son and his son's wife, his three daughters, and Margaret Giggs. The figure behind young John More is thought to be Henry Pattison, for some years a well-known member of the household; he was a late survival of the medieval jester or fool; it surprised Erasmus that More should encourage this primitive form of amusement. Pattison was allowed to join in the family conversation after meals, which began with a reading from Scripture by one of the daughters of the house, continued with a discussion of this, and usually ended with some light and amusing topic, in general merriment. When More became Chancellor, he transferred Pattison to the service of Sir John More, and after his death to that of the Lord Mayor.

A sketch or copy of this painting was sent by Holbein's own hand to Erasmus, who wrote of it to Margaret Roper: 'Holbein's picture showed me your whole family almost as faithfully as if I had you before my eyes; I seem to behold through all your beautiful household a soul shining forth still more beautiful.' He concludes:

'I am writing in bad health and in the midst of overwhelming work, therefore I must leave it to your tact to convince all your sisters that this is a fair and adequate letter, and written to each one of them no less than to yourself. Convey my respectful and affectionate salutations to the honoured lady Alice your mother. I kiss her picture as I cannot kiss herself. To my godson, John More, I wish every happiness, and you will give a special salutation on my part to your honourable husband, so justly dear to you.

'May God keep you all and give you every prosperity by his Almighty Grace.

'From Fribourg, 6th September 1529.'[3]

Dame Alice More and Erasmus were better friends apart, and Margaret, in a beautifully composed complimentary letter 'to the old and faithful friend of my father', did not omit to send the cordial salutations of her mother, with those of her husband, brother, and sisters.[4]

[1] See frontispiece.
[2] This is described in the preface by Dame Elizabeth Wordsworth, and reproduced here.                    [3] Bridgett, *Life of More*, p. 150.
[4] London, 4 Nov. 1529, ibid., p. 151.

More's three daughters, with their husbands, Roper, Daunce, and Heron, and, in course of time, eleven grandchildren, all lived together in the greatest harmony; there was no idleness and no quarrelling in his house. More ruled over all by kindness and love, and maintained a strict discipline with no apparent effort. It is only fair to say that his wife helped him considerably in matters of detail. Though she had no comprehension of his ideals, took no share in his intellectual interests, and did not always understand his jokes, yet she did her best to carry out his wishes, even when they were different from her own, and even though she could not refrain from contradictory argument.

The following well-known letter seems to show her as a capable vicegerent in her husband's absence, and also indicates the reasons which caused More to be loved by all his neighbours. It was written on his return from Cambrai in 1529, when the ill-news reached him of great losses by fire on his Chelsea farm.

'Mistress Alice, in my most hearty wise, I recommend me to you.

'And whereas I am informed by my son Heron, of the loss of our barns and our neighbour's also, with all the corn that was therein, albeit, (saving God's pleasure) it is great pity of so much good corn lost, yet sith it hath liked him to send us such a chance, we must and are bounden, not only to be content, but also to be glad of his visitation.

'He sent us all that we have lost: and sith he hath by such a chance, taken it away again, his pleasure be fulfilled. Let us never grudge thereat, but take it in good worth, and heartily thank him, as well for adversity as for prosperity. And peradventure we have more cause to thank him for our loss, than for our winning. For his wisdom better seeth what is good for us than we do ourselves.

'Therefore I pray you be of good cheer, and take all the household with you to Church, and there thank God, both for that he hath given us, and for that he hath taken away from us, and for that he hath left us which, if it please him, he can increase when he will. And if it please him to leave us yet less, at his pleasure be it.

'I pray you to make some good ensearch what my poor neighbours have lost, and bid them take no thought therefor: for and I should not leave myself a spoon, there shall no poor neighbour of mine, bear any loss happened by any chance in my house.

'I pray you be with my children and your household merry in God. And devise somewhat with your friends, what way were best to take, for provision to be made for corn for our household, and for seed this year coming, and if ye think it good that we keep the ground still in our hands. And whether ye think it good that we so shall do or not, yet I think it were not best suddenly thus to leave it all up, and to put away our folk off our farm, till we have somewhat advised us thereon. Howbeit if we have more now than ye shall need, and which can get them other masters ye may then discharge us of them. But I would not that any man were suddenly sent away he wot ne'er whither.

'At my coming hither I perceived none other, but that I should tarry still with the King's grace. But now I shall (I think) because of this chance, get leave this next week to come home and see you: and then shall we further devise together upon all things what order shall be best to take.

'And thus as heartily fare you well with all our children as ye can wish.

'At Woodstock the third day of September, by the hand of your loving husband, Thomas More, Knight.[1]

[1] More's *English Works* (1557), p. 1419.

# CHAPTER XV

# AFFAIRS OF STATE

## 1523–1527

THE renewed enterprise of war against France forced the King to summon a Parliament in 1523, for the purpose of voting supplies. On the 15th of April he took his seat on the throne in the Parliament chamber, with Wolsey and Warham at his right hand; the usual oration was made by Tunstall. On the 18th, the Commons presented Sir Thomas More to the King as their Speaker; his election was favoured by Henry, and probably proposed by Wolsey.

In a long oration More begged the King's grace to take in good part any future mistakes of his own, and secondly, to allow the usual liberty of speech in the House. On the 29th, Wolsey came in person to the Commons to recite the ill-deeds of the French king, and to urge the necessity of providing for the war by the enormous subsidy of £800,000, to be raised by a tax of four shillings in the pound on all men's goods and lands.

The Commons, in protest, sent a deputation to the Cardinal to beseech him to move the King to accept a smaller sum, but this Wolsey dared not do. He feared the King, though he feared no man besides. With a great retinue he descended on the House to enforce his demands. Roper describes the ensuing scene in the House.

'After long debating there, whether it were better but with a few of his lords, as the most opinion of the House was, or with his whole train royally to receive him there among them: "Masters", quoth Sir Thomas More; "forasmuch as my Lord Cardinal lately, ye wot well, laid to our charge the lightness of our tongues for things uttered out of this House, it shall not in my mind be amiss to receive him with all his pomp, with his maces, his pillars, his poll-axes, his crosses, his hat and the Great Seal too, to the intent that if he find the like fault with us hereafter, we may be the bolder from ourselves to lay the blame upon those that his grace bringeth hither with him." Whereunto the House wholly agreeing, he was received accordingly.'[1]

The Cardinal-Archbishop, coming straight from the King, with almost Royal pomp and more than Royal pride, confidently expected to bear down all opposition. It lay with More, as Speaker, to avert a breach between the Crown and the indignant

[1] Roper, p. 18.

Commons; it was a difficult situation, but even here, his mocking humour found an irresistible target in the 'proudest prelate that ever breathed'—with his 'maces, his pillars, his poll-axes, his crosses, his hat and the Great Seal too'. He arranged that the Cardinal's speech should be received in dead silence by the House. In some surprise, Wolsey addressed one member after another, but 'none of them all would give him so much as one word'. 'Masters,' quoth the Cardinal, 'unless it be the manner of your House, as of likelihood it is, by the mouth of your Speaker whom ye have chosen for trusty and wise—as indeed he is—in such cases to utter your minds, here is without doubt a marvellous obstinate silence.'

He then turned to the Speaker for a reply, and More solemnly fell upon his knees and with misleading humility, explained that the House was 'abashed at the presence of so noble a personage'. Moreover it was not according to precedent that any member should make answer, except himself as Speaker. But here was an insuperable difficulty—for 'except every one of them could put into his one head all their several wits, he alone in so weighty a matter was unmeet to make his Grace answer'.

Obviously then, there was nothing to be said by any one, and Wolsey, in excusable exasperation 'suddenly arose and departed', with all his following. Later, he said irritably to More, 'Would to God you had been at Rome, Mr. More, when I made you Speaker', to which More replied amiably that *he* wished so, too—he had long wanted to see Rome! But then, with his usual tact, he turned the subject, and contrived to 'wind such quarrels out of the Cardinals head' and 'wisely break off his displeasant talk' by complimenting him on his fine gallery at Whitehall.

Some of More's biographers, following Roper, have traced to this incident a feeling of enmity between Wolsey and More, but there is ample proof in the State Papers that they were on friendly terms long after this.[1]

More, having maintained the privilege of the Commons 'not to reason, save among themselves', did his best loyally to further the proposals of the Court, in the debates which followed. At last, on the 13th of May, the Commons proposed a grant much smaller than that demanded by the Crown, and on the 21st, Parliament

[1] Owing to lack of corroboration from any other source, Dean Hutton throws great doubt on Roper's story, saying, 'It can hardly be conceived that Wolsey would be so ignorant of the privileges and customs of the House of Commons as he appears in this scene' (*Sir Thomas More*, p. 159). But Wolsey would gladly have swept aside the 'privileges and customs' of the House; it seems that Roper may have given the facts correctly, though his inferences from them were mistaken.

was prorogued till the 10th of June. The resentment felt at
Wolsey's heavy exactions and high-handed conduct was echoed
in the country; after the recess, the debates continued hotly;
tempers rose and fierce recriminations between burgesses and
knights were only composed by the persuasive powers of the
Speaker, who worked long and earnestly to keep the peace and
to secure the passage of the measure.[1]

It was in this Parliament that More first found himself opposed
by Thomas Cromwell, who was one of the strongest critics of the
proposed subsidy.[2] By a strange anomaly, Cromwell—utterly
self-seeking as he always was—appeared as the champion of the
poor against excessive taxation, and the opponent of an English
invasion of France, while More was forced by his loyalty to the
Crown to uphold an unpopular and oppressive measure and
to countenance the aggressive foreign policy which he greatly
deplored. He knew it was useless for him to utter any public
protest, or to thrust upon Wolsey 'such advice as he was sure
would never be listened to'.

When the Parliament was dissolved, Cromwell wrote a cynical
account of its proceedings in a letter to John Creke.

'By long time,' he said, 'I amongst other have endured a parliament
which continued by the space of seventeen whole weeks; where we com-
muned of war, peace, strife, contention, debate, murmer, grudge, riches,
poverty, penury, truth, falsehood, justice, equity, deceit, oppression,
magnanimity, activity, force, temperance, treason, murder, felony,
counsel—and also how a commonwealth might be edified and also continued within our realm. Howbeit, in conclusion we have done as our
predecessors have been wont to do, that is to say, as well as we might,
and left where we began.'[3]

After the session, Wolsey wrote expressly to the King, to move

[1] The grant agreed to amounted to two shillings in the pound from incomes
of twenty pounds and upwards; one shilling in the pound from incomes between
twenty pounds and two pounds, and a poll-tax of fourpence on incomes below
two pounds, the payments to be spread over two years. This being thought
insufficient by the Court party, Sir John Hussey proposed a tax of one shilling
in the pound on land of fifty pounds value and upwards to be paid for three
years. After the recess it was proposed that a similar tax be levied on goods
in the fourth year (H. A. L. Fisher, *Political History of England*, v. 246). The
tax fell much more heavily on the clergy, being no less than 50 per cent. income
tax, to be paid by instalments in five years (Brewer, *Reign of Henry VIII*, i.
481, 494). Convocation, summoned concurrently with Parliament, agreed
reluctantly to this heavy taxation, which increased Wolsey's unpopularity.
The Parliament of 1523 was also employed in regulating the sale of woollen
cloths, the reform of coinage, the incorporation of the physicians of London,
and other minor matters (ibid. i. 491).

[2] Roger Bigelow Merriman, *Life and Letters of Thomas Cromwell* (Oxford,
1902), i. 30.

[3] Ibid., p. 313.

that the Speaker should be granted a reward of £100, above the customary remuneration. He added:

'I suppose Sir, that the faithful diligence of the said Sir Thomas in all your causes treated in this your late Parliament, as well as for your subsidy right honourably passed, as otherwise considered, no man could better deserve the same than he hath done, wherefore, your pleasure known therein, I shall cause the same to be advanced to him accordingly, ascertaining your Grace that I am the rather moved to put your Highness in remembrance thereof, because he is not the most ready to speak and solicit his own cause.'[1]

This request was instantly granted, and More wrote to Wolsey that he 'would be very unkind if he ever forgot, and blind if he did not perceive, the gracious favours that the Cardinal had done him with the King'.[2]

Although More supported the demands of the King, and refrained from all but the most guarded comments on his ambitious policy, he was troubled at heart when he heard the reports of the Earl of Surrey and of his successor, the Duke of Suffolk, who commanded the English forces in France. They recorded no creditable achievements, but told a pitiless tale of ruined villages and shattered towns, of burning cornfields and helpless peasants left to starve without home or hope. He was not consulted on questions of policy, but was constantly employed in secretarial work, and conveyed to the Cardinal the King's approval of Wolsey's 'politic counsel' concerning the campaign.

At Wolsey's command, More read to the King the dispatches received from Richard Pace, relating the disaster suffered by Francis I in his invasion of Italy, which culminated in the capture of the French king by Imperial troops at Pavia in February 1525. More related to Wolsey how he told the King that Wolsey wished to show the dispatches to other members of his council, 'as also to John Joachim, for the contents be such as will do him little pleasure'. '"Marry," quoth his Grace, "I am well apaied thereof", and so fell in merrily to the reading of the letters of Mr. Pace . . . and thanked your Grace most heartily for your good and speedy advertisement, and forthwith he declared the news and every material point (which upon the reading his Grace well noted) unto the Queen's Grace and all other about him, who were marvellous glad to hear it.'[3]

Though Henry was delighted to hear of the misfortunes of

---

[1] *State Papers Henry VIII*, i, pt. i, no. lxix, p, 124, 24 Aug. 1523.
[2] *Letters and Papers*, iii, nos. 3270, 3363, 26 Sept. 1523, cf. p. 171, *infra*.
[3] More to Wolsey. Ellis, *Original Letters*, 2nd edition, i. 254. 'John Joachim' was an agent in London for the French Court.

Francis, he was jealous of the success of the Emperor, his own ally. A joint invasion of France was again proposed; Charles was to recover Burgundy, and Henry to seize the French Crown. This ambitious scheme was made impossible by lack of funds. Wolsey proposed an 'amicable loan' in 1525, but roused such acute discontent throughout the country that the project of invasion was perforce abandoned; a change of policy ensued and relations with the Emperor became strained. An incident occurred which caused great annoyance to the Imperial Ambassador in London, the Sieur de Praet. A packet of his letters was intercepted by the watch on the night of the 11th of February; this in due course came into the hands of More, who sent it in the morning to Wolsey in the Chancery. Wolsey read the letters without scruple and took a high hand with the Ambassador, whom he accused, before the Council, of making false reports, forbidding him to communicate with the Emperor. 'For a thousand years,' said de Praet indignantly, 'there is no instance on record of allied and friendly powers having their correspondance violated and divulged, much less of their being forbidden to write to their kings and masters!'[1]

The Emperor had little interest in prolonging an alliance no longer reinforced by a supply of English gold; Wolsey, for his part, saw the necessity for making peace with France, and secret negotiations were begun in London with an agent of Louise of Savoy, mother of Francis I.

More was employed during 1525 to interview this agent, Passano, a Genoese, known as John Joachim, and in August he was associated with the Bishop of Ely in drawing up the terms of a truce arranged with the French agents;[2] on the 30th of the month he was a signatory to the Treaty of the More, in Hertford-shire,[3] on the occasion of which he was granted, probably at Wolsey's request, a French pension of a hundred and fifty crowns.[4] A sum of 2,000,000 crowns was demanded from France as the price of Henry's friendship.

Wolsey's anxiety was renewed by the Treaty of Madrid, made between Charles and Francis in January 1526, whereby Francis regained his liberty at the cost of sending his two sons as hostages to Spain. More was again employed by the Cardinal to bargain with the French agents and to draw up the terms of a fresh treaty.[5]

[1] Brewer, op. cit. ii. 34; *Letters and Papers*, iv, no. 1083; and *Cal. S. P. Spanish*, iii, no. 50, February 1525.
[2] *Letters and Papers*, iv, no. 1570.
[3] Ibid. iv, no. 1600 (Rymer, xiv. 48).
[4] Ibid. iv, no. 3619.    [5] Ibid. iv, no. 2382, 8 Aug. 1526.

When a French embassy came to England in the early spring of 1527, More was present at some of the interviews which Wolsey conducted with his usual dexterity;[1] once again a matrimonial alliance was proposed between the Royal Houses of England and France, for Henry was ready to offer his daughter's hand from time to time to the Emperor—to the Dauphin—to the King of France—to the Duke of Orleans—father or son, it mattered not which, provided the momentary needs of diplomacy were served. The welfare of the Princess was of no consideration in this strange game of deceit played by rival statesmen. After numerous conversations an agreement was concluded and a treaty of alliance drawn up between Henry and Francis, in which Henry engaged himself to assist in the recovery of the captive French princes. More, among others, signed the treaty on the 30th of April 1527.[2] It was out of the question to send an English army to resist the designs of the Emperor Charles in Italy, but Wolsey encouraged with fair words the league formed between Francis, the Pope, Venice, and Florence, and More was commissioned, with Stephen Gardiner, to make an agreement with the Bishop of Tarbes and John Joachim for the 'entertainment' of foreign troops in Italy.[3]

The tortuous negotiations of these years constitute a striking example of the unscrupulous foreign policy which More had criticized with unsparing irony in *Utopia*;[4] it is easy to guess how uncongenial to him much of his work for Wolsey must have been, but their correspondence indicates that the Cardinal appreciated his loyal support on many occasions. Though the two ministers never were on terms of intimate friendship, they worked together with every appearance of cordiality, and More expressed his thanks because 'his services were so well liked'.[5]

Wolsey, as Papal Legate, felt that he derived his highest honour from the Holy See. His fidelity to papal policy caused him to oppose the pretensions of Francis and Charles in Italy, and led him more than once to engage his own country in war.[6]

Some years afterwards More spoke to his daughter Margaret of the warlike policy of Wolsey which 'did in his days help the king and the realm to spend many a fair penny'. 'In times past,' he said, 'when variance began to fall between the Emperor and

[1] *Letters and Papers*, iv, no. 3105, Dodieu's narrative, 8 May 1527. The Bishop of Tarbes was the principal French negotiator. The Dukes of Norfolk and Suffolk, the Bishops of London and Ely, Lord Rochford and Sir William Fitzwilliam, besides More, accompanied Wolsey (Brewer, op. cit. ii. 1139).
[2] *Letters and Papers*, iv, no. 3080.
[3] Ibid. iv, no. 3138, 29 May 1527.
[4] *Utopia*, pp. 91, 92.
[5] *Letters and Papers*, iii, no. 3302.
[6] Pollard, *Wolsey*, pp. 120–5.

the French king, in such wise as they were likely and did indeed,
fall together at war', some of the Council 'thought it wisdom, that
we should sit still and let them alone: but ever more against that
way . . . said his grace, that if we would be so wise that we would
sit in peace while the fools fought, they would not fail after, to
make peace and agree and fall at length all upon us. I will not
dispute upon his grace's counsel, and I trust we never made war
but as reason would. . . . But that gear is passed, and his grace
is gone our Lord assoil his soul.'[1]

There appears to be no ground but that of prejudice for the
statements of Roper and of Stapleton that Wolsey feared and
disliked More, and 'in revengement of his displeasure, counselled
the King to send him Ambassador unto Spain', where the climate
was so unsuitable, that 'if his grace sent him thither he should send
him to his grave'. Probably the subsequent death of Sir Richard
Wingfield at Toledo gave rise to the suspicion in Roper's mind that
a like fate had been designed for More, but Wolsey had no reason
to wish for the disappearance of so useful a colleague. It was not
unnatural that he should recommend for the embassy a man
whose discretion and experience he had learned to value, and who
was well known and liked, not only by Tunstall, his intended
colleague, but also by many continental diplomatists.

The diplomatic service abroad, however, was still very unpopular; it was considered an unpleasant duty rather than a
privilege to be chosen as ambassador; members of the nobility
disliked the discomforts of travel and the insufficiency of reward;
the payment of envoys or residents abroad was dependent on the
King's liberality, usually irregular and often in arrears.

When the King learned that More was reluctant to accept
a post so far from home, in a climate which he dreaded, he
graciously conceded the point, and in his most pleasant manner,
said to him: 'It is not our pleasure, Master More, to do you hurt,
but to do you good we would be glad. We will therefore, for this
purpose devise upon some other, and employ your service otherwise.' The mission to Spain was entrusted to Tunstall and Sir
Richard Wingfield, with whom More had been associated at Calais
in 1517. Roper adds: 'And such entire favour did the king bear
him, that he made him Chancellor of the Duchy of Lancaster upon
the death of Sir Richard Wingfield who had that office before.'[2]

At the same time he was employed in the negotiations with the
French already noticed.

---

[1] More, *English Works* (1557), pp. 1435–6, and Roper, appendix, p. 133. The
context indicates that More did not approve of the policy of war.
[2] Roper, p. 21. This was in 1525.

Henry indeed was very willing to keep More at home. When regulations were issued in 1526 for the reform of the Royal Household, it was provided that he should be one of the members of the council of whom two were to wait on the King 'every day in the forenoon by ten of the clock at the furthest, and at afternoon by two o'clock in the King's dining-chamber' or other place appointed as council-room.[1] He was also among the Councillors appointed to hear the complaints and petitions presented to the King as he moved from place to place.[2] Besides this, he had judicial duties connected with his posts of High Steward of Oxford University, to which he was appointed in 1524, and of Cambridge, in 1525. The High Stewards had special power to try members of the University who were accused of serious criminal offences in the limits of the University, where they also held a leet. These offices brought him into contact with many Oxford and Cambridge men, who came to him, either 'for suits of the Universities', or for the pleasure of his conversation. He was famous in argument or 'disputation', but rather than discourage young students, if he saw 'they could not without some inconvenience hold out much further disputation against him, then, lest he should discomfort them, would he by some witty device courteously break off into some other matter and give over'.[3]

The delight of the King in his society continued to be slightly embarrassing to More; even the peace of his own home was invaded by the irrepressible monarch, while, with his extraordinarily clear and prophetic vision, he was beginning to perceive the worthlessness of Henry's apparent affection. The simple hospitality offered to the King at Chelsea made a piquant contrast to the magnificence of Wolsey's entertainments to the sovereign, when two hundred costly dishes adorned the table,

[1] The reason for this regulation was that the King 'should not be any season unfurnished of an honourable presence of counsellors about his grace with whom his highness may confer upon the premises at his pleasure' (Brewer, op. cit. ii. 54). More is noted in 1527 as 'belonging to the King's Chamber' (*Letters and Papers*, iv, no. 2972, 20 Mar. 1527; assessment of Sir Thomas More in lands and fees, £340).

Dr. A. F. Pollard (*English Historical Review* (1922), xxxvii. 359) writes: 'There is no evidence that this scheme (the Eltham ordinances) was carried into effect in 1526.' The Chancellor, Treasurer, and Privy Seal, and others were often necessarily absent on their judicial and other administrative duties, and Wolsey, in the Star Chamber, was often better provided with counsel than the King, if he were absent from London. The regulations show a tendency to differentiate the Council with the King from the Council in the Star Chamber, but not until 1540 is it possible to treat them as two distinct entities (ibid., pp. 358–60). More, though usually with the King, was sometimes detained at Westminster.

[2] *Letters and Papers*, iv, no. 1939, p. 864, 1 Jan. 1526. In the same year he was again appointed commissioner of sewers by the coast of Thames, from East Greenwich to Gravesend (ibid. iv, no. 2758).          [3] Roper, p. 22.

and 'banquettes were set forthe, masks and moumeries in so gorgeous a sorte and costly manner that it was a heaven to behold'.[1]

At Chelsea the chief attraction was the conversation of Sir Thomas. Roper relates a well-known incident, saying:

'For the pleasure he took in his company, would his grace suddenly sometimes come home to his house at Chelsey to be merry with him. Whither, on a time, unlooked for he came to dinner, and after dinner, in a fair garden of his, walked with him by the space of an hour, holding his arm about his neck. As soon as his grace was gone, I rejoicing thereat, told Sir Thomas More how happy he was whom the King had so familiarly entertained, as I never had seen him do to any before except Cardinal Wolsey, whom I saw his grace walk once with arm in arm. "I thank our Lord, son," quoth he, "I find his grace my very good lord indeed; and I believe he doth as singularly favour me as any subject in this realm. Howbeit, son Roper, I may tell thee I have no cause to be proud thereof, for if my head could win him a castle in France, *it should not fail to go*." '[2]

The office of Chancellor of the Duchy of Lancaster was held by Sir Thomas More from July 1525 until October 1529, when he relinquished it on his appointment as Lord Chancellor.

The inheritance of the House of Lancaster was held by the Crown 'separately from all other hereditaments', and the affairs of the Duchy had an independent administration.

The Chancellor of the Duchy was a judicial officer who presided over a court which sat at Westminster and heard appeals from the Chancery Court of the County Palatine. This court, known as the Court of Duchy Chamber, exercised an equitable jurisdiction over all the tenants of the Duchy, which included many lands and possessions outside the boundaries of the County Palatine.[3]

It was the business of the Chancellor, as representative of the Crown, to supervise the management by the Duchy officials of all the estates and lands belonging to the Duchy; in September 1526 More was occupied in viewing some of these lands at the King's command.[4] Suits brought before the Chancellor of the Duchy comprised disputes about lands, houses, boundaries, trespass, assault, robbery, murder, tolls, customs, fairs, deer-

[1] Cavendish, *Cardinal Wolsey* in *Eccles. Biography*, (ed. Wordsworth) i. 357.
[2] Roper, pp. 21–2. Roper interpolates after 'France' the words, 'for then was there war between us'. War against France had been declared in 1522. Peace was agreed in negotiations between 1525–7.
[3] W. S. Holdsworth, *History of English Law* (1922), i. 116. 'This jurisdiction did not exclude the equitable jurisdiction of the King's Chancery and the Court of Exchequer, but was concurrent with it' (ibid.).
[4] *Letters and Papers*, iv, no. 2536, 30 Sept. 1526.

killing; claims for getting coals and cutting turf, and disturbances of all kinds.[1]

Appeals to the Chancellor for justice were made on various grounds; sometimes the plaintiff pleaded that he was a poor man, and the person complained of, one of great power in his part of the country. In some cases a *viva voce* examination before the Duchy Court would suffice, in others the Chancellor would consider carefully drawn-up depositions. He would sometimes order an investigation *in situ* by a number of local gentlemen who were instructed to take depositions of the parties concerned; in other cases the Sheriff was directed to impanel a jury of twenty-four to inquire into the dispute.[2]

The larger number of suits brought before More as Chancellor related to disputes concerning the possession of land; other complaints refer to the wrongful digging of coal, the refusal to pay rent, the distraint and impounding of cattle, and cases of assault and disturbance at Church Services.[3]

One of the few decisions in this Court which have been preserved relates to a case concerning the alleged enclosure of common land at Hindley (Hyndeley) in the County of Lancaster in 1528-9.[4] The decree of the Chancellor followed a report submitted by certain gentlemen, whom he had commissioned to take the depositions of numerous freeholders and tenants concerned. The tenants claimed the right of 'common of pasture and turbary in the said waste', and pulled down some buildings erected upon it. The case was examined in great detail by the Chancellor and Council, who finally ordered 'by the assent of the said parties' that certain 'encroachments lately built and made upon the said common shall be utterly put down and laid open again'. On the other hand, certain cottages and 'parcels of land' supposed to be encroachments on the common, were to be 'used kept and held in severalty by the owners thereof, forasmuch as it hath been so

---

[1] The Records of the proceedings of this Court consist of pleadings by way of bills and answers, depositions and surveys, and interrogatories relating to suits brought before the Court. The Records were transferred to the Public Record Office in 1868 (Lieut.-Col. Henry Fishwick, F.S.A., *Pleadings and Depositions in the Duchy Court of Lancaster; time of Henry VII and Henry VIII*, vol. i. Record Society for the Publication of original documents relating to Lancashire and Cheshire, vol. xxxii (1896)).

[2] Ibid., introduction, p. vii.

[3] Ibid., pp. 146-55. A case occurred in which Richard Townley, farmer of the King's coal-mines in Burnley, complained of the unlawful digging of coal by the King's tenants and others, and prayed for a writ under the Privy Seal, commanding them to answer the charge. The writ was issued, and after inquiry an order was signed by More to the effect that a number of persons named should pay 3d. for each 'fother' (19 cwt.) of coal. Ibid., pp. 138-44.

[4] Ibid., pp. 160-71 (from 'Decrees and Orders Henry VIII', book 5, f. 422).

used by a long time past'. It was also ordered that no one should hereafter 'claim or pretend to be lord of the said waste . . . but suffer the same to be open for common for ever', the tenants to be allowed 'common of pasture, common of turbary, and coals for their own fuel'.

With his usual practical good sense, the Chancellor ordered that a committee including some of the tenants should be appointed annually to supervise the digging of coals and turf, 'forasmuch as by the wilfulness of the said tenants great hurt and damage might be done upon the said waste and common, by reason of digging of coals and turbary upon the same'. His consideration for the public welfare in this vexed question of encroachment on common land is seen in a clause which ordered 'the ground and encroachments to a smithy-house belonging, to be set at large, but the house to stand still, with a little garden to it'.

The Chancellor of the Duchy received a salary of only £21 annually,[1] but this was exclusive of fees. More retained his Councillor's fee of £100 annually, and was given a grant of land in Oxfordshire, in partial compensation for the loss of his salary as Under-Treasurer, which he relinquished in January 1525/6.

[1] *Letters and Papers*, iv, no. 3380, p. 1533.

# CHAPTER XVI

## AMIENS AND CAMBRAI

### 1527–1529

MORE had been so closely occupied with the French negotiations from 1525–7 that it followed naturally that he should accompany Wolsey when he went to France in the summer of 1527, with the ostensible purpose of settling further details of agreement between the two Crowns. He must have been well aware, however, that Wolsey had another and secret object, for he knew that Henry had begun to seek a pretext for the dissolution of his marriage, and that the Cardinal was instructed to further the project in every possible way. More had heard, of course, the discussions at the time of the King's marriage in 1509 with Catherine of Aragon, the widow of his brother, Prince Arthur, and knew that the validity of such marriages was disallowed by Canonical Law. The Pope, Julius II, was doubtful of his own power to grant a dispensation in such a case;[1] Archbishop Warham's opinion had been against it in the beginning; but even those who held that the marriage ought not to have been made, felt most strongly that, having been made, it ought not to be undone. The Queen had won the respect and affection of all who knew her well; her unaffected goodness and intelligence, her cheerfulness and kindliness were acknowledged and esteemed.

During all the years that More spent at Court he entertained the highest regard for the Queen, and with profound misgiving he heard that Henry, after eighteen years of marriage, now professed to find scruples of conscience concerning the sufficiency of the papal dispensation of 1509. It was, probably, early in 1527, when rumours of a projected Royal divorce[2] were already current, that More spoke of his forebodings to his son-in-law, who recorded the following incident:

'On a time walking with me along the Thames side at Chelsey, in talking of other things, he said unto me: "Now would to our Lord, son Roper, upon condition that three things were well established in Christendom, I were put in a sack and here presently cast into the Thames." "What great things be those Sir," quoth I, "that should move you so to wish?" "Wouldst thou, son Roper, know what they be?"

[1] T. M. Lindsay, *History of the Reformation*, (1907), ii. 322.
[2] The term 'divorce' is used for convenience. Henry was really seeking a declaration that his marriage was null and invalid; this he eventually obtained from Cranmer's Archiepiscopal Court, having failed to do so from the Pope.

quoth he? "Yea marry, with goodwill Sir," quoth I, "if it please you."
"In faith son, they be these", said he. "The first is, whereas the most
part of Christian princes be at mortal war, they were all at universal
peace.

'"The second, that where the Church of Christ is at this present sore
afflicted with many errors and heresies it were well settled in a perfect
uniformity of religion.

'"The third, that where the matter of the king's marriage is now
come in question, it were to the glory of God and quietness of all parties
brought to a good conclusion." 'Whereby, as I could gather', continued Roper, 'he judged that otherwise it would be a disturbance to
a great part of Christendom.'[1]

It was by no means remarkable for a Royal marriage to be
dissolved for reasons of State. It has been urged in Henry's
defence that it was of the utmost importance for the country to
secure an undisputed succession to the throne. His only surviving
child was the Princess Mary and Englishmen were as yet unaccus-
tomed to the idea of a Queen regnant. Mary was frequently
betrothed to a foreign prince, and neither a French nor Spanish
consort would be welcomed by the nation. Henry's life alone
seemed to stand between his people and a civil war which would
bring disaster to the realm and would destroy the benefits of
nearly half a century of progress under Tudor sovereignty.

It was unfortunate for Henry's reputation that the awakening
of his conscientious scruples should coincide with his burning
passion for Anne Boleyn, the 'little, lively, sparkling brunette,
with fascinating eyes and long black hair', for whom he appeared
eager to repudiate a loyal and devoted wife, whose only fault lay
in being 'of a modest countenance', short, stout, and forty. But,
in whatever light his aims might appear to other people, Henry
persuaded himself, as usual, that he was obeying the command
of conscience; the cause was just, because it was his own. 'The
capacity for convincing himself of his own righteousness is the
most effective weapon in the egotist's armoury, and Henry's
egotism touched the sublime.'[2] He entertained a confident hope
of persuading Clement VII to overrule the dispensation granted
by Julius II. Was not Henry known to all Christendom as the
favoured son of the Church—champion of the Holy See with
sword and pen—acknowledged Defender of the Faith? How
should he doubt that the Pope would respect the scruples of his
upright conscience, would pronounce his marriage void, and give
a blessing to whatever union he might choose to contract?

Most unfortunately for his aims, Clement VII, at that very

---

[1] Roper, pp. 24-5.    [2] Pollard, *Henry VIII*, p. 209.

time, fell into the hands of the Emperor, after the capture of
Rome by Imperial troops in 1527. Charles V, the nephew of
Queen Catherine, made it a point of honour to oppose the humilia-
tion of a princess of the Royal House of Spain, and he urged the
Pope, who was virtually in his power, to refuse Henry's demand.
It was to the interest of Charles that his cousin Mary, half Spanish
by birth and sympathy, should succeed to the English throne.

When Wolsey, accompanied by More, went to France in July,
he was instructed to divulge Henry's purpose to Francis I, as far
as he could safely do so 'in a cloudy and dark sort', with the hope
of securing the moral support of France. Above all, he was to
ascertain the best means of communicating with the Pope, and
of counteracting the influence of the Emperor. In these schemes,
Wolsey's confidence was given, not to More, but to Stephen
Gardiner, who from this time onwards rapidly gained favour at
Court.

On the way to the coast Wolsey was instructed to investigate
the 'talkings rumours and seditious speakings' which were spreading against the divorce, though the question was supposed to be
still secret. He was ordered also to persuade Warham and Fisher
that the King 'had nothing intended nor done but only for the
trying out of the truth' and that he was really acting in the best
interests of the Queen herself.

Warham had never been able to withstand Wolsey and was
easily overcome by his arguments, but Fisher refused to discuss
the question of the papal dispensation. Wolsey and More stayed
two days at Rochester, and there can be little doubt that the
Bishop would turn in his perplexity to his old and trusted friend.
Fisher lived very much out of the world, devoting himself to his
diocese, his prayers, and his books. It was hard for him to
distinguish the true from the false in Wolsey's subtle arguments;
More, with a greater experience of men, must have had a clearer
insight into the true state of affairs, and though he still tried
desperately to believe in the King's honesty, both he and Fisher,
after long consideration, came to conclusions in favour of the
Queen's cause.

After staying a few days at Canterbury, Wolsey, accompanied
by a number of officials and a retinue of nine hundred horsemen,
reached Calais on the 11th of July, but it was not until the 4th of
August that Francis arranged to meet the Cardinal and his company at Amiens. Here they were graciously entertained by the
King's mother, Louise of Savoy, 'who', wrote Wolsey, 'in most
loving pleasant manner encountered, welcomed and embraced
me . . . and most part of such gentlemen as came with me'.

On Sunday the 18th of August the peace between England and France was confirmed by the Treaty of Amiens; Princess Mary was pledged to the Duke of Orleans and it was agreed that Henry and Francis should urge upon Charles the deliverance of the Pope.

At the end of September Wolsey returned with his companions to England, apparently successful indeed, but only to find that Anne Boleyn was paramount in the King's favour, and by her insinuations was undermining the influence of the Cardinal and preparing the way for his disgrace.

It was inevitable that More should be consulted by the King in his 'great matter', which now occupied all Henry's thoughts. While he was walking one day with Sir Thomas in the gallery at Hampton Court, Henry suddenly announced that he had found his marriage with his brother's wife to be so contrary to Divine Law 'that it could in no wise by the Church be dispensable'. He produced an open Bible to prove his point by the Levitical law, and invited the opinion of More, who excused himself as best he could, as 'un-meet many ways to meddle with such matters'. Henry, however, required a definite answer, and 'so sore still pressed upon him therefore' that he could only ask for time to consider the question. The King commanded him to confer with the Bishops of Durham and Bath, and other learned men of his Council, but when More returned to Court he told the King that neither he nor they could be such impartial advisers as he might find in St. Jerome, St. Augustine, 'and divers other old· holy doctors, both Greeks and Latins; and moreover showed him what authorities he had gathered out of them. Which although the King, as disagreeable to his desire, did not very well like of, yet were they by Sir Thomas More—who in all his communication with the King in that matter had always most discreetly behaved himself—so wisely tempered, that he both presently took them in good part, and often time had thereof conference with him again.'[1]

In all the tedious negotiations with Clement VII concerning the King's divorce More took no part; when a bull of commission was granted by the Pope to Wolsey and Campeggio to try the case in England, he must have watched the proceedings with painful interest—his friends, Fisher and Vives, were among the Queen's counsel—but, with all the tact and dexterity which he could command, he strove to keep aloof from the whole question, and occupied himself in the controversial writings in which he could count on the King's approval, for Henry was still the champion

[1] Roper, pp. 32–3, and More's letter to Cromwell, ibid., appendix v, p. 116.

of orthodox doctrine and the greatest opponent to the diffusion of heretical teaching in England.[1]

If the Pope had decided in Henry's favour, no doubt More would have acquiesced, regretfully, in the decision.[2] Clement VII, however, could not for a long time be induced to give a decision of any kind, and so the miserable affair dragged on. He had little sympathy for Catherine; he was unwilling to offend Henry, but he dared not oppose Charles. The Papal Legates, Wolsey and Campeggio, implored the Queen to retire to a convent and effect an honourable retreat from an impossible position, but Catherine, with all her gentleness, was immovable as Henry in his fury; she would not yield her just rights for the sake of Pope or Church, king or country. The Pope wept and wished he were dead—he wished Catherine in her grave—he feared her obstinacy would 'lose all England for the Spirituality'—he wished Henry would take two wives at once—he repeatedly told the Bishop of Tarbes that he would be glad if the new marriage were made by any means, provided he were not held responsible.[3] At last he made the fatal move of citing the case to Rome, whereby he awakened Henry's proud resentment and turned many of Catherine's sympathizers to the King's side.

All this time More maintained the most discreet silence, only assuring the King of his own unalterable loyalty. For a time Henry appeared satisfied, and promised to employ him in other matters. In July 1529 More was sent with Tunstall to represent the King at an international conference at Cambrai.[4]

At the Treaty of Amiens in 1527 Wolsey's diplomacy had appeared to be triumphant; the friendship of Francis seemed assured, but, while Henry was absorbed in personal matters, negotiations were again set on foot between the two enemies, Francis and Charles, to the practical exclusion of England. It was arranged by them that Louise of Savoy and Margaret, Regent

[1] More's controversial writings will be alluded to in a subsequent chapter.

[2] More, as a Catholic, could not recognize any dissolution of marriage except by a Papal decree. In his *Utopia*, however, he had written: 'When a married couple do not agree in their dispositions, and both find others with whom they hope they would live more agreeably, they separate by mutual consent and contract fresh unions, but not without the sanction of the Council, which allows no divorce until the members of it and their wives have carefully gone into the case. Even then they do not readily consent, because they know that it is a very great drawback to cementing the affection of married couples, if they have before them the easy hope of a fresh union. Breakers of the conjugal tie are punished by the strictest form of slavery' (p. 87).

[3] *Letters and Papers*, iv, nos. 6290, 6627.

[4] Ibid. iv, no. 5744, 30 June 1529. A commission given to Tunstall, Bishop of London and Privy Seal, and More, Chancellor of the Duchy, to treat with the Imperial and French ambassadors. Dr. William Knight and Mr. John Hackett were associated with them.

of the Netherlands, should meet at Cambrai to settle the differences between the two monarchs. Meanwhile, the Pope came to
terms with the Emperor in the Treaty of Barcelona on the 29th of
June. It was a situation with which Wolsey's genius alone could
have dealt successfully; he was the only English statesman whose
ability might have turned the transactions to the advantage of his
King. He wished to be present at the negotiations to maintain
the interests of England; up till now his absence would have been
incredible—but now his star was setting; he had lost the confidence of the King and no longer was he to direct the councils of
Europe.

A feeble excuse was made that Wolsey would not be able to
reach Cambrai in time; Tunstall and More were hurried off in his
stead, and a message was sent requesting Francis to defer proceedings until their arrival, 'for considering their age and quality
they could not be expected to travel post'.[1]

Both Tunstall and More were experienced and able men, but
the master-hand was missing, and details of the agreement
between the French and Imperial powers were kept secret from
them. A general peace was proclaimed, however, between the
Pope, Charles V, Francis I, Ferdinand of Bohemia, and Henry
VIII, and a separate treaty was made between Henry and Charles,
as well as a financial agreement with the French plenipotentiaries.
Wolsey had advised Tunstall and More to refuse any more
English loans, and they were largely occupied in negotiations
concerning the financial obligations of Charles and Francis to
Henry VIII.[2] The Treaties of Barcelona and Cambrai between
the Continental powers emphasized the defeat of Wolsey's foreign
policy.

On the return to England, Tunstall had a fall from his horse
and could not proceed to Court, so More went alone on the 1st
of September to make a verbal report to the King and Council.
He told the King that although he had found Madame (Louise)
and the French councillors 'ready to do all that a perfect friend
could do', nevertheless, when they came to the specification of
the articles granted in the treaty, 'they never could obtain a copy
of it or have it read'.

The King, it was reported, was dissatisfied because he was not
informed when the French and Imperial ambassadors were to

[1] *Letters and Papers*, iv, nos. 5733, 5741. More was granted for his 'diets'
26s. 8d. per diem. No account by More of the embassy has been found. The
date of the embassy is given erroneously in *D.N.B.* as 1528.

[2] Ibid. iv, nos. 5818, 5829, 5832, 5833, 5862, 5891, 6067, 6231. A copy of the
Treaty of Cambrai, signed by Margaret and Louise of Savoy, is in Rymer's
*Foedera*, vi. 129 seq.

meet to ratify the treaty,[1] but he did not impute blame to Tunstall or More. Roper stated that in this mission Sir Thomas More 'worthily handled himself, procuring in our league far more benefits unto this Realm than at that time by the King or his Council was thought possible to be compassed'.[2]

[1] *Letters and Papers*, iv, no. 5911. Bishop of Bayonne and Langey to Francis I.
[2] Roper, p. 36.

# CHAPTER XVII

# LORD CHANCELLOR OF ENGLAND

## 1529–1532

IN the autumn of 1529 Wolsey's fall was imminent. For the first time seemingly, in many years of intense devotion and unremitting services he had failed to gain for the King the fulfilment of a desire. Henry was amazed and infuriated by the unexpected check to his plan in the matter of the divorce; his resentment of the insult that he had incurred from the Papacy drove him to dismiss the loyal servant who had been powerless to prevent it, and to embark on a series of measures designed to coerce the Pope and to transfer to his own hands the authority exercised by the ecclesiastical powers. The hesitation of the Pope caused the ruin of Wolsey, and Wolsey's fall removed the strongest support of the Papal power in England.

On the 9th of October the attorney-general preferred a bill of indictment for *praemunire* against Wolsey; he was condemned in the Court of King's Bench on the ground that he had used illegally his authority as Papal Legate; he was deprived of the office of Lord Chancellor, ruthlessly stripped of most of his enormous wealth and all his political power, but allowed to retain the Archbishopric of York and to retire to the palace of Esher.[1]

The Great Seal was taken from Wolsey on the 17th of October; the French ambassador wrote on the 22nd: 'Wolsey is accused of so many things that he is quite undone; the Duke of Norfolk is made chief of the Council, Suffolk acting in his absence; at the head of all, Mademoiselle Anne. It is not yet known who will have the Seal; I expect the priests will never have it again, and that in this Parliament they will have terrible alarms.'[2]

It was not without discussion that More was chosen as Lord Chancellor to succeed Wolsey. Tunstall had been suggested, but Henry would have no more Bishops, although it was said that the post had been offered to Warham and declined by him. The Duke of Norfolk objected to the appointment of Suffolk. More's name alone met with no opposition. Even Wolsey, himself the 'last of the great ecclesiastical Chancellors', admitted that no one could be more worthy; but the appointment of a layman, though not unprecedented, gave a hint of Henry's determination to subjugate the ecclesiastical power in England.

---

[1] For the fall of Wolsey see A. F. Pollard, *Wolsey*, ch. vi, 'The Nemesis of Power'.  [2] *Letters and Papers*, iv, no. 6019. du Bellay to Montmorency.

On the morning of the 25th of October the Great Seal was delivered to Sir Thomas More by the King in his privy chamber at East Greenwich; on the following day Sir Thomas took the oath as Chancellor.[1]

Roper has described the scene, when More, escorted by the Dukes of Norfolk and Suffolk, came through Westminster Hall to his place in the Chancery, and Norfolk, at the King's special command, declared 'openly in presence of them all, how much all England was beholden unto Sir Thomas More for his good service and how worthy he was to have the highest room in the realm, and how dearly his Grace loved and trusted him, for which, said the Duke, he had great cause to rejoice'. More, in his answering speech, declared his deep gratitude to the King for his 'singular favour', though he felt himself to be 'unmeet for that room, wherein, considering how wise and honourable a prelate had lately before taken so great a fall, he said he had no cause thereof to rejoice'.[2]

Stapleton attributed to More a long oration on this occasion, in which he alluded to Wolsey's 'incomparable prudence, his skill and experience of affairs', saying: 'Following after a man of such power of intellect, such prudence, influence and splendour . . . I shall be as a torch compared to the sun!' He went on to compare himself with Damocles, for the sudden and unlooked-for fall of such a man was a fearful warning to himself not to be dazzled by his new honours.[3]

When More accepted the Great Seal he made the fatal mistake, against his own true judgement, of trusting to Henry's promise to allow him to remain silent on the question of the divorce. There were people who said that the King made him Chancellor in the hope of persuading him to give a favourable opinion in the 'great matter', but More himself was dismayed when Henry again urged him to 'weigh and consider it'. More fell upon his knees and assured his sovereign that 'there was nothing in the world so grievous unto his heart' as to find that he was not able in this matter to content his grace 'as he willingly would with the loss of one of his limbs'. He reminded Henry of his own most gracious words when he first entered the royal service: 'the most virtuous lesson that ever prince taught his servant, willing him first to look unto God and after God unto him'. Again the King renewed his promise, assuring him that 'he was content to accept his service

---

[1] Ibid. iv, no. 6025.                                    [2] Roper, p. 39.
[3] Stapleton, *Tres Thomae* (1588), pp. 33–5; cf. Hallett's ed., pp. 22–5. The speech as given by Stapleton is not authenticated. He makes More allude to the 'inglorious end' of Wolsey, who was still living in 1529; but the substance of the speech may be fairly accurate.

otherwise and would nevertheless continue his gracious favour towards him, and never with that matter molest his conscience afterward'.[1] For some time after this Henry kept his word.

One of More's earliest duties as Chancellor was to attend the opening of Parliament, which met on the 3rd of November 1529,[2] and which was to last for seven years, carrying out, before its close, many far-reaching measures.

In the course of this Parliament Henry VIII contrived to effect an entire change in the relations between the Church and the Crown. A series of statutes limited ecclesiastical privileges; at the same time the clergy in Convocation were induced to submit to the King's demands and to accept the theory of the Royal Supremacy over both State and Church; the long division of sovereignty between the Crown and the Papacy was brought to an end by the imperious will of the King.

Standing at the King's right hand the Chancellor made his opening speech. He began by praising the King for his labours for the cause of peace and the good of his people. The Parliament, he continued, was called together to advise the King on matters concerning the welfare of the kingdom, and especially the reform of justice and of ecclesiastical affairs. He then went on to speak of the fallen Cardinal in terms of scorn and reproach so greatly out of harmony with More's usual charity and his former friendliness with Wolsey, that doubt has been thrown by his defenders on the truth of the reports of the speech.[3]

According to the *Chronicle* of Hall (never very favourable to More) he pictured the King as the shepherd of his people, and Wolsey as 'the great wether of the flock', of late fallen, who 'so craftily, so scabbedly, yea and so untruly juggled with the King', presuming that his grace would not perceive his 'crafty doing' nor see 'his fraudulent juggling and attempts.' . . . 'But his grace's sight was so quick and penetrable that he saw him, yea and saw through him . . . and according to his desert he hath had a gentle correction, which small punishment the King will not to be an example to other offenders.'[4]

The simile of the prince as shepherd of the flock was one which

[1] Roper, p. 48, and More's letter to Cromwell, ibid., pp. 117–18 (appendix v).
[2] Several of More's relatives had seats in this Parliament. William Roper represented Bramber in Sussex, conjointly with Henry See of 'Chelchythe'. William Dawnsye (or Daunce) and Giles Heron sat for Thetford in Norfolk. Thetford belonged to the Duchy of Lancaster; it had not returned members before 1529, and disappeared from the Norfolk returns for the rest of the reign. (A. F. Pollard, 'Thomas Cromwell's Parliamentary Lists', *Bulletin of the Institute of Historical Research*, ix. 25 June 1931).
[3] Bridgett, *Life of More*, p. 232; Hutton, *Sir Thomas More*, p. 175.
[4] Hall's *Chronicle*, (1809), p. 764.

More may well have used; even if Hall's account were incorrect, there is besides, the evidence of the new Imperial Ambassador, Chapuys, according to whose report the Chancellor asserted that 'the Cardinal had committed many things against the royal authority and many acts of gross and flagrant injustice', for which he had been tried and condemned in a court of law. The King (he said) had long trusted the Cardinal and only lately had discovered that his confidence was misplaced.[1]

Dr. Brewer accepted the reported speech as authentic and condemned it as being foreign to the gentleness of More's character and to the justice which he usually upheld. ' It is', he said, ' little creditable to the candour, good sense and good taste for which Sir Thomas was on the whole remarkable. . . . On this occasion More, unlike himself, was overbearing both law and conscience, forgetting how differently Wolsey had acted towards himself in other and more prosperous days. The King looked on and made no sign.'[2]

Was this speech, then, mere time-serving hypocrisy; a piece of ingratitude to Wolsey, and, as Bishop Creighton suggested, a proof that More could not withstand 'the temptation to catch a passing cheer by unworthy taunts at a defeated adversary'?[3]

No one who has studied the life of More could suspect him of stooping to snatch a cheap popularity, or of making deliberate accusations which he believed to be unjust. The only explanation appears to be that he spoke in obedience to an express command of the King, who sat listening to his words. As Chancellor, he was the 'voice of the King' in Parliament; he may have been misled by Henry as to the extent of Wolsey's guilt, which had 'lately been discovered'. His language—as reported—was intemperate —but it was the custom of his day to use intemperate language, either in reprobation or praise; if More remembered his own words to Wolsey in 1523, he must have regretted the necessity of deserting him in his troubles, but his duty to the State came before his personal gratitude to the Cardinal.[4] In political matters, the King's will was absolute; More would not assert his own feeling against it, if his conscience did not forbid compliance. He gave way to the King perhaps too far, but the force which opposed him was very hard to resist.[5] No one knew better than

[1] Cal. S. P. Spanish, no. 211, pp. 323-4. Chapuys to the Emperor, 8 Nov. 1529.                          [2] Brewer, op. cit. ii. 391.
[3] Creighton, Wolsey, p. 190.                          [4] Cf. p. 153 supra.
[5] Cf. Nisard, Renaissance et Réforme, ii. 26. 'Morus fut saisi par la fortune presque malgré lui . . . il ne céda jamais tout à fait, quoique cédant toujours beaucoup trop. Morus ne sut ni se défendre de la cour ni s'y engager tout à fait. Un tel homme devait être . . . deshonoré s'il cédait jusqu'au bout, tué à quelque point qu'il s'arrêtât. Sa mort fut le seul acte libre et volontaire de sa vie.'

Wolsey that the King's commands must be obeyed, and that More was bound to Henry by a strong though anxious loyalty almost equal to his own.

The Lord Chancellor was a member of the committee in the Upper House which presented to the King forty-four articles enumerating Wolsey's alleged misdeeds; these articles, however, were not in the form of a bill of attainder; they did not accuse Wolsey of treason nor ask for his execution, but merely requested that 'he be so provided for, that he never have any power, jurisdiction or authority hereafter to trouble, vex and impoverish the Commonwealth'.[1] More had good reason to believe at that time that Henry intended to do the Cardinal no further harm, but would be content with the 'gentle correction' of his fall from power and wealth.

The perplexing question of More's relations with Wolsey is complicated by the prejudices of his early biographers, Roper and Harpsfield, followed by the anonymous 'Ro Ba' and Cresacre More. All these, ardent Catholics, attributed to Wolsey the responsibility for the royal divorce and the subjection of the clergy to the Crown. A connexion of ideas led them to depict Wolsey and More as adversaries and the opinion has been accepted generally; it gains force from More's action in the Parliament of 1529, and it has been assumed that after this time relations ceased between them. Yet a small but significant event indicates that they were not at enmity.

With Wolsey's fall before his eyes, as early as 1530 More was beginning to prepare himself for a like fate and to make provision for the scattering of the several families gathered under his own roof. He asked and obtained from Wolsey the use of his house at 'Batirsey', for 'young Daunce', More's son-in-law, 'if any death or other inconvenience compelled him to remove from his own house'.[2] It is hardly credible that More would have asked, or Wolsey have granted, the favour, had there been rancour between them.

It is evident also that Wolsey counted on More's sympathy in a matter very near to his heart—the fate of the two great colleges which he had designed, at Oxford and Ipswich, to be his noblest and most lasting memorial. These two foundations were threatened with destruction after Wolsey's fall, and More associated himself with Stephen Gardiner, by whose influence the Cardinal's

[1] A. F. Pollard, *Wolsey*, p. 261. The charges against Wolsey are discussed in Chapter VI, ibid.

[2] *Letters and Papers*, iv, no. 6484. A difficulty arose because Daunce claimed possession of the house before Wolsey's tenant wished to leave (Wolsey to Cromwell).

college at Oxford was ultimately rescued to survive as Christ Church. The college at Ipswich it was impossible to save from the rapacity of the King. A deputation from Oxford appealed to More to intercede with the King, and Dr. Tresham reported to Wolsey:

'The Chancellor is very good in this matter, he entertained me very lovingly.'[1] . . . 'I hope to obtain Mr. Baynton by the promise of a fee and so consequently my lord of Norfolk, for that is the chief way. . . . My lord Chancellor fears that the King will in conclusion have your grace's college for all the *supersedeas*, but he added that Mr. Secretary [Gardiner] was active for its continuance and he thought the King could not make it less than you intended. . . . I trust it shall continue as we shall now be impartially heard by the Chief Justice.'[2]

Wolsey and More had but little in common; Wolsey exemplified the arrogant pride, the avarice, and the extravagant display of wealth and power which More vigorously and consistently condemned. Yet he admired Wolsey's great qualities and sympathized with some of his projects; he felt no triumph in Wolsey's fall from power and assuredly made no effort to supplant him. 'Glorious was he very far above all measure,' said More, 'and that was great pity, for it did harm and made him abuse many great gifts that God had given him.'

As Lord Chancellor of England, Sir Thomas More became the King's chief officer in the State and in the law, with functions both administrative and judicial. To him was entrusted the Great Seal, by which acts of state were authenticated; its guardianship constituted him the head of the English legal system.[3]

The Chancellor was the chief official adviser of the Crown and 'keeper of the King's conscience'; he acted as Secretary of State for all departments.[4] Royal justice must be called into action by original writs issued by him; royal commands, grants, and treaties passed under his review; his duties were of immense range and variety. Petitions to the Crown were frequently referred by the Council to the Chancellor;[5] gradually it became the Chancellor's province to exercise the royal right to modify the strict administration of justice on equitable or moral grounds.[6] The Chancellor presided over the Courts held in the Chancery and in the Star Chamber, which in the Tudor period became separate from the King's Council, though still closely connected with it.[7]

[1] *Letters and Papers*, iv, no. 6666, 7 Oct. 1530.
[2] Ibid. iv, no. 6679, 11 Oct. 1530.
[3] Holdsworth, op. cit. i. 396.
[4] Pollard, *Wolsey*, p. 61.                               [5] Ibid., pp. 62–3.
[6] Holdsworth, op. cit. i. 398 and 446; ibid. iv. 252 and 276.
[7] Ibid. i. 404–5; iv. 273–7; and v. 219; and cf. Pollard, *Wolsey*, ch. iii.

The rules of equity were not yet developed into a settled system, but the Court of Chancery, with the Chancellor at its head, was becoming recognized as a court of equity, acting independently of the Council, with powers to mitigate hardships which might be caused in various cases by the harshness, inadequacy, or complicated procedure of the Common Law.[1]

Appeals might be made to the Chancellor from the judgements of any other tribunal, but from the equitable decisions of the Chancellor at this time no appeal was allowed.[2]

The power and jurisdiction of the Court of Chancery had been increased by Wolsey,[3] but the number of suits which came before it during More's term of office—from the 25th of October 1529, to the 16th of May 1532—was smaller than five hundred; the numbers increased enormously in the following century,[4] though, owing to political causes, the development of a system of equity did not make rapid way till after the Restoration.[5]

More has been described as the 'first of the lawyer chancellors of the modern type', and in spite of the distractions of other duties he set himself to clear off the arrears of work left by the neglect of his predecessor, who, though a great Chancellor, was not a lawyer.[6]

The *Court of Chancery*, from the early years of the sixteenth century, became a separate court, possessed of both a common law and an equitable jurisdiction, the latter being by far the more important (Holdsworth, i. 409). The *Star Chamber* also came to be regarded as the Chancellor's court. Wolsey made it famous for vigour of administration, but after his time it was gradually subordinated to the Privy Council (Pollard, 'The Star Chamber under the Tudors', *Eng. Hist. Review* (1922), p. 532). The Court of the Star Chamber tended to become a court of criminal equity, to a large extent separate from the Council acting as an executive body, though nominally consisting of the Lords of the Council sitting in the Star Chamber for the exercise of the judicial powers of the Council (Holdsworth, op. cit., i. 409, 497, 499; ibid. iv. 273 and v. 156, 163).

[1] The 'general laws' laid down by the Common Law courts were sometimes so narrow and technical as to make the interference of the Chancellor peculiarly necessary, in cases which they did not cover (ibid. i. 453). 'In the Common Law jurisdiction only the legal rule could be considered, but in the equitable jurisdiction of the Chancellor considerations of fairness and the claims of conscience could also be weighed. There followed a necessary difference in the procedure employed. The ideally fair decision could not be arrived at by the verdict of a jury. It could only be arrived at by a patient examination of the parties and the witnesses and all other relevant circumstances' (ibid. i. 450). Jurisdiction in uses and trusts formed a large part of the work of Chancery, especially with regard to land (ibid. iv. 417–21).

[2] Stapleton (Hallett's ed., p. 20) says 'not even to the King himself'. It was laid down in 1459 that error lay to Parliament from the *Common Law* side of the Chancery, but the decisions of the Chancellor in matters of *equity* were only subject to review by himself. The claim of the House of Lords to interfere with the decisions of the Chancellor began in 1621 (Holdsworth, op. cit., i. 372–3).

[3] Pollard, *Wolsey*, p. 66; Holdsworth, op. cit. v. 219.

[4] Ibid. i. 409 (quoting C. P. Cooper, *Public Records*, i. 356 n.).

[5] Ibid. v. 254.                                  [6] Pollard, *Wolsey*, p. 59.

It was said that there were cases pending in the Chancery which had been introduced twenty years before;[1] it was considered a remarkable event when, for the first time on record, no suits remained on the list, and More ordered that the occurrence should be inscribed in the registers of the Chancery. This incident gave occasion for the popular rhyme:

> When More some time had Chancellor been
> No more suits did remain.
> The like will never more be seen
> Till More be there again.

More, as Chancellor, was scrupulously conscientious in the matter of granting writs of *subpoena*.[2] He found that writs were issued often on insufficient grounds, and made an order that no *subpoena* should issue till a bill had been filed, signed by the attorney, and approved by himself;[3] 'whose manner was', as Roper says, 'also to read every bill himself, ere he would award any *subpoena*, which bearing matter worthy a *subpoena* would he set his hand unto, or else cancel it'.[4] Cresacre More relates that one bill, signed by an attorney 'A. Tubbe', was disallowed by More, who wrote above the man's signature the words 'a tale of ——'. The attorney, thinking he had obtained the Chancellor's endorsement, went away without looking at it, only to discover too late what had been written.[5]

The increasing jurisdiction of the Chancellor in the early Tudor period was beginning to awaken the jealousy of the Courts of Common Law. 'It had become clear that the law could not be modified upon equitable principles unless the Chancellor possessed the power of restraining the parties from proceeding at law; or, if they had already done so, from enforcing judgement.'[6] The judges were naturally hostile to a claim to set aside or modify their decisions by means of 'injunctions' in Chancery, and many complaints were made by the Common lawyers.

More, himself trained in the Common Law,[7] took steps to

---

[1] Stapleton (Hallett's ed.), p. 27.
[2] i.e. writs commanding the appearance in court, as defendants or witnesses, of the persons on whom they were served.
[3] Campbell, *Lives of the Lord Chancellors* (1845), i. 540.
[4] Roper, pp. 41–2; cf. Holdsworth, op. cit. v. 223.
[5] Cresacre More, op. cit., p. 182.
[6] Holdsworth, op. cit. i. 459. Wolsey did a good deal by means of injunctions in Chancery (Pollard, *Wolsey*, p. 96).
[7] He made this an excuse for not 'meddling' in the King's divorce suit which was tried in the Legates' court. 'I never meddled there, nor was a man meet to do, for the matter was in hand by an ordinary process of the spiritual law, whereof I could little skill.' (More to Cromwell, Roper, appendix, p. 117).

improve the relations between the Chancery and the Common Law judges, and urged upon them the infusion of equity into their administration of the law. He granted few injunctions, Roper stated, 'yet were they by some of the judges of the law misliked'. The Chancellor took the characteristic step of inviting all the discontented judges to dine with him. Having caused a list to be made of all his injunctions, after dinner, in his persuasive manner, he put the cases before them so plainly 'that upon full debating of those matters they were all enforced to confess that they in like case, could have done no otherwise themselves'.

The Chancellor then offered that, if the judges would, 'as they were, he thought, in conscience bound, mitigate and reform the rigour of the law themselves, there should from thenceforth by him no more injunctions be granted'.

The judges, however, would not agree to this, and More told them that they drove him to the 'necessity for awarding out injunctions to relieve the people's injury'. He remarked privately to Roper that the judges preferred to put their responsibilities on to the juries.[1] He succeeded, however, in restoring harmonious relations between the Chancery and the Common Law courts, which lasted till the revival of the struggle in the latter part of the sixteenth century.[2]

He was the most accessible of Chancellors, and in his own great hall would hear the complaints or petitions of any suitors who chose to come. One day a beggar-woman arrived, to claim the ownership of a little dog which Lady More had lately bought. By the Chancellor's order the dog was placed in the middle of the hall; the claimant stood at one end, the Chancellor's lady at the other, both calling the dog. It ran to the plaintiff and was awarded to her, but she gladly relinquished it to Lady More in exchange for a gold piece, 'enough to buy three dogs'. So all the parties concerned were satisfied—the beggar with her coin, dame Alice with her dog, and the dog, presumably, with an excellent home. Incidents of this kind caused More's son-in-law, William Daunce, to complain jokingly that he found it most discouraging —Sir Thomas was 'so ready himself to hear every man, poor or rich, and kept no doors shut from them'—that there was no profit in being related to the Chancellor, for although people sometimes offered him gifts to obtain an introduction, he felt obliged to decline them, 'for that they might do as much for themselves as he could do for them'.

More's impartiality was above suspicion, though he was ready

[1] Roper, pp. 43–4.
[2] Holdsworth, op. cit. v. 224.

to help his friends or relatives in ways not regarded as legitimate in more formal times.[1]

He replied to the protest of his son-in-law:

'You say well, son; I do not mislike that you are of conscience so scrupulous; but many other ways be there, son, that I may both do you good, and pleasure your friend also. For sometime may I by my word stand your friend in stead, and sometime may I by my letter help him: or if he have a cause depending before me, at your request I may hear him before another. Or if his cause be not all the best, yet may I move the parties to fall to some reasonable end by arbitrament. Howbeit this one thing, son, I assure thee on my faith, that if the parties will at my hands call for justice, then all-were it my father stood on the one side and the devil on the other, his cause being good, the devil should have right.'[2]

He exemplified his principles by making a decree against another son-in-law, Giles Heron, who presumed too far on his favour.[3] Several anecdotes are related of his firm though tactful refusal of gifts offered to him by grateful or expectant suitors in his Court.[4]

His integrity was the more remarkable by contrast with his predecessor in office, who 'took as Chancellor a commission for every favour he conferred',[5] and whose underlings followed his example.

More's close attendance on affairs of state had destroyed his own private legal practice; he was almost entirely dependent on his official salary and allowances, with the exception of about £60 a year from his landed property. As Chancellor, his annual salary was £142 15s. with £200 a year for his attendance in the Star Chamber, with other customary allowances.[6] The emoluments consisting of fees were probably much smaller in his case than the £2,000 or so a year received by Wolsey under this head;[7] his income, though large, was little more than his expenditure.

The Chancellor was called upon to decide, in the Courts over

[1] Sir James Mackintosh, in his *Sir Thomas More* (p. 73), criticized these methods as 'breaches of equality ... altogether dishonest'. He takes the story from Cresacre More, and suggests that the 'biographer not being a lawyer, might have misunderstood the conversation'. But it was first told by Roper, who *was* a lawyer, and probably well informed.

[2] Roper, pp. 40–1.

[3] Ibid., and Harpsfield, *Life of More* (1932 ed.), p. 53.

[4] Ibid., pp. 60–2.

[5] Pollard, *Wolsey*, p. 321.

[6] *Letters and Papers*, iv. 6079, 2 Dec. 1529. Warrants issued to the Treasurer of the Exchequer to allow the above to Sir Thomas More as Chancellor, and also to the chief butler to allow him £64 a year for the price of 12 tuns of wine and to the keeper of the great wardrobe £16 for wax.

[7] Pollard, *Wolsey*, p. 324.

which he presided, questions of disorder, riot, and 'actions tending but not extending to crime'. Many new opportunities for
wrong-doing were produced by the development of civilization,
for which the Common Law courts provided no remedy. With the
increase of education came a larger number of cases of forgery,
libel, slander, and perjury, which were brought before the Chancellor. The greatly disputed question of the enclosure of land was
subject to his jurisdiction.

One of the first cases heard by More in the Star Chamber was
the subject of litigation carried on from 1494 to 1538.[1] The Star
Chamber, the Court of Requests, the Court of Chancery, and the
Common Law courts were all invoked in turn by the aggrieved
inhabitants of the Manor of Thingden in Northamptonshire, who
complained that their rights of common had been encroached
upon by the lords of the Manor. Wolsey had issued a writ for the
destruction of the disputed enclosures; the lord of the Manor,
Thomas Mulsho, protested that the decree was issued without due
examination; he complained of the violence of the villagers who
had broken his gates and torn up his trees. More investigated the
matter, and finally reversed Wolsey's decision, allowing Mulsho
to retain his enclosures, in accordance with a previous decree of
the Star Chamber in 1510.[2]

The statement that 'the unfortunate villagers were by this
decision made the victims of a change of agrarian policy',[3] rests
on evidence insufficient without further confirmation. The impli-
cation that More had forsaken his early sympathy for a poor and
oppressed peasantry is not borne out by his action in another case
of the same kind, in the same year, when, as Chancellor of the
Duchy of Lancaster, he decreed that the lands then in question
should 'be open for common for ever'.[4]

His decisions in both cases suggest that he was guided by the
practical consideration of long-established custom; that he wished
to inflict the least possible hardship on all concerned, and that he
judged each case on its merits, not in accordance with any
changed agrarian policy, but 'as his conscience dictated'.

Very little precise information is available concerning More's
work as Chancellor,[5] but his reputation undoubtedly was very

[1] *Select cases before the King's Council in the Star Chamber*, edited by I. S.
Leadam (Selden Society, 1911), ii, p. lix seq.
[2] Ibid. The defendant at first concerned was John Mulsho. He was followed
by his grandson and heir.
[3] Ibid., p. lxxv.
[4] p. 160, *supra*.
[5] The vast bulk of MS. Records of the work in Chancery for the period are
not yet sifted and published; the whole of the decrees of the Star Chamber
have disappeared (Holdsworth, op. cit, v. 162, and cf. Pollard, *Wolsey*, pp.

high. It was generally agreed that no one could be better fitted for his difficult post, and justice was to be expected at his hands by suitors either poor or rich. The Venetian, Ludovico Falier, described him as 'the most just and virtuous Chancellor More, a most eminent and lettered doctor of laws, fitted for the most intricate negotiations; a man full of goodness and religion, so that the sentences of other courts are deservedly judged and ratified aright by his excellency'.[1] When More was made Chancellor, Erasmus said that he himself received numerous letters from English friends, 'congratulating the King, the Kingdom, themselves, and even me!'

The opinions of More's contemporaries were almost universally in his favour; it remained for modern critics to object that 'More the Chancellor, never attempted to introduce into the country which he helped to govern, the reforms which he had sketched as a younger man'.[2] 'He acquiesced', says Sir Sidney Lee, 'in a system of rule which rested on inequalities of rank and wealth and made no endeavour to diminish poverty.'[3]

Such criticism appears to over-estimate the power that was actually in his hands. More was Chancellor for only two years and seven months; for not more than half that period had he the confidence of the King on whose authority his high position depended. Neither time nor occasion was his to carry out great reforms; from the first he realized how precarious was his position; how warily he must balance himself to maintain it. He had neither the ambition nor the force of Wolsey, who had been Chancellor for fourteen years and yet had not found time to put into effect the reforms in Church and State which he had in mind. Besides this, Wolsey possessed vast powers which never pertained to his successor; he was not only Lord Chancellor and Archbishop of York, he was also for many years the King's principal minister for foreign affairs, and beyond all this, he was Papal Legate *a latere*, with authority to supersede the ecclesiastical courts in all the kingdom.

It was this power which gave to Wolsey his jurisdiction in heresy; he could and did override the episcopal courts in a way which his successor could not emulate, even if he would.[4]

---

66–8 notes). It is not until the middle of the seventeenth century that reports of cases decided in the Court of Chancery begin to get into print (Holdsworth, v. 262).

[1] *Cal. S. P. Venetian*, iv, p. 296, 10 Nov. 1531. The writer states erroneously that More, as Chancellor, presided in the Court of King's Bench.

[2] Joyce Oramel Hertzler, Ph.D., *The History of Utopian Thought* (1923), p. 127.

[3] Sidney Lee, Litt.D., *Great Englishmen of the Sixteenth Century* (1904), p. 33.

[4] Pollard, *Wolsey*, pp. 209, 213–14.

# CHAPTER XVIII

# THE CHANCELLOR'S RESIGNATION

## 1529–1532

THE Parliament which met in 1529 quickly set to work on measures designed to limit clerical fees and privileges. A blow had been struck at the papal authority by the disgrace of Wolsey, the legate and representative of the Pope; now the King determined to make use of Parliament in an attack on the power and property of the Church at home. Through Parliament, he appealed to his own people for approval of his assertion of independence, and he obtained a large measure of popular support for the bills which were passed in the first session.[1] 'Now with the Commons is nothing but "down with the Church!"' exclaimed Fisher indignantly in the House of Lords; but Henry manipulated both Houses with great dexterity and successfully demonstrated the power of the Crown; the financial demands of ecclesiastical courts had become extremely unpopular.

Henry for some time had no wish to separate himself or his country from the papal Church, but his examination of papal claims led to the assertion of the Royal Supremacy; he discovered in his kingdom a divided allegiance and, worse still, a divided revenue. In January 1531 the whole body of the English clergy were accused of having violated the statutes of Provisors and Praemunire, by their recognition of the legatine authority of Wolsey. Under the weak leadership of Warham—old, infirm, and bewildered—Convocation was coerced into submission, and on the 11th of February reluctantly acknowledged the King to be 'Supreme Head' of the Church, 'as far as the law of Christ allows'.

'This', wrote the Imperial ambassador, 'implies in effect as much as if they had declared him Pope of England. The Chancellor is so mortified at it that he is anxious above all things to resign his office.'[2]

It has been seen that More was anxious for reforms in the life of the Church, though not in its teaching, and he did not oppose the first measures in Parliament, which were political and financial, rather than religious in motive. He was, however, genuinely shocked by Henry's claim to authority in spiritual questions, and foresaw only too clearly the extremes to which he would go.

[1] Bills were drafted concerning the probate of wills, mortuary fees, non-residence, pluralities, and the farming of church lands.
[2] *Letters and Papers*, v, nos. 105, 112, Chapuys to Charles V, 14 and 21 Feb. 1531

The King was determined to secure his divorce at no matter what cost, and for a time subordinated all other aims to this purely personal matter, which became strangely and inextricably interwoven with the social, political, and ecclesiastical revolution which marked the beginning of the religious reformation in England.

During 1530 he had sent out messengers to Oxford, Cambridge, and a number of foreign universities, to canvass their opinion on the question of the papal power to dispense with the law against marriage with a deceased brother's wife. On the 30th of March 1531 the Chancellor was commanded to announce to both Houses of Parliament the result of the inquiry.

The event was reported to Charles V by Chapuys, who wrote:

'On Thursday, the Chancellor set forth by command that there were some who had said that the king pursued this divorce out of love for some lady, and not out of any scruple of conscience, and this was not true, for he was only moved thereto in discharge of his conscience, which, through what he had read and discovered, was in bad condition from his living with the Queen, as would appear by the seals of the Universities, which he would show them. . . . Some one asked the Chancellor for his opinion, on which he said that he had many times already declared it to the King, and he said no more. . . . When the matter was thus finished in the House of Lords, the Chancellor, with the Dukes of Norfolk and Suffolk, the Bishops of London and Lincoln, Brian Tuke and many others, descended to the hall of the Commons, where the whole thing was read and set forth as before the Lords, except that the Chancellor added that the King had wished them to be advertised of this matter, that when they returned to their houses they might inform their neighbours of the truth. When the reading was over, the Bishops of London and Lincoln, with great ceremony, took it on their conscience that the marriage of the King and Queen was more than illegal. . . . The Chancellor and the others retired without a word from the Commons . . . and so far as I can learn, the King is mistaken if he thinks that by these helpers he has justified his intentions with the people, for they are less edified than ever.'[1]

The next day the King himself went to the Parliament, and told the members, by the Chancellor, that he was well satisfied with them.

The Chancellor in Parliament was the voice of the Sovereign, who spoke 'by the Chancellor' even when present in person. On this occasion, as in the speech about Wolsey, More's words were dictated by the King. He did not 'show of what mind himself was therein'; he merely delivered the Royal message, but he began to feel that his position was untenable.

[1] Ibid. v, no. 171, p. 84, Chapuys to Charles V, 2 Apr. 1531.

When he accepted the Great Seal he had taken care, as he thought, to make it clear to the King that he could not serve him in the matter of the divorce; he had received the Royal promise that he should not be asked to do so. When, in spite of this, Henry again appealed to him for an expression of his approval, he could only plead that nothing but conscience should deter him from obeying his Sovereign with the most scrupulous particularity.

His plea was unlucky in the extreme. Could anything be more exasperating to a monarch who felt himself fully competent to supply the place of conscience to all his subjects? It was simply incredible to Henry that More should honestly consider his actions wrong; he began to attribute his opposition to obstinate ill will. He was eager to enlist the support of all his subjects in the struggle. Although his attack on clerical and papal claims had a large measure of public approval, in the question of the divorce popular sympathy was with the Queen. It was not enough for Henry to impose his will on his people; he required their admiring approbation for all that he did, and there was no one whose support he desired more greatly than that of More; no opinion in the country would carry greater weight than his. 'His learning, his reputation, his legal acquirements were sure to point him out to the King as the one man above all others in his Kingdom whose judgment on the question none would venture to impugn and few would be inclined to dispute.'[1] More, the most learned layman, Fisher, the saintliest Bishop—these were the two men whose support he most desired, and the only two men in high public position who dared to withhold it.

More's opinion of the divorce was known to Henry, but to all others he maintained a strict neutrality. He did not, however, put his name to a memorial to the Pope, which was signed by many prelates, temporal peers, and others, begging him to meet the King's wishes and dwelling on the dangers of delay, and Chapuys reported: 'The Chancellor, I hear, has spoken so much in the Queen's favour, that he has had a narrow escape of being dismissed.'[2] In all other possible ways, however, he strove to conciliate the King. He would not even read an opinion adverse to the King's purpose; he refused rigidly to discuss it; not one word could he be induced to utter against it to any one but Henry himself. His discretion and fidelity were complete and should have been undoubted, but he thought it necessary to beg the Imperial ambassador not to visit him, lest his loyalty to the King be suspected.

[1] Brewer, op. cit. ii. 161.    [2] Cal. S. P. Spanish, iv, pt. i, nos. 354, 433, and 460.

Chapuys wrote to the Emperor:

'I have sent to tell the Chancellor that I have letters for him from your Majesty and that I wished to visit him. He begged me for the honour of God to forbear, for although he had given already such proof of his loyalty that he ought to incur no suspicion, whoever came to visit him, yet considering the time, he ought to abstain from everything which might provoke suspicion, and if there were no other reason, such a visitation might deprive him of the liberty which he had always used in speaking of those matters which concerned your Majesty and the Queen.[1] He said he would not hold them in less regard than his life, not only out of the respect that is due to your Majesty and the Queen, but also for the welfare, honour and conscience of his Master and the repose of his kingdom.'

Chapuys goes on to say that More had begged him to keep the Emperor's letter for a more propitious time, as 'if he received it he must communicate it'.[2]

It is not easy to realize the immense temerity that was needed to oppose, or even to criticize, the actions of the King. It was not only that the Sovereign was the sole giver of honour and promotion, or that ruin and even death might, and often did, follow the loss of his favour. He was a tyrant, but his rule was tyranny by consent. The extraordinary domination of a strong personality over men of many types has never been exemplified more remarkably than in the case of Henry VIII. He inspired an intense and devoted loyalty; none of his ministers dared or wished to oppose him, he fascinated or overawed them all; even Wolsey had literally trembled before him and said he would 'rather have his tongue torn out with red-hot pincers' than make a proposal unwelcome to the King. His victims made no murmur against his authority, and went to the block praying for the welfare of their 'gentle prince'.

Among all his courtiers no one but More ventured even to hint at criticism, and it was beyond the power of his mild persuasion to influence the Royal will. It was deeply distressing to him to find that he could no longer approve the actions of the master to whom he was bound by the ties of gratitude and long-standing affection; he had promised and desired to serve the King in every possible way; again and again he bowed to his commands, but in the end Henry tried him too far, and found in More's sense of right and justice a barrier which he could not break.

After the events of the 30th of March 1531 More decided that he must as soon as possible retire into private life: 'seeing the

[1] Presumably to the King himself, as he refused to speak of them to any one else.
[2] *Letters and Papers*, v, no. 171, Chapuys to Charles V, 2 Apr. 1531.

King fully determined to proceed forth in the marriage of Queen Anne and . . . doubting lest further attempts should follow, which, contrary to his conscience, by reason of his office, he was likely to be put unto'.[1] He enlisted the help of the Duke of Norfolk, now the most influential man at Court, to persuade the King to accept his resignation, though for some time without avail.

The events of the following year only strengthened his resolve. Parliament reassembled in January 1532 to begin a fresh campaign against ecclesiastical powers, the object of which was 'to intimidate the Pope, to enrich the Crown and to subject the Church'.[2] The clergy were required to submit to measures which forbade them to enact any ordinances without the Royal assent, until it seemed to Chapuys that 'Churchmen would be of less account than shoe-makers'. The King announced his discovery that 'the clergy of our realm be but half our subjects—yea, and scarce our subjects, for the prelates at their consecration make an oath to the Pope clean contrary to the oath they make to us, so that they seem his subjects and not ours'. He said, it was reported, that the bishops ought not to lay hands on persons accused of heresy—they were only doctors of souls, and should not meddle with bodies.[3] In the House of Lords the Chancellor and the Bishops raised some objections to the King's measures, but Convocation, on the 15th of May, accepted the articles which subordinated all ecclesiastical legislation to the pleasure of the Crown.

On the day following this 'submission of the Clergy', More at last obtained leave to lay down his office. Accompanied by the Duke of Norfolk he went to his appointment with the King in the garden of York Place at three in the afternoon; he carried with him the Great Seal in its white leather bag, enclosed in another of crimson velvet, and surrendered it to his Sovereign.[4] Four days later it was given to Sir Thomas Audley, who was, however, not styled Lord Chancellor until January 1533.

The King, it was rumoured, was very angry with the Chancellor, but it was Henry's way to conceal his resentment until the time came to strike. He was still gracious in speech and manner,

[1] Roper, pp. 48–9.
[2] H. A. L. Fisher, *Political History of England*, v. 311. A bill was passed to abolish the annates, of first-fruits of benefices, paid to the Pope on every vacancy. The King reserved the power to give or withhold his consent to the Act, which More apparently did not oppose.
[3] *Letters and Papers*, v, no. 1013, Chapuys to Charles V, 13 May 1532. The statement did not imply any tenderness towards heretics on the part of Henry, but merely his desire to control by royal writ the execution of sentence.
[4] Ibid. v, no. 1075.

thanking Sir Thomas courteously 'with thanks and praise for his
worthy service', and promising to be his 'good and gracious lord'
in any suit or future request that he might make 'that should
either concern his honour or that should appertain unto his
profit'.[1] The plea of ill health made by More to excuse his
resignation was not altogether without foundation, and it was
nominally accepted by the King, who ordered that an 'honourable testimony' should be given to the late Chancellor, on the
installation of his successor, and also in Parliament.[2] It still
remained for More to break the news of his resignation to his wife.
It seems incredible that she should not have known of it at once,
but Roper writes:

'Whereas upon the holydays, during his high chancellorship, one of
his gentlemen, when service at the church was done, ordinarily used to
come to my lady his wife's pew door, and say unto her "Madam, my
lord is gone"; the next holiday after the surrender of his office and
departure of his gentlemen, he came unto my lady his wife's pew himself, and making a low courtesy, said unto her, "Madam, my lord is
gone."'[3]

Probably it was not the first intimation to the poor lady that—
as Pattison the Fool said—'the Chancellor More was Chancellor
no more'. More's resignation of office was a great disappointment
to Dame Alice.[4] She had enjoyed the importance of being the
'Chancellor's lady', in her velvet gowns, her 'gay girdle and her
golden beads'—the capable mistress of a large house and estate
with ample means to maintain a standard of dignified comfort
and generous hospitality. We do not hear that she went to Court,
but she entertained the King himself in her own house, and saw
him walking in her garden with a ponderous arm thrown affectionately round her husband's shoulders—a weighty honour indeed.
His grace had sent a walking-staff wrought with gold to Sir
Thomas, no later than last New Year's day, and still showed him
every favour. Constantly he was summoned to Court and she
saw him almost daily leave his water steps to enter his stately
barge, rowed by eight stalwart watermen. She heard of his
progress through the law courts, 'on his right a golden sceptre
surmounted by the Royal crown, as a sign of his supreme power
under the King, on his left a book, as a sign of his knowledge of
the law; the royal seal carried before him'.[5] Now all this honour
and wealth were thrown away, as it seemed, for a quixotic whim.

[1] Roper, p. 50.
[2] More to Erasmus, 1533, Bridgett, *Life of More*, p. 249.
[3] Roper, pp. 53–4.
[4] 'Dame Alice More' was a usual form of address, as well as 'my Lady More'
and even 'Lady Alice More'.          [5] Stapleton (Hallett's ed.), p. 20.

The loss of office brought serious loss of income. More had not enriched himself, as his predecessor had done, by taking gifts and exorbitant fees; his father, Sir John More, had left his estates for life to his widow, who still survived; Sir Thomas had no great property in land or in gold and silver plate; he gave to all who asked his help, and all Dame Alice's economy had not prevailed over his generosity. No savings had been made, and after his resignation he was faced with comparative poverty. 'He was not able, for the maintenance of himself and such as necessarily belonged to him, sufficiently to find meat, drink, fuel, apparel and such other necessary charges.'

He called all his children together and told them that he had now but little over a hundred pounds a year, so that 'he could not, as he was wont, and gladly would, bear out the whole charges of them all himself, from thenceforth be able to live and continue together as he wished we should'. It would be necessary for all to contribute to the common fund, and even so, to descend to a lower scale of living—and, if all else failed—why, he said, they might yet 'with bags and wallets go a-begging together' and sing on good folks' door-steps, 'and so still keep company and be merry together'.[1] So the serious discussion ended, after all, with a laugh.

Not long afterwards, however, More arranged that his children should settle in homes of their own, keeping the Ropers near his own house at Chelsea.

As soon as he found leisure, he resumed the correspondence with Erasmus which had been long interrupted by the stress of public life. Soon after his resignation, he wrote:

'From the time of my boyhood, dearest Desiderius, I have longed that I might some day enjoy what I rejoice in *your* having always enjoyed—namely, that being free from public business, I might have some time to devote to God and myself. This, by the grace of a great and good God, and by the favour of an indulgent prince, I have at last obtained. I have not, however, obtained it as I hoped, for I wished to reach that last stage of my life in a state which, though suitable to my age, might yet enable me to enjoy my remaining years healthy and unbroken, free from disease and pain. It remains in the hand of God whether this wish—perhaps unreasonable—shall be fulfilled. A disorder, of I know not what nature, has attacked my chest; I suffer less from this in present pain than in fear of the consequence. For when it had troubled me continuously for some months, the physicians whom I consulted gave their opinion that the long continuance of it was dangerous, and the speedy cure impossible, but that it must be dealt with by time, proper diet and medicine. Neither could they fix the period of my

[1] Roper, pp. 51-3.

recovery nor ensure me a complete cure. Considering all this, I saw that I must either lay down my office or fail in the performance of its duties. I could not carry out all the tasks imposed by my position without endangering my life, and if I were to die, I should have to give up my office as well as my life. So I determined to give up one rather than both!

'Wherefore for the benefit both of public business and my own health, I humbly appealed, and not in vain, to the goodness of my noble and excellent Prince. . . .

'I am good for nothing when I am ill. We are not all Erasmuses! Here are you, in a condition which would break the spirit of a vigorous youth, still bringing out book after book, for the instruction and admiration of the world. What matter the attacks upon you ? No great writer ever escaped malignity. But the stone which these slanderers have been rolling so many years is like the stone of Sisyphus, and will recoil on their own heads, and you will stand out more grandly than ever. You allow frankly that if you could have foreseen these pestilent heresies you would have been less outspoken on certain points. Doubtless the Fathers, had they expected such times as ours, would have been more cautious in their utterances. They had their own disorders to attend to, and did not think of the future. . . . The bishops and the king try to check these new doctrines, but they spread wonderfully. The teachers of them retreat into the Low Countries, as into a safe harbour, and send over their works written in English. Our people read them, partly in thoughtlessness, partly from a malicious disposition. They enjoy them, not because they think them true, but because they wish them to be true. Such persons are past mending, but I try to help those who do not go wrong from bad will, but are led astray by clever rogues.'[1]

He wrote in the same strain to Cochlaeus, saying:

'I could not attend to my duties as Chancellor without allowing my health to become daily more impaired. . . . The leisure which the kind favour of my noble Prince has graciously granted at my petition, I intend to devote to study and prayer.'[2]

More was far too discreet to put into writing, even to Erasmus, the principal reasons which moved him to retire from Court. Among these reasons may well have been the growing influence of the man whose principles were the very antithesis of his own.

Thomas Cromwell, once Wolsey's servant, was steadily pushing his way into the King's favour, and it is possible that the intimidation of the clergy and the break with Rome were first proposed by him.[3]

---

[1] More to Erasmus, from Chelsea, 14 June 1533. Part of this letter is translated by Bridgett, op. cit., p. 245, and also by Froude, *Life and Letters of Erasmus*, pp. 374–5. Stapleton also gives it in part, *Tres Thomae* (1588), p. 99 and Hallett's ed., p. 78.

[2] Stapleton, *Tres Thomae* (1588), p. 200; cf. Hallett's ed., p. 79.

[3] Roger B. Merriman, op. cit. i. 90. I have adopted the usual spelling of Cromwell's name, though he himself wrote it 'Crumwell', as it was probably pronounced.

# CHAPTER XIX

# MORE AND THE REFORMATION

## 1523–1533

IN nothing has More been criticized with greater disapproval than in his attitude to the religious Reformation. When he resigned the chancellorship, he determined to devote himself more intensely to the controversial writing which already had occupied a great deal of his scanty leisure.

It has been noted that he entered the dispute over Lutheran teaching in 1523 in defence of the King's book. Before this he had shown himself to be, to some extent, in accord with the principles of reformation, and had criticized those who 'relied more on the ceremonies of their own order than on the grace of God'. He deprecated, however, the extreme application of the tenet that 'Faith alone justifies before God', when it led to the disparagement of a worthy life. Later, he deplored the development of reformed teaching on the Sacraments, and the refusal to pray for the dead.

In a private letter to Bugenhagen in 1525 More wrote:

'You insinuate that we put works in the place of Christ. . . . The Church both believes and teaches that man's works cannot be well done without the grace of God, or be of any merit without faith in Christ. . . . But they fight against faith and deny Christ, who, while they extol only grace and faith, deny the value of works, and make men callous to living well.'[1]

One of More's correspondents on the Continent was Cochlaeus, Luther's bitter opponent, who drew the blackest possible picture of events in Germany, the Anabaptist insurrection and the excesses of the Peasant War. More believed that these excesses were directly due to the teaching of Luther's followers. 'Do you contend', he asked Bugenhagen, 'that it is false to say that your faction has wasted Germany by tumult, slaughter and rapine? Do you dare to call those liars who affirm that your doctrine is the cause of it all?'

The terrible story of the sack of Rome and the cruelties ascribed to Luther's adherents among the Imperial troops confirmed More in his belief that the new doctrines were subversive

---

[1] This was written in reply to a letter addressed to the 'Saints in England' by the Lutheran reformer Bugenhagen (John of Pomerania). More's reply is discussed in an interesting article in the *North British Review*, vol. xxx (1859), 'Sir Thomas More and the Reformation', attributed to Prof. Seebohm.

of all morality and good order; his sympathies were estranged by violence and excess. He dreaded the future outcome of such teaching, fearing that when 'those folk fell once to their horrible heresies . . . they shall at the last fall in a new rage . . . and much harm shall hap upon many good men's heads'. 'For remember now good reader', he wrote again, 'that . . . Christ's church can be but one. Whereupon it must needs follow, that there can none go out of it to begin any new church of Christ. But those therefore that go out thereof, must needs be churches of heretics.'[1]

He urged Erasmus to carry on with his powerful pen the fight against Luther and to let nothing interfere with this work. Erasmus, standing between the opposing camps, deplored the bitter spirit which destroyed all hopes of reconciliation. He was urged to declare himself for the reformers, but would not, lest he should seem to side against the Pope; nor was he willing at first to denounce Luther, 'lest he might be found to fight against the Spirit of God'. Some of his friends sympathized with Luther's cause; he still hoped that a way of fellowship might be opened; he feared that forcible repression of revolt would crush all hope of the peaceful settlement which was the aim of his own life. He grieved to see the uncompromising violence of Luther and his endeavour to replace one tyranny by another. He wrote to Beraldus:

'No one denied that the Church was oppressed by tyranny, ceremonies and human ordinances, instituted for gain. Many people wish for, and are considering, reform, but often reforms begun with too little skill lead to a worse condition and their supporters are brought back into harsher slavery. If only the man would stop altogether, or would only attempt what is more moderate and circumspect! I do not trouble myself about Luther, but I work for the glory of Christ.'[2]

Against his own wish, Erasmus was drawn into the struggle. He was encouraged by More to produce the 'brilliant works in promotion of Christian piety' which were anxiously awaited, and to let nothing—not even illness—interrupt the completion of his *Hyperaspistes* in reply to Luther.[3] More wrote to him, lamenting that the long-standing disease from which Erasmus had suffered was found to be stone, which was fatal to Linacre, and hoping nevertheless soon to see his book completed.

'Truly you can scarcely believe how eagerly all good men are awaiting it, while certain evil men, who either favour Luther, or are envious of you, seem to rejoice in the delay of your reply. If you have stopped for

---

[1] More's *English Works* (1557), p. 628.
[2] Louvain, 16 Feb. 1521, Allen, iv, no. 1185 (abridged).
[3] A treatise written in reply to Luther's *De Servo Arbitrio*.

a time, while finishing other works, such as the *Institutio Christiani Matrimonii*, which her Majesty the Queen esteems so highly—as I hope you will shortly experience—I can bear the delay with resignation. And if you are giving more accurate study to the subject, I rejoice—But if, as some allege, the fear of danger has stopped your work, and you dare not proceed, then I cannot sufficiently express my surprise nor moderate my grief. God forbid, sweetest Erasmus, that you, who have endured such Herculean labours for the benefit of the world, should now begin to cherish the years of sickness, and rather than lose the stone, would desert the cause of God! I cannot doubt that you will keep that fine strength of mind even to the last act of your life, even if it should come about by a most stormy catastrophe, for you can never cease to trust in God.'[1]

Erasmus replied to the persuasions of More and Tunstall, now Bishop of London, that he found it hard to differ from two such friends, but he saw little use in stirring up a hornet's nest as he had done before. 'I cannot be the leader of any earthly party. There are many fitted to take the lead in this struggle for which I am neither fitted in character, spirit nor aptitude. I am of the opinion that the whole controversy is a matter of words rather than of subject. It does not conduce to piety.' A change of life, he considered, was more desirable than a change of dogma; he was reluctant to embark on a discussion concerning free will and grace; if he had treated the subject in the spirit of the monks and theologians, he would be speaking against his own conscience, and would darken the glory of Christ.[2]

To his friends, however, Erasmus seemed the most fitting leader of their cause. Probably at the suggestion of Tunstall or More, an invitation was sent to him by Henry VIII to make England his head-quarters in an attack on heresy. The King reminded him that he had once spoken of England as the chosen refuge of his old age, and referred to his services to letters and religion. 'You will easily understand', he continued, 'how necessary it is to attack these evils. No way seems better than for you to leave Italy and Germany and to come over to our kingdom. If it seems pleasant and acceptable to you, it will not only be very pleasing to us, but you shall come on the best of terms, which you will find both liberal and honourable.'[3]

Erasmus wrote to More to make his excuses to the King—he did not wish to leave the protection of the Emperor for that of Henry, and looked to More to express his gratitude while declining the offer. He added that 'it was indeed about time for him to

[1] More to Erasmus, 18 Dec. 1526, from Greenwich, Allen, vi, no. 1770 (abridged).
[2] Erasmus to More, Basel, 30 Mar. 1527, Allen, vii, no. 1804.
[3] Henry VIII to Erasmus, 18 Sept. 1527, Allen, vii, no. 1878.

look round for a sepulchre—a dead man at least may be allowed the quiet which is denied to a live one!' At the same time Erasmus spoke of the great increase of the Anabaptist heresy.[1]

The anxiety of the English bishops grew as controversial writings came pouring into England from the Continent. Tunstall was anxious to check their influence, especially in his diocese of London, where forbidden works were secretly but widely read. There was no one more capable than More of putting the orthodox case in a popular and convincing manner; his high character, his literary distinction, his skill in argument, his wit, and not least his popularity, pointed to him as the best advocate that could be found.

Tunstall authorized More to read heretical books in order to refute them, and wrote:

'Because you, most dear brother, are able to emulate Demosthenes in our vernacular tongue no less than in Latin, and are an ardent defender of Catholic truth whenever you hear it attacked, you cannot spend the occasional hours that you can steal from your official duties better than in composing in our own language such books as may show to simple and unlearned men the cunning malice of the heretics, and fortify them against these impious subverters of the Church, for it is of great help towards victory to know the plans of the enemy, for if you try to refute what they protest they do not hold, you lose your pains. Engage therefore courageously in this holy work, by which you will benefit the Church of God.'[2]

In response to this appeal, More produced a number of controversial works in support of the orthodox teaching of the Catholic Church.[3]

In his study of the proscribed writings which were being brought secretly into England, More found that the chief of his

[1] Erasmus to More, Basel, 29 Feb. 1528, Allen, vii, no. 1959.
[2] Bridgett, *Life of More*, p. 281 (abridged).
[3] One of the principal of these was *The Dialogue concerning Tyndale*, a Platonic dialogue described as 'a masterpiece of its kind' which appeared in 1528. It was printed in Rastell's edition of More's *English Works* (1557), and has lately been re-edited by W. E. Campbell (1927) with introductions and notes by the editor and by Dr. A. W. Reed. It was followed by a second work, *The Supplication of Souls* (1529), in answer to a tract by Simon Fish, called the *Supplication of Beggars*, directed against the mendicant friars. During his Chancellorship, More found time to write his *Confutation of Tyndale's answer* (1532). After his resignation he answered by a letter a treatise by John Frith on the doctrine of the Eucharist; and composed also his *Apology* (1533), *The debellation of Salem and Byzance*, and *The Answer to the Poisoned Book which a nameless heretic hath named the Supper of the Lord*. The discussion of these writings is outside the scope of the present volume. They are competently summarized, from More's own point of view, by Father T. E. Bridgett in his *Life of More*, p. 281 seq. An interesting account of them, from a different angle, is given by the Rev. R. Demaus, in his *William Tyndale*, ch. ix.

opponents was William Tyndale, whose translation of the New Testament was sold in ever-increasing numbers.

Tyndale in his youth, like More, was influenced by the teaching of Colet and of Erasmus, whose *New Testament* inspired the great aim of his own life—the translation of the Bible into the English tongue. There was nothing in this ambition hostile to the teaching of leading English churchmen; nothing, certainly, contrary to the principles of More, who wrote:

'Nor I never yet heard any reason laid, why it were not convenient to have the Bible translated into the English tongue, but all those reasons seemed they never so gay and glorious at the first sight . . . might . . . as well be laid against the holy writers that wrote the Scripture in the Hebrew tongue, and against the blessed Evangelists that wrote the Scripture in Greek and against all those in likewise that translated it out of every of those tongues into Latin, as to their charge that would well and faithfully translate it out of Latin into our English tongue.'[1]

More himself translated into English many passages from the Gospels; he spoke of the Bible as 'the Queen of all books'. The need for an English version was acknowledged, but the Bishops took no steps to supply one. 'And surely', said More: 'how it hath happed that in all this while God hath either not suffered, or not provided that any good virtuous man hath had the mind in faithful wise to translate it, and thereupon either the clergy, or at the leastwise some one bishop to approve it, this can I nothing tell.'[2]

Tyndale, as early as 1523, sought the approval of the Church in his great work, but in vain. To Tunstall, Bishop of London, renowned for enlightened culture, friend of Erasmus and More, Tyndale came, full of hope, asking for sympathy and help—but Tunstall turned away the eager young scholar; he had not the vision to see the opportunity that was at his door, nor did he guess what a noble work he might have furthered, if only he had given his approval to Tyndale's great design, and had enlisted on his behalf the help of More and his School in the production of an English version of the Scriptures. Great bitterness might have been avoided had Tyndale and More been associated in this work, instead of being driven into enmity with one another.

The opportunity was lost; the Church did not act, and the reformers could not wait. Tyndale went abroad where he came under the influence of men whose hatred of the Papacy made an ever-widening breach between orthodox churchmen and themselves. With no help from his own country, without the support he had sought from the Church, Tyndale laboured to produce the

---

[1] More's *English Works* (1557), p. 243 (*Dialogue*).   [2] Ibid., p. 241.

beautiful and treasured version of the Scriptures which was destined to have an immeasurable influence on the literature and on the spiritual life of the English people.[1]

The scornful hostility of More to this noble work is one of the saddest incidents in his literary life. So great was his horror of the heretical tenets of the reformers that he could accept nothing from their hands. In unmeasured words he denounced Tyndale's translation of the New Testament, seeing, in many of the terms used, the intention of the translator to disparage the authority of the Church and to 'corrupt and change from the good and wholesome doctrine of Christ to devilish heresies of his own'. He contended that the Church alone had authority to interpret the Scriptures, whereas the reformers appealed to the Scriptures against the authority of the Church, by the light of individual reason. He compared Tyndale's version to 'poisoned bread' which could not be scraped clean again, and declared that 'the faults be as ye see so many and so spread through the whole book, that likewise as it were as soon done to weave a new web of cloth as to sew up every hole in a net, so were it almost as little labour and less to translate the whole book all new, as to make in his translation so many changes as needs must be ere it were made good'.[2]

More was frankly prejudiced against Tyndale's work, and a controversy ensued in which neither was capable of giving justice to the other. More's indignation was roused by the pamphlets, in which Tyndale assailed the papal system and the general practices of the Church with implacable hostility and bitter sarcasm.[3]

Tyndale regarded More as one who had seen the dawning light of reform and had turned from it deliberately to the darkness of old superstitions. He believed, sincerely though mistakenly, that More had sold his pen for money and was bribed by the Bishops to write against his own conscience. 'He knew the truth and for covetousness forsook it again', Tyndale asserted: 'Covetousness blinded the eyes of that gleering fox more and more and hardened his heart against the truth.' He included More among those whom he described as 'poisoned spiders', which spread 'a dark stinking mist of devilish glosses on the clear text of Scripture'.[4]

More's denunciation of Tyndale—'that beast and hell-hound of the devil's kennel'—was equally vindictive. It was indeed

---

[1] It was not until 1534 that Convocation petitioned the King for an authorized English Bible. The Authorized Version, issued under Cranmer, owed much to the work of Tyndale (cf. Demaus, op. cit., p. 485).

[2] More's *English Works* (1557), p. 224 (*Dialogue*).

[3] *The Obedience of a Christian Man* and the *Parable of the Wicked Mammon*.

[4] Demaus, op. cit., p. 355.

a pitiable thing to see those two noble and saintly souls, each pouring out upon the other violent abuse in the name of Christ, the one upholding the Church and the other the Bible as the supreme arbiter of morals and the only authoritative guide to the Christian life. In this tragic controversy More defended with all his force the authority and unity of the Church, while Tyndale was ready to make any sacrifice to spread the free light of the Gospels through all the land.

The charge made against More of accepting bribes for his writing was due to a mistaken report. The bishops and clergy had offered him a large sum of money as a recompense for his literary work on behalf of the Church, but he had instantly refused this offer, nor would he accept anything on behalf of his wife or children. 'Not so my lords,' he replied, when the Bishops begged him to do so: 'I had liever see it cast into the Thames than either I or any of mine should have thereof the worth of a penny.'[1] He wrote: 'I am both over proud and over slothful also, to be hired for money to take half the labour and business in writing, that I have taken in this gear since I began.'[2]

More's vehement controversial writings naturally drew upon him the bitter resentment of the reformers. He made no secret of his dread of heresy, which, in his days, was regarded not merely as the holding of unorthodox religious views, but as a species of high treason against the Church.[3] He feared it as a form of poisonous epidemic, which, if allowed to spread unchecked, would overthrow all government, whether secular or ecclesiastical, and lead to the moral and material ruin of the Christian world. 'As touching heretics,' he said, 'I hate that vice of theirs and not their persons, and very fain would I that the one were destroyed and the other saved.' But this was a distinction difficult to remember in the heat of battle, and he admitted to Erasmus that he took pride in describing himself as 'troublesome to heretics'; 'for I so entirely detest that race of men that there is none to which I would be more hostile—unless they amend. For every day more and more I find them to be of such a sort, that I greatly fear for what they are bringing on the world.'[4]

Largely owing to his own writings, he came to be regarded as the responsible and active leader of the religious persecution that was renewed after the fall of Wolsey. As soon as More became Chancellor, stated Froude, 'the Smithfield fires recommenced',

[1] Roper, p. 46.        [2] *English Works* (1557), p. 867 (*Apology*).
[3] Holdsworth, op. cit. i. 616.
[4] More to Erasmus, 1533, Bridgett, op. cit., p. 250.

the 'genial philosopher' became the 'merciless bigot'.[1] The accusations of Foxe, who was followed by Burnet and Froude, were repeated by other writers; it was even said, in a popular history, that More's Chancellorship was '*chiefly* notable for his persecution of heretics . . . burnings at Smithfield became numerous'.

In more recent years the facts concerning these alleged 'numerous burnings' have been investigated; it has been demonstrated that, for the first two years that More was Chancellor, no burnings for heresy took place at Smithfield;[2] in the last few months of his term of office, when he was already losing favour and power, there were three.[3] It is possible that John Frith was arrested on a warrant issued by More, as Chancellor,[4] though it is not clear that he returned to England from the Continent while More was still in office. When Frith was examined by Cranmer and the Council in June 1533, the Lord Chancellor who was present was not More but Thomas Audley, and More can have had no legal responsibility for the condemnation by Bishop Stokesley of Frith, who suffered martyrdom in July 1533.[5]

The question arises, how far was More responsible for the three martyrdoms at Smithfield in the last year of his Chancellorship?

It was laid down by the canon law that the penalty for heresy was death by burning; the common law recognized this rule, and it was required by statute that all secular officials from the Chancellor downwards should assist the ecclesiastical courts in the repression of heresy.[6] The Chancellor might issue writs for the arrest of heretics, but the responsibility for deciding on the fate of a person condemned in the episcopal court rested on the Bishop.

The authority of Wolsey, as Papal Legate *a latere*, was superior to that of the episcopal courts and enabled him to restrain their severity; More, though the highest magistrate in the land, had no jurisdiction in heresy by law. Wolsey's biographer has

---

[1] An account of More's alleged cruelties is given by Froude, *History of England* (1868), ii. 76–88.

[2] There was one at Norwich, when Bilney was burned, 19 Aug. 1531.

[3] These were Bayfield, Tewkesbury, and Bainham, who relapsed into heresy (Gairdner, *The English Church in the sixteenth century*, pp. 128–30). Also *North British Review*, xxx (1859), 'Sir Thomas More and the Reformation'.

[4] It is so stated in *D.N.B.* ('John Frith'), but it is said that Frith returned 'about the middle of the year' (ibid.) and More had resigned in May. Foxe (*Acts and Monuments*, v. 6 (4th ed.)) speaks in general terms of the 'great hatred and deadly pursuit' of Sir Thomas More, who 'persecuted him [Frith] both by land and sea', and offered rewards for 'any tidings of him'. More was still a member of the Council till 1534, though living in retirement.

[5] *Letters and Papers*, vi, nos. 661 and 761.

[6] Holdsworth, op. cit. i. 617.

pointed out that the comparison often made between the two Chancellors is fallacious.

'Confusion mainly arises from remembering that both were Chancellors but forgetting that one was the highest ecclesiastic in the land, while the other was only a layman. That was the essential difference: Wolsey could have burnt as many heretics as he wished, and it is to his credit that he refrained; but the law gave no jurisdiction in heresy to laymen, however exalted. . . . More therefore had and could have legally nothing to do with any sentence of death for heresy. . . . Wolsey's legatine authority overrode episcopal jurisdiction; it was in his legatine court that heretics were condemned in penalties which were often preliminary to the harsher fate they encountered when the bishops recovered their liberty; the diocesan courts of Stokesley in London, Nix at Norwich and Vesey in Exeter account for all the burnings during the chancellorship of Sir Thomas More.'[1]

The revival of persecution was in fact not due to More's succession to Wolsey but to the liberation of the episcopal courts from the legatine supremacy of Wolsey, and to the succession of Stokesley to the Bishopric of London in place of Tunstall. The responsibility of More was limited to the possible issue of writs for the arrest or execution of heretics,[2] and to his support of the authority of the ecclesiastical courts to exercise jurisdiction in cases of heresy. The law was explicit; the notorious statute *de haeretico comburendo* directed that a person convicted of heresy should be burned to death by the civil power;[3] the only possible respite was for the victim to be detained in the bishop's prison until he abjured. The King was as great an opponent of heresy as the Bishops.

More, as Chancellor, at times had the custody of persons accused of heresy, pending their committal to the Bishops' Court; in some cases he assisted at their examination, but this is not, in itself, evidence of cruelty.[4] His anxiety was not to convict but

[1] A. F. Pollard, *Wolsey*, pp. 209, 213–14. Erasmus believed that More possessed the power to condemn heretics and refrained from using it; but he was no longer in close touch with English affairs.

[2] Cf. Pollard's *Wolsey*, pp. 211–12 and note. 'How far More usurped the function of issuing writs to burn depends upon Foxe's casual and contradictory remarks that writs were received before the burning of some of the half-dozen martyrs who suffered that death during More's Chancellorship. The absence of any confirmation of Foxe on this point suggests that he is wrong.'

[3] 2 Hen. IV, c. 15.

[4] Cf. Gairdner, *The English Church in the sixteenth century*, p. 130. Tewkesbury was sentenced by the Bishop of London at More's house, Chelsea, and was burned at Smithfield, 20 Dec. 1531. Bainham was also examined there and persuaded to submit to the Church, but revoked his submission. Foxe told a story, first of Tewkesbury and then of Bainham, that More had the prisoner whipped and tortured, but 'the story is in fact one of those malicious lies which began to be circulated about More even in his own days and which More himself

to convince them, and his own word for it may be accepted, that he used 'favour and pity' towards them, striving 'in the most hearty loving wise that he could' to persuade them to conform to the law, and so save themselves—as he sincerely believed—from both present and eternal fire.

When More was imprisoned in the Tower, having refused to deny the papal supremacy, he described how Cromwell taunted him with his former conduct towards heretics, while he was Chancellor. 'He said that I then, *as he thought, and at the leastwise bishops*, did use to examine heretics whether they believed the Pope to be head of the Church, and used to compel them to make a plain answer thereto.'

More neither admitted nor denied the charge, but observed that, at that time, the authority of the Pope was universally acknowledged and accepted in England and all other Christian countries. He made a distinction between the case of contumacious heretics and his own, when he would not accept the Royal supremacy, which was a 'law local', recently made in England only, contrary to the long-established law of 'the whole corps of Christendom'.[1]

When More went with Tunstall to Antwerp in 1529, and a search for English heretics was set on foot, the object was not to hunt down harmless fugitives, but to prevent the exportation to England of proscribed books. The methods which More preferred to use were those of reason first, and then ridicule. When Tyndale's brother and an associate were brought before More in the Star Chamber, on a charge of selling copies of the forbidden New Testament, he sentenced them to be exhibited in Cheapside, seated on horses, their faces to the tail, and hung round with the prohibited volumes.[2]

The charges of cruelty to prisoners accused of heresy brought against More in his life time, he answered in his *Apology*. Of the two petitions extant in the Public Record Office, which accused him of illegal imprisonment, one was not substantiated; the other does not appear to have been a case of heresy at all.[3] Wild stories were circulated of the 'cruel tormenting' of heretics in More's house—he had invented a new torture, it was rumoured, burning the soles of his victim's feet 'in new boots'—others were reported

expressly denounces as such. . . . More was undoubtedly a great enemy to heretics . . . but he gave effect to his enmity in methods strictly legitimate, and nothing that he ever did was tainted with inhumanity' (ibid.).

[1] *English Works* (1557), p. 1454; Roper, appendix, 156–7.
[2] Demaus, op. cit., pp. 18 and 293.
[3] The first case was that of Phillips (*Proceedings of British Academy*, xii. 193). The second, that of John Field (*Letters and Papers*, vi, no. 1059). Froude accepts the charges as true: *History of England* (1856 ed.), ii. 76–83.

to be bound to a tree in his garden and 'piteously beaten', or chained with heavy irons like wild beasts.

In reply to these charges, More admitted that he had sometimes sanctioned a prison flogging in the Marshallsea and elsewhere, in cases of robbery, murder, and sacrilege, committed by 'desperate wretches as else had not failed to have gone farther abroad, and to have done to many good folk, a great deal much more harm'. Yet he was more humane in these cases than most magistrates of his time, for he stipulated that punishment should not be so severe as to cause permanent injury to the offender.

With regard to heretics, however, More declared most earnestly, that except in two instances, he had never in his life used any force, 'saving only their sure keeping'. In one of these instances, a boy who was a servant in his house had been whipped 'like a child before my household, for amendment of himself, and ensample of such other', because he had repeated to another child in the house heretical teaching which he had heard at home, and which was proscribed by law. There were few houses besides More's in which the beating of children was an unusual occurrence. As to the case of the half-witted fellow who disturbed the church-goers of Chelsea, the following is More's own account.

'He used, in his wandering about to come into the church, and there to make many mad toys and trifles, to the trouble of good people in the divine service, and specially would he be most busy in the time of most silence, while the priest was at the secrets of the Mass about the levation. And if he spied any woman kneeling at a forme, if her head hung any-thing low in her meditations, then would he steal behind her, and if he were not letted [prevented], would labour to lift up all her clothes, and cast them quite over her head. Whereupon I being advertised of these pageants, and being sent unto and required by very devout religious folk, to take some other order with him, caused him as he came wander-ing by my door, to be taken by the constables, and bounden to a tree in the street before the whole town, and there they striped him with rods therefore till he waxed weary, and somewhat longer. And it appeared well that his remembrance was good enough, save that it went about grazing till it was beaten home. For he could then very well rehearse his faults himself, and speak and treat very well, and promise to do afterward as well. And verily God be thanked I hear none harm of him now.'

The rather callous humour of this tale has proved itself a little shocking to a generation which tends to regard crime as insanity, whereas in the sixteenth century, insanity was treated as crime. More's action was at any rate more merciful than a recommittal

---

[1] More's *English Works* (1557), p. 901 (*Apology*).

of the culprit to Bedlam, and it can hardly be counted as religious persecution.

'Of all that ever came into my hand for heresy,' More wrote, 'as help me God, saving as I said the sure keeping of them, and yet not so sure neither, but that George Constantine could steal away, else had never any of them any stripe or stroke given them, so much as a fillip on the forehead.'

This explicit statement, made by a man of such high character as More's, may be held to outweigh unsubstantiated rumour. The specific charges of cruelty and of illegality brought against him are either disproved or 'not proven', but on the other hand it must be admitted that he acquiesced in the barbarous law against heresy, and that he defended the authority of the epis- copal courts, which might be expected to administer it with severity. He could make no allowance for the burning zeal which inspired the reformers to speech and action. 'I neither will nor can cease to speak', Frith exclaimed: 'for the Word of God boileth in my body, and will needs have issue!' He offered, for Tyndale and himself, to write no more, if only the Bishops would 'grant that the Word of God, I mean the text of Scripture, may go abroad in our English tongue, as other nations have it in their tongues'. Failing this, he said, they must needs continue, and 'so at the least, save some'.

In their fearless eagerness for truth they could not bring them- selves to accept the liberty of silence which was all that More could offer them, and, in the end, all that he asked for himself, when he too came into conflict with the authority of the State.

# CHAPTER XX

# ANXIOUS YEARS

## 1532–1534

SOON after More resigned the office of Lord Chancellor, there came to him at his house at Chelsea, with a message from the King, Thomas Cromwell, the former retainer of Wolsey, who, at the Cardinal's disgrace, had shed tears of anxiety—for himself; and had ridden off alone from Esher to London, as he said, 'to make or mar'. Now, quietly and assiduously, he was gaining influence at Court, and making his own fortune, while he promised to help the King to become 'the richest prince that ever was in Christendom'. Cromwell's large heavy face gave little hint of his subtle brain; his thoughts were secret to himself, but at times his shifty eyes would light up with a look of extraordinary cunning, as he threw a sly, oblique glance at his interlocutor, to see the effect of an unexpectedly witty remark.[1] Though he was one of the most harsh and unfeeling of men, he could assume a pleasing and flattering manner when he thought it expedient; he made no show of enmity against the man whom he laboured to destroy, but posed for a long time as his friend.

When their business was done More ventured to offer him a piece of prescient advice.

'Master Cromwell,' he said, 'you are now entered into the service of a most noble, wise and liberal prince; if you will follow my poor advice, you shall, in your counsel-giving to his grace, ever tell him what he ought to do, but never what he is able to do. So shall you show yourself a true faithful servant and a right wise and worthy counsellor. For if a lion knew his own strength, hard were it for any man to rule him.'[2]

The advice was wasted on Cromwell, the student and follower of Machiavelli, whose whole policy was opposed to the principles inculcated by More. It is impossible to know how far Cromwell was the originator of the far-reaching changes effected by Henry VIII, but there is little doubt that his insinuating whispers constantly impressed upon the King 'what he was able to do', and showed him ways and means of achieving the concentration of supreme power in the Crown.

In pursuance of this policy the severance from Rome was made irrevocable. An act was passed forbidding appeals to Rome from

[1] Cf. Roger Bigelow Merriman, op. cit. i. 84–5.
[2] Roper, p. 55.

PLATE 13

THOMAS CROMWELL. Earl of Essex
*National Portrait Gallery*

the Courts in England; it was declared that all spiritual cases
henceforth should be 'finally and definitely adjudged and determined within the King's jurisdiction and authority and not
elsewhere'.[1]

Early in 1533, in defiance of papal authority, Anne Boleyn was
married secretly to the King. Cranmer, the new Archbishop who
had succeeded Warham, pronounced Henry's first marriage null;
in June, Queen Anne was crowned with great magnificence at
Westminster. Sir Thomas More, watching these things from
Chelsea, said to his son-in-law forbodingly, 'God give grace, son,
that these matters within a while be not confirmed with oaths.'
Roper adds: 'I, at that time seeing no likelihood thereof, yet
fearing lest for his fore-speaking it would the sooner come to
pass, waxed therefore for his so saying much offended with
him.'[2]

Some of his old friends, Bishops Tunstall, Gardiner, and Clarke,
made an attempt to bring him to the ceremony. They begged
him to accompany them to the Abbey, and to accept twenty
pounds to buy a gown for the occasion. The money he kept, but
the coronation day saw him quietly 'at home still tarrying', and
he told the three bishops 'merrily' when next he met them that
as he had granted them *one* of their requests, he thought he might
be the bolder to deny the other!

The enmity of the new Queen's party was made inevitable by
his absence from the Coronation, which showed all too plainly
the disapproval which he was careful not to express in words.

After the marriage Henry gave up all attempts to compromise
with the Papacy; it was announced that the Pope was to be
spoken of as 'Bishop of Rome'; his authority in England was
denied, his jurisdiction forbidden. Parliament met on the 15th of
January 1534; the final measures were passed in March.[3]

By the Act of Succession of 1534 the succession to the throne
was vested in the heirs of Henry and Anne. In the preamble to
the Act, which has been described as 'a treatise on the canon law,
a constitutional enactment and a political manifesto', it was
stated that the King's marriage with Catherine was invalid, his
marriage with Anne, valid. Catherine was to be called princess
'dowager to Prince Arthur'.

As More had feared, Henry was not content to enforce his will
in Parliament. It was decreed that all his subjects should swear

---

[1] February 1533.                          [2] Roper, p. 56.
[3] The 'act for the restraint of annates'; an act forbidding the payment of
'Peter's pence' and all other pensions or fees to Rome; an act embodying the
submission of the clergy to the Crown, and reaffirming the act in restraint of
appeals (H. A. L. Fisher, *Political History*, v. 325–6).

before Royal Commissioners that they would 'observe and maintain' the Act; the penalties of refusal were those of misprision of
treason. Cranmer, Audley, Norfolk, and Suffolk were the Commissioners first appointed. The oath was taken by the members
of both houses of Parliament on the 30th of March.

The imposition of the oath was intended as a test of loyalty to
the King's revolution; it reflects the nervousness felt by Cromwell
lest the new measures should be followed by rebellion. A veritable
reign of terror ensued, which lasted while Cromwell was in favour.
His spies were everywhere; private conversations were reported;
arrests were made on the slightest pretext. The King was irritated
by the long-delayed and useless verdict at last given by the Pope
in favour of Catherine; he was determined to be master in his
own country and to exact from his subjects an express repudiation
of papal authority.

More knew himself to be in the greatest danger. He was
charged, early in 1534, with writing a pamphlet against a proclamation of the King's Council, which was made in justification
of the marriage with Anne. He cleared himself easily of this
charge, and he wrote earnestly to Cromwell: 'I know my bounden
duty to bear more honour to my prince and more reverence to his
honourable council, than that it could become me for many
causes to make an answer, or to counsel any man else to do it.'[1]
Other grounds of accusation against him were sought out; he
was summoned before the King's Council to answer various
frivolous charges of receiving bribes while he was Lord Chancellor.
He admitted that he had indeed been offered by a lady 'a fair
great gilt cup' which he had accepted. Whereupon Lord Wiltshire, Anne Boleyn's father, called out joyfully, 'Lo my lords, did
I not tell you, my lords, that you should find this matter true?'
But after all, it was only one of More's jokes—he could not give
them up, to save his life—he had merely pledged the giver, and
returned the cup to her again. And thus, observes Roper, 'was
the great mountain turned scant to a little mole-hill'.[2]

The next attempt made against him was a groundless charge
of complicity in the notorious affair of the 'Holy Maid of Kent'.
Many people, including Bishop Fisher, believed that divine
inspiration was the source of the prophecies uttered by Elizabeth
Barton, a poor girl who became a nun at Canterbury and who
gained an immense reputation for her revelations and miracles.
Unfortunately she was drawn into politics and declared herself commissioned by God to protest against the Royal divorce.

---

[1] *Letters and Papers*, vii, no. 149, 1 Feb. 1534. Roper, appendix, p. 100.
[2] Roper, p. 61.

A political plot was suspected by the government; the nun and several associates were arrested, and subsequently executed.

In the face of all the evidence, the name of More, as well as that of Fisher, was included in a bill of attainder on a charge of misprision of treason. Cromwell tried craftily to cross-examine William Roper, in the hope of getting from him an admission that More had 'declared favour' to the nun, and had 'given her advice and counsel'; on hearing of this More wrote to Cromwell a long letter giving a complete vindication of his own part in the matter.[1]

He had indeed acted with the utmost prudence. He had been interested in the reports he heard of the marvellous sayings of the nun, but he had utterly refused to hear from her anything concerning the King; he had advised her not to meddle with the affairs of princes 'but only to commune and talk with any persons high or low, of any such manner things as may to the soul be profitable for you to show and for them to know'.[2]

Again he was summoned to appear as a culprit before the King's Council, of which he had been an honoured member for sixteen years. It was evident that the charge of conspiring with the nun was the merest excuse; the King's hope was that the bill of attainder would be to Sir Thomas 'so troublous and terrible that it would force him to relent and condescend to his request'— in other words, to announce his approval of the divorce, and his denial of papal authority.

From friendly persuasion the Councillors turned to threats, and unfairly reproached him with his part in the King's book against Luther, published thirteen years before. To their threats he replied quietly, 'My lords, these terrors be for children, and not for me'. He reminded them of the true circumstances of his advice to the King concerning the supremacy of the Pope, and said that he trusted his highness would 'call to his gracious remembrance my doings in that behalf, and clear me thoroughly therein himself'.

The four Councillors who heard his defence were Cranmer, who inclined to be friendly towards him; the Duke of Norfolk, whose former friendship was giving way before his anxiety to stand well with the King; Cromwell, the King's secretary, who was working secretly for More's destruction; and Audley, the new Chancellor, a poor creature, hand in glove with Cromwell. Before the interview, William Roper earnestly advised his father-in-law 'to labour unto those Lords for the help of his discharge out of that

[1] Roper, appendix, p. 101 seq.
[2] Ibid., p. 107; and cf. *Letters and Papers*, vii, nos. 265, 287, 288, 289, 296.

Parliament Bill'. Sir Thomas answered that he would do so, but Roper, who met him on the way home, wrote afterwards:

'Then took Sir Thomas More his boat towards his house at Chelsey, wherein by the way he was very merry, and for that I was nothing sorry, hoping that he had gotten himself discharged out of the Parliament bill. When he was landed and come home, then walked we twain alone in his garden together; where I, desirous to know how he had sped, said: "I trust Sir, that all is well, because that you be so merry."

'"It is so, indeed son Roper, I thank God," quoth he.

'"Are you then put out of the Parliament bill?" quoth I.

'"By my troth, son Roper," quoth he, "I never remembered it."

'"Never remembered it Sir!" said I: "a case that toucheth yourself so near, and us all for your sake! I am sorry to hear it, for I verily trusted, when I saw you so merry, that all had been well."

'Then said he: "Wilt thou know, son Roper, why I was so merry?"

'"That would I gladly Sir," quoth I.

'"In good faith, I rejoiced son," said he, "that I had given the devil a foul fall, and that with those lords I had gone so far as without great shame I could never go back again."

'At which words waxed I very sad, for though himself liked it well, yet liked it me but a little.'[1]

When the result of the interview was reported to the King, Henry broke into furious anger; he deprived More of his salary as Councillor,[2] and determined that nothing should save him from being attainted in Parliament. With the utmost difficulty Audley and Cromwell persuaded Henry that the Lords of the Upper House were 'so precisely bent to hear him in his own defence make answer himself, that if he were not put out of that Bill, it would without fail be utterly an overthrow of all'. They added, says Roper, that 'they mistrusted not in time, against him to find some meeter matter to serve his grace's turn better'.[3]

The counsels of prudence prevailed; on the following day, Cromwell, meeting Roper in the Parliament House, smoothly pretended friendship, and told the good news of More's discharge. 'He willed me', continues Roper's narrative, 'to tell my father that he was put out of the Parliament Bill. But because I had appointed to dine that day in London, I sent the message by my servant to my wife to Chelsey. Whereof when she informed her father; "In faith, Meg," quoth he, "*Quod differtur non aufertur.*"'

[1] Roper, p. 67.
[2] *Letters and Papers*, vii, no. 296, Chapuys, 7 Mar. 1534. The last instalment of More's salary was paid at Easter 1534 (*P.R.O.* E 405, nos. 104, 202).
[3] Roper (pp. 67–8) does not give his authority for the account of this interview.

PLATE 14

Mother Iak.

MARGARET GIGGS. Wife of John Clement. *By* HOLBEIN

Soon after this the Duke of Norfolk came to Sir Thomas with a rough but friendly warning, and

'as they chanced to fall in familiar talk together, the Duke said unto him; "By the Mass, Master More, it is perilous striving with princes; therefore I would wish you somewhat to incline to the King's pleasure; for by Gods body, Master More, *Indignatio principis mors est.*"[1]

'"Is that all, my Lord?", quoth he; "then in good faith the difference between your grace and me is but this, that I shall die to-day and you to-morrow."'[2]

So Norfolk, who had said no more than the truth, went away offended, for, though he liked Sir Thomas, he set more value on the King's favour than on the claims of friendship.

Fisher, who alone of all the Bishops had dared to oppose the King, was already condemned to imprisonment in the Tower, on a charge of misprision of treason; More was well aware that very soon he should share the fate of his old friend. He realized the shock which the dreaded summons would cause to his own family, and in the midst of his own mental struggle, he did all in his power to prepare them for the blow. He was no iron saint, secure in an armour of self-righteousness, but very human, very much afraid; yet never for one moment wavering in his steadfast obedience to the call of conscience. He was not one of those who sought martyrdom; he said truly that he would have rejoiced to believe the King's cause just and his own judgement mistaken. He confided afterwards to his daughter Margaret:

'I found myself (I cry God mercy) very sensual and my flesh much more shrinking from pain and from death than methought it the part of a faithful Christian man.'[3]

And in another letter:

'That you fear of your own frailty, Margaret, nothing misliketh me. God give us both twain grace to despair of ourselves and wholly to hang upon the strength of God. . . . Surely Meg, a fainter heart than thy frail father hath, thou canst not have. And yet I verily trust in the great mercy of God that he shall of his goodness so stay me with his holy Hand that he shall not finally suffer me to fall wretchedly from his favour.'[4]

On Sunday the 12th of April he went with William Roper to hear the sermon at St. Paul's; after the service he went to the house of John and Margaret Clement, his own old home in Bucklersbury; one of the King's officers followed him there and he was cited to appear on the following morning before the

---

[1] This was a saying often repeated in warning to Queen Catherine by Archbishop Warham.  [2] Roper, pp. 68–9.
[3] *English Works* (1557), p. 1448.  [4] Ibid., p. 1449.

Commissioners at the Archbishop's palace at Lambeth for the purpose of taking the new oath.

He returned home at once, and that evening bade farewell to
all his dear ones, whom he scarcely expected to see again; he
knew the consequences of the refusal upon which he was determined. The next morning he went early to Church, to confess, to
hear Mass, and to receive the Sacrament, as he had done always
before any important event in his life. His words of farewell to
his family remained between himself and them; but William
Roper's touching narrative gives an incomparable account of his
last departure from his Chelsea garden, the scene of so many
happy hours.

'And whereas he evermore used before at his departure from his wife
and children whom he tenderly loved, to have them bring him to his
boat, and there to kiss them all and bid them farewell, then would he
suffer none of them forth of the gate to follow him, but pulled the wicket
after him and shut them all from him; and with a heavy heart, as by his
countenance it appeared, with me and our four servants there took boat
towards Lambeth. Wherein sitting still sadly awhile, at the last he
rounded me in the ear, and said, "Son Roper, I thank our Lord the
field is won." What he meant thereby I then wist not, yet loath to
seem ignorant I answered, "Sir, I am thereof very glad." But as I
conjectured afterwards, it was, for that the love he had to God wrought
in him so effectually, that it conquered all his carnal affections utterly.'[1]

Arrived at Lambeth, More passed alone through the familiar
gateway, known to him from his boyhood. Very often as a young
man he had entered it in cheerful company with Colet, Erasmus,
Linacre, Grocyn, or Lilly, to share the genial hospitality of
Warham. Now, Cranmer sat in Warham's place; with him were
the Lord Chancellor, Audley, William Benson, abbot of Westminster, and Cromwell, the King's secretary. These were the
Commissioners now appointed to administer the oath. The form
of this had not been determined by statute, but was prescribed
in terms devised by Audley and Cromwell, involving an acceptance of all the propositions contained in the Act of Succession.
More, having asked to see both the Act and the oath, declared
that he did not wish to find fault with the Act, with those who
made it, or with those who swore to it. He was willing himself to
be sworn to the Succession, but he could not find it in his conscience to assent to the clauses which implied a repudiation of
papal authority in England and asserted the invalidity of the
King's marriage with Catherine. Audley then said 'they were all
very sorry to hear him say this, and they said all, that he was

---

[1] Roper, p. 70: *rounded me in the ear* = whispered to me.

the very first that ever refused it'. On the same day the oath was taken by a number of the London clergy, and More, looking into the palace garden, saw an excited crowd of them, talking and laughing; he heard that those who had sworn were 'sped apace to their great comfort: so far forth that master Vicar of Croydon, either for gladness or dryness, or else that it might be seen, *Quod ille notus erat pontifici*, went to my lord's buttery bar, and called for drink, and drank *valde familiariter*'. 'When they had played their pageant,' continued More, 'and were gone out of the place, then was I called in again. And then it was declared unto me, what a number had sworn even since I went aside, gladly without any sticking. Wherein I laid no blame in no man, but for mine own self answered as before.'

The Commissioners tried in vain to move him. They gave him time to reflect, but he had reflected long enough—'neither suddenly nor slightly, but by long leisure and diligent search for the matter'. He would give no reason for his refusal, except that in his conscience the truth seemed on the other side.

'Upon this,' said More ironically, 'Master Secretary, as he that tenderly favoureth me, said and sware a great oath, that he had leiver that his own only son . . . had lost his head, than that I should thus have refused the oath. For surely the king's highness would now conceive a great suspicion against me, and think that the matter of the nun of Canterbury, was all contrived by my drift. To which I said that the contrary was true and well known. And whatsoever should mishap me, it lay not in my power to help it without the peril of my soul. . . . Howbeit, as help me God, as touching the whole oath I never withdrew any man from it, nor never advised any to refuse it, nor never put nor will put any scruple in any man's head, but leave every man to his own conscience. And me thinketh in good faith that so were it good reason that every man should leave me to mine.'[1]

The account of the interview was written by More in the form of a letter to Margaret Roper.

He recognized the right of Parliament to settle the Succession; he would accept the union with Anne as an accomplished fact. He had told Cromwell that since the King was now married again, and 'this noble-woman really anointed queen', he would neither murmur at it nor dispute upon it, but 'faithfully pray to God for his grace and hers both long to live and well, and their noble issue, so in such wise as may be to the pleasure of God, honour and surety to themselves, rest, peace, wealth and profit unto this noble realm'.[2] Cranmer was ready to accept the compromise.

---

[1] More's *English Works* (1557), pp. 1428–30.
[2] *Letters and Papers*, vii, no. 289.

There was no danger that More would contest the Succession, and Cranmer thought it would suffice if he and Fisher were allowed to take a modified form of the oath, for 'it would be a good quietation to many other within this realm, if such men should say that the succession is good according to God's laws'.[1] For four days after his refusal of the oath, More was kept in the custody of the Abbot of Westminster, while Cranmer made one more effort to save him and Fisher, who, like More, refused to take the oath, though he, too, was ready to accept the Royal Succession as determined by Parliament.

Some members of the Council agreed with Cranmer, but Cromwell, disappointed of the hoped-for triumph of carrying More's submission to the King, gave his own account to Henry of More's demeanour before the Commissioners. He replied to to Cranmer's reasoning that the King considered 'if their oath should be so taken, it were an occasion to all men to refuse the whole, or at the least, the like'.[2]

Another enemy of More, even nearer to Henry than Cromwell, was Queen Anne. Probably Roper wrote truly that she 'did by her importunate clamour so sore exasperate the King against him' that no compromise was allowed. More 'was forthwith committed to the Tower'.

[1] *Letters and Papers*, vii, no. 499, Cranmer to Cromwell, 17 Apr. 1534.
[2] Merriman, op. cit. i, letter 71; *Letters and Papers*, vii, no. 500.

# CHAPTER XXI

# IN THE TOWER

## 1534–1535

ON the 17th of April, with indomitable cheerfulness, More disembarked at the Tower steps on his way to lifelong imprisonment. At the gate the porter demanded as toll his 'upper garment'. More, knowing well the custom, handed his cap to the man, saying: 'Master porter, here it is; I am sorry it is no better for thee.' 'No sir,' objected the porter, stolidly; 'I must have your gown.'

For a time he was treated with some leniency. He was allowed the services of one of his own men, John a Wood; the Lieutenant of the Tower, Sir Edmund Walsingham, an old acquaintance, apologized that he was not permitted to offer him better cheer, to which More replied that he believed, and thanked him for, his good intention: 'and assure yourself, Master Lieutenant, I do not mislike my cheer, but whensoever I so do, then thrust me out of your doors!' His friend of forty years standing, Antonio Bonvisi, the Italian merchant, sent him a warm camlet gown and presents of wine and meat, to supplement the meagre prison fare for which Lady More paid a heavy charge of 15s. a week—10s. for her husband and 5s. for his servant.

Before long, Margaret Roper obtained leave to visit her father; to her he said:

'I may tell thee Meg, they that have committed me hither for the refusing of this oath not agreeable with the Statute, are not by their own law able to justify mine imprisonment; and surely, daughter, it is great pity that any Christian prince should, by a flexible council ready to follow his affections, and by a weak clergy lacking grace constantly to stand to their learning, with flattery be so shamefully abused.'[1]

After this, More received a visit from his wife. The poor woman, bewildered by the turn of events, her temper sharpened by anxiety and grief, came into his cell in great perturbation—she, unlike her husband, was often 'in a fume'. Probably Margaret accompanied her, and related the following scene to William Roper, who wrote:

'When Sir Thomas More had continued a good while in the Tower, my lady his wife obtained licence to see him. Who at her first coming, like a simple ignorant woman, and somewhat worldly too, with this

[1] Roper, p. 74.

manner of salutation bluntly saluted him: "What the good year, Master More," quoth she: "I marvel that you, that have been always hitherto taken for so wise a man, will now so play the fool to lie here in this close filthy prison, and be content thus to be shut up among mice and rats, when you might be abroad at your liberty and with the favour and goodwill both of the King and his Council, if you would but do as all the Bishops and best learned of this realm have done. And seeing you have at Chelsey a right fair house, your library, your gallery, your garden, your orchard and all other necessaries so handsome about you, where you might in the company of me your wife, your children and household, be merry, I muse what a'God's name you mean here still thus fondly [i.e. foolishly] to tarry."

'After he had a while quietly heard her, with a cheerful countenance he said unto her: "I pray thee good Mistress Alice, tell me one thing." '"What is that?" quoth she. "Is not this house", quoth he, "as nigh heaven as mine own?" To whom she, after her accustomed homely fashion, not liking such talk, answered, "Tille valle, tille valle!" "How say you, Mistress Alice," quoth he; "is it not so?" "Bone Deus, Bone Deus, man, will this gear never be left?" quoth she.

'"Well then, Mistress Alice," quoth he; '"if it be so it is very well; for I see no great cause why I should much joy in my gay house, or in anything thereunto belonging, when if I should but seven years lie buried under the ground, and then arise and come thither again, I should not fail to find some therein that would bid me get out of doors, and tell me it were none of mine. What cause have I then to like such an house as would so soon forget his master?" So her persuasions moved him but a little.'[1]

Another visit from his wife was described, with slight disguise, by More, to whom she afforded at least some amusement.

'I wist a woman once that came into a prison to visit of her charity a poor prisoner there; whom she found in a chamber (to say the truth) meetly fair, and at the leastwise it was strong enough, but with mats of straw the prisoner had made it so warm, both under the foot and round about the walls, that in these things for the keeping of his health, she was on his behalf glad and very well comforted, but among many other displeasures that for his sake she was sorry for: one she lamented much in her mind, that he should have the chamber door upon him by night, made fast by the jailer that should shut him in. "For by my troth," quoth she, "if the door should be shut upon me, I would ween it would stop up my breath."

'At that word of hers the prisoner laughed in his mind, but he durst not laugh aloud nor say nothing to her, for somewhat indeed he stood in awe of her, and had his finding there much part of her charity for alms, but he could not but laugh inwardly: why he wist well enough, that she used on the inside to shut every night full surely her own chamber to her, both door and windows too, and used not to open them of all the long

[1] Roper, pp. 78–9.

night. And what difference then as to the stopping of the breath whether they were shut up within or without?'[1]

The testimony of William Roper, and that of More's own writings, makes it clear that he was not altogether unhappy in his prisoner's life. He resigned himself cheerfully to the loss of wealth and honours, imagining himself in the monastic cell which he had once wished to enter; though he missed sadly the intercourse with his friends and his children which had been his chief pleasure in the world. It was now that his true greatness showed itself. He set himself resolutely to turn his hardships into stepping-stones to a higher spiritual life. Above illness, discomfort, loneliness, anxiety, and fear, his faith rose, strong and unwavering, until, 'by his gracious demeanour in tribulation, appeared it that all the trouble that ever chanced to him, by his patient sufferance thereof, were to him no painful punishments, but of his patience profitable exercises'.[2] He found by prayer 'grace to help in time of need', and it was he who comforted his children and friends. He planned and wrote for them in his prison cell the *Dialogue of Comfort in Tribulation* which is one of his greatest works. He wrote to Margaret Roper letters full of loving encouragement and consolation, and of thoughtful care for the welfare of his family. Even when pens or ink failed him, he contrived to get little pieces of charcoal to write with, that she might not be without news of him. One of these letters, carefully preserved by her, is the following.

'Mine own good Daughter, our Lord be thanked I am in good health of body, and in good quiet of mind: and of worldly things I no more desire than I have. I beseech him make you all merry in the hope of heaven. And such things as I somewhat longed to talk with you all, concerning the world to come, our Lord put them into your minds, as I trust he doth and better too by his Holy Spirit: who bless you and preserve you all. Written with a coal by your tender loving father, who in his poor prayers forgetteth none of you all, nor your babes, nor your nurses, nor your good husbands nor your good husbands' shrewd wives, nor your father's shrewd wife neither, nor our other friends. And thus fare ye heartily well for lack of paper.

Thomas More, knight.

Our Lord keep me continually true faithful and plain, to the contrary whereof I beseech him heartily never to suffer me live. For as for long life (as I have often told thee Meg) I neither look for nor long for, but I am well content to go, if God call me hence to-morrow. And I thank our Lord, I know no person living, that I would had one fillip for my sake: of which mind I am more glad than of all the world beside.

[1] More's *English Works* (1557), p. 1247.          [2] Roper, p. 73.

'Recommend me to your shrewd Will, and mine other sons, and to John Harris my friend, and yourself knoweth to whom else, and to my shrewd wife above all, and God preserve you all and make and keep you his servants all.'[1]

To one of her father's letters Margaret replied:

'Mine own most entirely beloved father,

'I think myself never able to give you sufficient thanks, for the inestimable comfort my poor heart received in the reading of your most loving and godly letter . . . which though it were written with a coal, is worthy in mine opinion to be written in letters of gold. Father, what moved them to shut you up again, we can nothing hear. But surely I conjecture that when they considered that you were of so temperate a mind, that you were contented to abide there all your life with such liberty, they thought it were never possible to incline you to their will, except it were by restraining you from the Church and the company of my good mother your dear wife and us your children and bedesfolk. But father, this chance was not strange [unexpected] to you. For I shall not forget how you told us when we were with you in the garden, that these things were like enough to chance you shortly after. Father I have many times rehearsed to mine own comfort and divers others, your fashion and words ye had to us when we were last with you: for which I trust by the grace of God to be the better while I live, and when I am departed out of this frail life. . . . Father, I am sorry I have no longer leisure at this time to talk with you, the chief comfort of my life, I trust to have occasion to write again shortly. I trust I have your daily prayer and blessing.

'Your most loving obedient daughter and bedeswoman Margaret Roper, which daily and hourly is bound to pray for you, for whom she prayeth in this wise, that our Lord of his infinite mercy give you of his heavenly comfort, and so to assist you with his special grace, that ye never in any thing decline from his blessed will, but live and die his true obedient servant. Amen.'[2]

In reply to this More wrote to Margaret:

'If I would with my writing (mine own good daughter) declare how much pleasure and comfort, your daughterly loving letters were unto me, a peck of coals would not suffice to make me the pens. And other pens have I (good Margaret) none here: and therefore can I write you no long process, nor dare adventure good daughter to write often. The cause of my close keeping again did of likelihood grow of my negligent and very plain true word which you remember . . . my mind so doth always give me, that some folk yet ween that I was not so poor as it appeared in the search, and that it may therefore happen, that . . . some new sudden searches may hap to be made in every house of ours, as narrowly as is possible. Which thing if ever it should so hap, can make but game to us

---

[1] More's *English Works* (1557), pp. 1430–1.
[2] Ibid., p. 1446 (abridged).

that know the truth of my poverty, but if they find out my wife's gay girdle and her golden beads. Howbeit I verily believe in good faith, that the king's grace of his benign pity, will take nothing from her. . . .

'Now have I heard since, that some say that this obstinate manner of mine, in still refusing the oath, shall peradventure force and drive the king's grace to make a further law for me. . . . But I am very sure that if I died by such a law, I should die for that point innocent before God. . . . And I thank our Lord (Meg) since I am come hither, I set by death every day less than other. . . . Nor never longed I since I came hither, to set my foot in mine own house, for any desire of or pleasure of my house : but gladly would I sometime somewhat talk with my friends, and specially my wife and you that pertain to my charge. But sith that God otherwise disposeth, I commit you all wholly to his goodness, and take daily great comfort, in that I perceive that you live together so charitably, and so quietly : I beseech our Lord continue it : And take no thought for me . . . whatsoever you shall hap to hear, but be merry in God.'[1]

It was no idle rumour that new laws were being devised, whereby More might be entrapped. As the summer wore on, those who loved him became increasingly anxious on his behalf. Margaret Roper conferred with her step-sister Alice, whose husband, Sir Giles Alington, had acted as first cup-bearer at Queen Anne's coronation, and who was on friendly terms with Audley, the Lord Chancellor. Alice Alington was no unworthy member of More's school; he had brought her up as one of his own daughters, and she gladly, though vainly, endeavoured to win the Chancellor's help for him. She wrote to Margaret:

'Sister Roper, with all my heart I recommend me to you, thanking you for all your kindness. The cause of my writing at this time is, to show you that at my coming home, within two hours after, my Lord Chancellor did come to take a course at a buck in our park, the which was to my husband a great comfort, that it would please him so to do. Then when he had taken his pleasure and killed his deer, he went to Sir Thomas Barneston's to bed: where I was the next day with him at his desire, the which I could not say nay to, for methought he did bid me heartily : and most especially, because I would speak to him for my father. And when I saw my time, I did desire him as humbly as I could, that he would (as I have heard say that he hath been) be still good lord unto my father. First he answered me, that he would be as glad to do for him as for his father,[2] and that (he said) appeared very well, when the matter of the nun was laid to his charge. And as for this other matter, he marvelled that my father is so obstinate in his own conceit.' . . .

Audley then proceeded, continued Lady Alington, to relate two long fables, to the intent that he considered More an obstinate fool. Having repeated these tales, the writer concludes ironically :

[1] Ibid., p. 1447–8.
[2] i.e. as if More were Audley's own father; ibid., p. 1433.

'Now my good sister, hath not my lord told me two pretty fables. In good faith they pleased me nothing, nor I wist not what to say, for I was abashed of this answer. And I see no better suit than to almighty God. For he is the comforter of all sorrows, and will not fail to send his comfort to his servants when they have most need.

Thus fare ye well mine own good sister.

Written the Monday after Saint Laurence in haste.

Your sister Alice Alington.'

As soon as Margaret saw her father again, she showed him the letter of her 'sister Alington', that he might see her 'loving labour taken for him'.[1] She found him in ill health indeed, but not much worse than before, and reported: 'and at that time I found him out of pain, and as one in his case might, meetly well minded, after our seven Psalms and the Litany said, to sit and talk and be merry, beginning first of other things, of the good comfort of my mother, and the good order of my brother and all my sisters'. After some further talk, she told him of her fears for his safety, unless he could 'content and please the king'. She added: 'I assure you father, I have received a letter of late from my sister Alington, by which I see well that if ye change not your mind, you are likely to lose all those friends that are able to do you any good. Or if you lose not their good wills, you shall at the leastwise lose the effect thereof, for any good that they shall be able to do you.'

Margaret's tale continues:

'With this my father smiled upon me and said: "What Mistress Eve (as I called you when you came first) hath my daughter Alington played the serpent with you, and with a letter set you a-work to come tempt your father again, and for the favour that you bear him labour to make him swear against his conscience, and so send him to the devil?" And after that, he looked sadly again, and earnestly said unto me. "Daughter Margaret, we two have talked of this thing ofter than twice or thrice. And the same tale in effect, that you tell me now therein, and the same fear too, have you twice told me before, and I have twice answered you too, that in this matter if it were possible for me to do the thing that might content the king's grace, and God therewith not offended, there hath no man taken this oath already more gladly than I would do. . . . I have ere I came here, not left unbethought nor unconsidered, the very worst and the uttermost that can by possibility fall. And albeit that I know mine own frailty full well, and the natural faintness of mine own heart, yet if I had not trusted that God should give me strength rather to endure all things, than offend him by swearing ungodly against mine own conscience, you may be very sure I should not have come here." '

[1] Margaret's conversation with her father is recorded in the form of a letter to Lady Alington, given in More's *English Works* (1557), pp. 1434-43, with a note by Rastell: 'whether this answer were written by Sir Thomas More in his daughter Roper's name, or by herself, is not certainly known'.

Carefully and slowly he read Alice Alington's letter, and then said to Margaret that he found her, as ever, a true daughter to him, and, he added:

'her take I verily for mine own too, since I have married her mother and brought up her of a child as I have brought up you, in other things and in learning both. . . . In this matter, she hath used herself like herself, wisely and like a very daughter toward me and in the end of her letter, giveth as good counsel as any man that wit hath would wish, God give me grace to follow it, and God reward her for it.'

He would not disclose, even to Margaret, for what reasons—'more causes than one'—he refused the oath. The example of others did not move him, even though they were men whom he had long honoured; he assured her that he intended never 'to pin his soul to another man's back'. He admitted that some men might think one way, and 'others of like learning and goodness think the contrary'; he would not take upon himself to define or dispute such matters; but he was very sure that all the causes which might move other men, were not such as would make any change in his own conscience.

'When he saw me sit with this very sad . . ., he smiled upon me and said: "How now daughter Marget? What how, Mother Eve? Where is your mind now? Sit not musing with some serpent in your breast, upon some new persuasion, to offer father Adam the apple once again!" "In good faith father," quoth I, "I can no further go, but am (as I trow Cresede saith in Chaucer) come to Dulcarnon even at my wits end. For sith the ensample of so many wise men, cannot in this matter move you, I see not what to say more, but if I should look to persuade you with the reason that Master Harry Pattison made.[1] For he met one day one of our men, and when he had asked where you were, and heard that you were in the Tower still, he waxed even angry with you, and said: 'Why? what aileth him that he will not swear? Wherefore should he stick to swear? I have sworn the oath myself.' And so I can in good faith go now no further neither, after so many wise men whom ye take for no sample, but if I should say like Mr. Harry: 'Why should you refuse to swear father? For I have sworn myself.'"[2] At this he laughed and said, "That word was like Eve too, for she offered Adam no worse fruit than she had eaten herself." "But yet father" quoth I, "by my troth, I fear me very sore, that this matter will bring you in marvellous heavy trouble. You know well that as I showed you, Master Secretary sent you word as your very friend, to remember that the parliament lasteth yet."

'"Margaret" quoth my father "I thank him right heartily. But as I showed you then again, I left not this gear unthought on. . . . I counted

[1] Pattison, Paterson, or Pattinson, formerly More's 'fool' or jester.
[2] She took the oath with the modifying clause: 'as far as would stand with the law of God'. More made no attempt to dissuade her, or any of his relatives, from this.

Marget full surely many a restless night, while my wife slept, and went
[thought] I had slept too, what peril were possible for to fall to me, so
far forth that I am sure there can come none above. And in devising
daughter thereupon, I had a full heavy heart. But yet I thank our Lord,
for all that, I never thought to change, though the very uttermost should
hap me that my fear ran upon. . . . For well I wot the change can not be
good for my soul, that change I say that should grow but by fear. And
therefore I pray God that in this world I never have good of such change.
Mistrust him Meg will I not, though I feel me faint. . . . But in good faith
Meg, I trust that his tender pity shall keep my poor soul safe and make
me commend his mercy. And therefore mine own good daughter, never
trouble thy mind, for any thing that shall ever hap me in this world.
Nothing can come, but that that God will.'' '

The Parliament which had been opened by More in 1529 met
for a further session in November 1534, in order to pass the 'Act
of Supremacy'. It was reaffirmed that the King 'rightfully is
and ought to be the only supreme head in earth of the Church of
England'. It was made high treason for any person 'maliciously'
to deprive the King or his heirs of the 'dignity title or name of
their Royal estates'.

In order to legalize the imprisonment of More and Fisher, the
oath which they had been asked to take was retrospectively
given the force of a statute; on the strength of the new laws, acts
of attainder were passed against them. Many misgivings were
felt at the inclusion of verbal offences in the category of high
treason.[1] The lands granted to More in 1523 and 1525 were
resumed by the King, to whom all his goods were forfeit.

The anxiety felt by More's family was acute. Margaret wrote
to her father once more urging him to submit to the King's
pleasure,[2] but he answered:

'If I had not been, my dearly beloved daughter, at a firm and fast
point, your lamentable letter had not a little abashed me, surely far
above all other things, of which I hear at divers times not a few terrible
towards me. But surely they all touched me never so near, nor were so
grievous unto me, as to see you my well-beloved child, in such vehement
piteous manner, labour to persuade unto me the thing wherein I have
of pure necessity for respect unto mine own soul, so often given you so
precise answer before . . . the matters which move my conscience, . . . I have
sundry times showed you that I will disclose them to no man. And therefore, daughter Margaret, I can in this thing no further. . . . A deadly
grief unto me, and much more deadly than to hear of mine own death, . . .
is, that I perceive my good son your husband, and you my good daughter,

---

[1] H. A. L. Fisher, *Political History of England*, v. 346.
[2] It was suggested that she wrote thus believing her letter would be read by
Cromwell, who would be the more ready to grant her access to her father. She
had, however, begged him to reconsider his opinion of the oath before this.

and my good wife, and mine other good children and innocent friends, in great displeasure and danger of great harm thereby.... I can no further but commit all to God.... Whose high goodness I most humbly beseech to incline the noble heart of the king's highness to the tender favour of you all, ... surely if his Highness might inwardly see my true mind such as God knoweth it is, it would, I trust, soon assuage his high displeasure....

'And thus my dear daughter, the blessed spirit of Christ for his tender mercy govern and guide you all, to his pleasure and your weal and comforts both body and soul.

Your tender loving father, Thomas More, Knight.'[1]

Margaret wrote in reply, saying that, since she could not talk with him, it was to her no little comfort, in the bitter time of his absence, to write to him, and to read again and again, his letter, 'the faithful messenger of your very virtuous and ghostly mind, fast knit only in the love of God and desire of heaven'. 'Father, what think you hath been our comfort since your departing from us? Surely the experience we have had of your life past and godly conversation and wholesome counsel and virtuous example.' She concludes on a note of resignation, looking forward to a meeting 'in the bliss of heaven'—but after this comes the heartfelt cry: 'Your own most loving obedient daughter Margaret Roper, which desireth above all worldly things to be in John a Wood's stead, to do you some service.'

In the meantime the oath to repudiate the Pope and to acknowledge the King as supreme head of the Church was administered throughout the realm, to clergy and laity alike. Submission was general, with only a few notable exceptions.[2] Tunstall subscribed to it 'for the peace of the Realm'.

During the winter of 1534–5 More's health failed rapidly; an appeal for his pardon and release was made by his wife and children, on the ground that he was likely to die, having been in the Tower eight months and more, 'in great continual sickness of body and heaviness of heart'. They besought the King to grant their petition, 'considering that his offence was not of malice or obstinacy but of such a long-continued and deep-rooted scruple as passeth his power to avoid and put away'. It was not to be expected that the repetition of this exasperating argument would soften Henry's heart, with its reminder of his own broken promise.

A further pathetic appeal was made to Cromwell by Dame Alice More, who begged him, 'of your most abundant goodness to show your most favourable help to the comforting of my poor

[1] Roper, app. x.
[2] The Observants of Richmond and Greenwich, the Carthusians of London, and the Brethren of Sion.

husband and me in this our great heaviness, extreme age and necessity'.[1] This appeal had no better effect than the last, for Cromwell had neither mercy nor justice to offer to those who brought him no bribes.

Though Cromwell showed no personal ill will to More, he was determined to achieve either his submission or his death. Already he was planning the plunder of the monasteries; rumours of threatening insurrection, even of foreign invasion, could not be disregarded. The King's revolution was successful, but not yet assured; while More and Fisher held out against it, many people would be the bolder to express their discontent. It might have been considered that the two helpless prisoners, safely lodged in the Tower, were harmless enough, but even their silence was bitterly resented by the King.

More explained to his daughter Margaret that this silence of his, which was made a grievance against him by the Council, was not, as they averred, 'for obstinacy' but only for prudence. He knew well that if he should 'open and disclose the causes why' he refused the oath, he should 'therewith but further exasperate his highness'. He offered indeed, to obey an express command of the King to announce his reasons, rather than be accounted obstinate, if he might be sure that his declaration would not offend his highness; but he was told by 'Master Secretary' that 'though the King would give him licence under his letters patent, it would not serve against the statute'. 'In this good warning,' said More, 'he showed himself my special tender friend. And now you see well, Margaret, that it is none obstinacy to leave the causes undeclared, while I could not declare them without peril.' He was only carrying out his own principle, that to protest publicly against the laws of the realm was an act of disloyalty, though his private opinion was well known to the King, and he could not change it against his conscience.

Cromwell taunted him with having said that 'he had as lief be out of the world as in it', and if so, 'why did he not then speak even plain out against the statute? It appeared well he was not content to die, though he said he was'. 'Whereto I answered,' said More, 'that I have not been a man of such holy living, as I might be bold to offer myself to death, lest God for my presumption might suffer me to fall.'

Early in May 1535 More wrote to his daughter an account of his examination in the Tower by members of the King's Council. Cromwell conducted these examinations, while the other Councillors sat and watched the duel between those two keen intellects:

[1] *Letters and Papers*, viii, no. 800.

Cromwell pressing his adversary to commit himself to an opinion which might be construed as treason, while More patiently and skilfully parried the thrusts. He was urged to say what he thought of the King's title as Supreme Head of the Church, but replied that he had discharged his mind of all such matters and 'would dispute neither king's titles nor pope's'. He was offered freedom and favour if he would submit, but answered that he 'would not, for the world, meddle with the world again'.

Still Cromwell plied him with questions and with threats, saying that his demeanour in that matter made others 'so stiff therein as they be'.

'Whereunto I answered,' wrote More to Margaret Roper, 'that I gave no man occasion to hold any point, one or other, nor never gave any man advice or counsel therein one way or other. "I am", quoth I, "the king's true faithful subject and daily bedesman and pray for his highness and all his and all the realm. I do nobody no harm, I say none harm, I think none harm, but wish everybody good. And if this be not enough to keep a man alive, in good faith I long not to live. . . . And therefore my poor body is at the king's pleasure. Would God my death might do him good." . . . And here am I yet in such case as I was, neither better nor worse. That that shall follow lieth in the hand of God.'

Margaret Roper was with her father on the 4th of May when he looked from his prison window to see Dr. Richard Reynolds and the three Carthusian Priors, Houghton, Webster, and Lawrence, going from the Tower to their barbarous execution, 'as cheerfully as bridegrooms to their marriage', after their condemnation for refusing the oath of Supremacy.[1]

A second band of Carthusians was executed in June. Some of these monks, arrested by order of Cromwell, were put to a most cruel imprisonment after refusing the oath; it was said they were chained upright so that they could not move for seventeen days. More's adopted daughter, Margaret Clement, contrived at great risk to herself to visit and help them as best she could; when she was shut out of the prison she made desperate attempts to feed them through a hole in the roof.[2]

Soon after the execution of the Carthusians, hoping that More might be intimidated by their fate, Cromwell again interviewed him in the Tower, still professing friendship for the prisoner. Another time he was accompanied by Cranmer, Suffolk, Audley, and

[1] Bridgett, *Life of More*, p. 404. With them was John Hale, vicar of Isleworth.

[2] Professor Chambers accepts the story as true. Harpsfield's *Life of More* (1932), introduction, cxxxi and pp. 235–6 (the Rastell fragments of Sir Thomas More's *Life*), and note p. 334 and pp. 361–2.

Wiltshire, members of the King's Council; More wrote again to Margaret:

'Verily, to be short, I perceive little difference between this time and the last. For as far as I can see, the whole purpose is, either to drive me to say precisely the one way, or else precisely the other.' Cromwell, who had reported the previous interview to the King, said, as More related,

'that the King's highness was nothing content nor satisfied with mine answer : but thought that by my demeanour, I had been an occasion of much grudge and harm in the realm, and that I had an obstinate mind and an evil towards him, and that my duty was . . . to make a plain and a terminate answer, whether I thought the statute lawful or not. And that I should either knowledge and confess it lawful, that his Highness should be supreme head of the Church of England, or else utter plainly my malignity. Whereto I answered, that I had no malignity, and therefore I none could utter. . . . Very heavy I was that the King's highness should have any such opinion of me. . . .'[1]

After a covert threat of torture, 'to compel him to make a plain answer', and a further lengthy argument, at last Cromwell, who before this had spoken 'full gently', 'in conclusion said that he liked me this day much worse than he did the last time. For then he said he pitied me much, and now he thought I meant not well.'

The only thing that remained was to contrive a pretext for the trial and condemnation of More and Fisher. It was discovered early in June that several letters had passed between More and his fellow prisoner in the Tower, and a long inquisition was made by the Council in the hope of finding grounds of prosecution.[2] Wilson, Fisher's servant, and John a Wood, More's man, were questioned, and admitted the carrying of little presents from one prisoner to the other. Apples and oranges, half a custard, some green sauce, an image or picture of St. John, were among the gifts exchanged.

Letters also had been entrusted to George Gold, servant to the Lieutenant of the Tower. More said he would have had George keep these, but George always said 'there was no better keeper than the fire'—he feared the Lieutenant who had ordered him not to meddle with such matters, and so burned them. There was no doubt of the passage of letters, but no proof could be obtained of conspiracy between the prisoners.

Fisher, however, had offended the King by devoting himself boldly to the defence of Catherine and the privileges of the Church; he had admitted imprudently that he would welcome

[1] *English Works* (1557), pp. 1453-4.
[2] *Letters and Papers*, viii, nos. 856, 858, 859, 867.

PLATE 15

JOHN FISHER. Bishop of Rochester. *By* HOLBEIN

a foreign invasion in their support. Even now he infuriated Henry by his willingness to accept the offer of a Cardinal's hat from the new Pope, Paul III. Henry swore that the Bishop should 'wear the hat on his shoulders, for head he should have none to set it on'.

Fisher was tried and condemned at Westminster on the 17th of June.[1] His execution, like that of More, was decided upon before he was brought to his so-called trial.[2] Cromwell, who 'ticked off lives' in his memoranda, was an adept in 'perpetrating murder under the name of the law', and in Henry's time 'Indignatio Principis mors est' was a true saying.

The King felt no regard for Fisher, one of the noblest characters in his kingdom; the earliest of his own counsellors; the partner in good works of Lady Margaret Beaufort. Fisher was universally revered as a scholar, a writer, and preacher of distinction, the friend of Erasmus and of 'good letters'; a man of exemplary life. He was loved for his self-sacrificing charity; he would stay for hours to comfort a dying labourer in a filthy chimney-less hovel, reeking with smoke, which no one else would enter; he had lived in his comfortless, ill-furnished palace, devoting himself to the care of his diocese in a way very exceptional at the time. Now he was old, and so ill and racked with pain that he could hardly be brought alive to the scaffold, when, on the 22nd of June, he was beheaded on Tower Hill. He faced death serenely, telling the pitying onlookers that he died for the faith of Christ's holy Catholic Church, and praying that God would send the King good counsel.

The fate of More was now only a matter of days. Soon after his last examination by the Council, he was deprived of the chief solace of his lonely hours; his books and papers were taken from him, and he could no longer write the loving letters treasured by his daughters and friends, nor the devotional reflections intended for their consolation and his own.[3]

[1] Fisher had asserted his willingness to 'be sworn unto that part of the oath concerning the succession' for he believed the King in Parliament had the right to appoint to this; but his conscience would not allow him to assent to other clauses included in the oath demanded of him.

[2] Letters and Papers, viii, no. 921, 25 June 1535. More's 'treason' was proclaimed before his trial took place.

[3] Many letters written by More from the Tower have been lost; among them those to his wife. In his English Works is preserved a long and very affectionate letter to Antonio Bonvisi (p. 1455) 'a little before he was arraigned'. He wrote also to William Leder, a priest, saying, 'if ever I should mishap to receive the oath ye may reckon sure that it were expressed and extorted by duresse and hard handling'. He asks for good folks prayers that he may have strength to stand if 'they will use violent forcible ways', ibid., p. 1450. He wrote two letters on the subject of the oath to Dr. Wilson, imprisoned in the Tower.

He closed his shutters after this, and passed his time in reflection and prayer. To the Lieutenant of the Tower, who found him sitting in the dark, he remarked drily that 'as the wares were gone and the tools taken away the shop windows might as well be shut'.

Most of his own writings had been taken into safety by Margaret Roper, or by John a Wood, when Cromwell sent his own servant, Palmer, with Sir Richard Southwell to bring away his books. With them came Richard Rich, newly appointed Solicitor-General. Rich was known to More as a man of contemptible character; lately he had basely procured evidence against Fisher by visiting him in prison and pledging Henry VIII's word that the conversation should be confidential.[1] Now, he was commissioned to entrap More into some statement that could be used against him.

'And while Sir Richard Southwell and Mr. Palmer were busy in the trussing up of his books, Mr. Rich, pretending friendly talk with him, among other things of a set course, as it seemed, said thus unto him: "Forasmuch as it is well known, Master More, that you are a man both wise and well learned as well in the laws of the realm as otherwise, I pray you therefore, Sir, let me be so bold, as of good will, to put unto you this case. Admit there were Sir," quoth he, "an act of Parliament that the realm should take me for king; would not you, Mr. More, take me for king?"

' "Yes, Sir," quoth Sir Thomas More; "that would I."

' "I put the case further," quoth Mr. Rich; "that were there an act of Parliament that all the realm should take me for pope, would not you then, Master More, take me for pope?"

' "For answer, Sir," quoth Sir Thomas More, "to your first case, the Parliament may well, Master Rich, meddle with the state of temporal princes, but to make answer to your other case, I will put you this case. Suppose the Parliament would make a law that God should not be God, would you then, Master Rich, say that God were not God?"

' "No, Sir," quoth he, "that would I not; sith no Parliament may make any such law." '[2]

The conversation ended in a significant silence; More saw and evaded the clumsy trap, yet, at his trial, Rich swore that he had replied: '*No more could the Parliament make the king supreme head of the Church.*' On the testimony of this man More was convicted of high treason and condemned to a traitor's death.

---

[1] *D.N.B.* Rich was made Lord Chancellor in 1548. He was an able lawyer, but notorious for his treachery on many occasions to those who had befriended him, and also for his cruelty to Protestants.

[2] Roper, pp. 80–1.

# CHAPTER XXII

# THE LAST DAYS

## 1535

O N the 1st of July, More was taken from the Tower to stand his trial at the bar of the Court of King's Bench, in Westminster Hall, on a charge of treason and misprision of treason. Under the lately passed Acts of Supremacy and of Treason[1] he was charged with traitorously and maliciously attempting to deprive the King of his title of Supreme Head of the Church of England.[2]

Fifteen months of imprisonment had injured his health, so that he walked feebly, leaning on a staff. He was not older than fifty-eight; only a few years earlier he had been young in appearance, with his slight active figure, his brown hair, clean-shaven face, and penetrating glance, but now the onlookers saw him greatly changed; an old man, with grey hair and long grey beard, with worn-out body but indomitable soul.

A long indictment was read, in which he was accused of corresponding with the Bishop of Rochester and agreeing with him in his treason. It was alleged that both More and Fisher had replied when questioned of the King's Supremacy: 'The act is like a two-edged sword, for if a man answer one way, it will confound his soul, and if the other way, it will confound his body.' It was alleged also that in conversation with Richard Rich, the Solicitor-General, he had denied the right of Parliament to confer on the King the title of Supreme Head of the Church, thus 'maliciously' depriving him of his title.

The evidence—or rather, the perjury, of Rich was the chief ground of More's condemnation, though it was in the highest degree unlikely that More, who had so long resisted all efforts to draw from him an expression of his opinion, would confide it at

---

[1] 26 Hen. VIII, c. 1 and 13.

[2] On 26 June 1535 a special commission of *Oyer and Terminer* for Middlesex was issued to Sir Thomas Audley, Chancellor; the dukes of Norfolk and Suffolk; the earls of Huntingdon, Cumberland, and Wiltshire; Lords Montague, Rochford, and Windsor; Thomas Cromwell, Secretary; Sir John Fitzjames, Chief Justice of the King's Bench, Sir John Baldwin, Chief Justice of the Common Pleas, Sir Richard Lister, Chief Baron of the Exchequer, Sir William Paulet, Sir John Porte, Sir John Spelman, Sir Walter Luke, Sir William FitzWilliam, Sir Anthony Fitzherbert, Justices.

The jury panel comprised Sir T. Palmer, Sir T. Spert, Gregory Lovell, Thomas Burbage, Geoffrey Chamber, Edward Stokwod, William Brown, Jaspar Leyke, Thomas Byllington, John Parnell, Richard Bellamy, and George Stokys. An account of the trial is in *Letters and Papers*, viii, nos. 974 and 996. See also Roper's account, pp. 81–90; and *Cal. S.P. Spanish*, v, pt. i, pp. 507–10.

last to such a man. The two witnesses, Southwell and Palmer, prudently said they had not heard nor heeded the conversation.

When the indictment had been read the Chancellor and the Duke of Norfolk invited More to 'repent and correct his obstinate opinion'. Having thanked them for their goodwill, More said: 'As to the accusations against me, I fear words, memory and judgment would alike fail me to reply to such a length of articles, especially considering my present imprisonment and great infirmity.' A chair was placed for him; in all his previous examinations by the Council he had refused to be seated, but now he was unable to stand. In spite of his weakness, he proceeded to make a long and closely reasoned reply to the indictment.

He was accused, he said, under a statute made since he was imprisoned, of refusing to the King, 'maliciously falsely and traitorously', his title of Supreme Head of the Church of England, in proof of which, there was alleged nothing but his reply to the Secretary and Council that, as he was dead to the world, he 'did not care to think of such things, but only of the Passion of Christ'. He claimed that the Statute could not condemn him to death for such silence, for neither it, nor any laws in the world could punish a man except for deeds or words—not, surely, for keeping silence. The King's proctor interrupted, saying that such silence was a proof of malice. More, with a flash of his old wit, instantly replied that if the legal maxim were true, 'Silence means consent' (*qui tacet, consentire videtur*), then his silence should rather be taken as approval, than contempt, of the Statute. He continued that conscience must be each man's guide, provided always that conscience did not raise scandal or sedition. He assured them once more that he had never disclosed what was in his conscience to any person living. He denied having conspired with the Bishop of Rochester; if they both had made a similar statement, it was not by arrangement, but because they held the same opinion. With regard to the perjurious statement of Rich, he denounced most solemnly 'this slanderous surmise by this man so wrongfully imagined against me'. He had never denied the King's Supremacy, though he refused to take the oath to support it; he had refused consistently to discuss the question or to give any opinion, one way or the other.

It is incredible that the jury could have believed the story told by Rich, unsupported, as it was, by the evidence of two witnesses of the scene, and contradicted by More's explicit statement. The jury however, knew what the King expected of them, and after a deliberation of only a quarter of an hour, they returned the verdict of guilty.

The Chancellor at once began to proceed in judgement, when More observed: 'My lord, when I was toward the law, the manner in such cases was to ask the prisoner before judgment why judgment should not proceed against him.' The usual permission to the prisoner was then given, and More at last allowed himself to speak out, saying: 'Since I am condemned, and God knows how, I wish to speak freely of your statute for the discharge of my conscience. For the seven years that I have studied the matter, I have not read in any approved doctor of the Church that a temporal lord could or ought to be head of the Spirituality.'[1]

The Chancellor interrupted him. 'What, More, you wish to be considered wiser and of better conscience than all the bishops and nobles of the realm?'

More replied: 'My lord, for one bishop of your opinion, I have a hundred saints of mine, and for one Parliament of yours, I have all the General Councils for a thousand years, and for one kingdom, I have France and all the kingdoms of Christendom.'

Norfolk told him that now his malice was clear.

He answered: 'What I say is necessary for the discharge of my conscience and satisfaction of my soul, and to this I call God to witness, the sole searcher of human hearts. I say further that your statute is ill-made, because you have sworn never to do anything against the Church, which, through all Christendom, is one and undivided, and you have no authority, without the common consent of all Christians, to make a law, or Act of Parliament or Council, against the union of Christendom. I know well that the reason why you have condemned me is because I have never been willing to consent to the King's second marriage. But I hope, in the divine goodness and mercy, that as Saint Paul and Saint Stephen, whom he persecuted, are now friends in Paradise, so we, though differing in this world, shall be united in perfect charity in the other. I pray God to protect the King, and give him good counsel.'

Sentence of death was pronounced by the Lord Chancellor, after consultation with the Lord Chief Justice of the King's Bench as to the sufficiency of the indictment.

No doubt More was right when he ascribed the bitter resentment of the Court party to his disapproval of the King's divorce and remarriage. Although he was willing to accept the accomplished fact, and to acknowledge the Succession as settled by Act of Parliament, neither Henry nor Anne could forgive his steady refusal to deny the queenship of Catherine. The question of the marriage, however, had become merged in the larger issue of the

[1] Some reports say 'ten years'. More's speech is considerably abridged here.

authority of the Pope. In both matters, More had already explained his position, which it may be convenient to recapitulate here. He had written to Cromwell after the King's marriage to Anne:

'I never have had against his Grace's marriage any manner demeanour whereby his highness might have any manner cause or occasion of displeasure toward me. I am not he whom it could become to take upon me the determination or decision of such a weighty matter . . . his Highness being in possession of his marriage [I] will most heartily pray for the prosperous estate of his Grace, long to continue to the pleasure of God.

'As touching the primacy of the Pope, I nothing meddle in the matter. Truth it is, I was myself sometime not of the mind that the primacy of that See should be begun by the institution of God, until I read in that matter those things that the King's highness had written in his most famous book against the heresies of Martin Luther.'

He continued that a long study of 'all the holy doctors, from Saint Ignatius unto our own days', had confirmed him in the belief that 'the primacy of the Pope was provided by God'. And even if this should be denied, it must be admitted 'that the primacy is at the leastwise instituted by the corps of Christendom'. He added that he had never thought the Pope to be above a General Council, and never in any English book had 'advanced greatly the Pope's authority'. He 'never intended any thing to meddle in that matter against the King's gracious pleasure, whatsoever mine own opinion were therein'.[1]

His own opinion was given, by the King's command, long before the breach with Rome, when he replied on Henry's behalf to Luther in 1523, under the name of William Ross.

'I am moved to obedience to that See,' he then wrote, 'by this fact especially, that every enemy of the Christian faith makes war on that See, while its declared enemies have always shown themselves to be enemies to the Christian religion. Another thing that moves me is this, that if the vices of men are to be imputed to the offices they hold, not only the Papacy, but every kind of government, law and order will be in danger. It is better for men to have bad rulers than no rulers at all. It is greatly to be wished that God may raise up Popes who will despise riches and honours, who will care only for heaven, will promote piety and seek peace. With one or two such Popes, it would be seen how much better it would be that the Papacy should be reformed, than that it should be overthrown.'[2]

It was impossible for More to defend the personal qualities of the Popes of his own time. The lives of Alexander VI, Julius II,

[1] More to Cromwell, Roper, appendix, pp. 114–22( abridged).
[2] Cf. Bridgett, *Life of More*, pp. 219–20 (abridged).

Leo X, Clement VII, were only too open to criticism; but he considered that the unity of the Church depended on the supremacy of the Pope, and it seemed to him that unity was of far greater importance than religious liberty. He had no sympathy with those who were convinced that the maintenance of unity meant the sacrifice of truth. In the cause of unity he gave his life.

The sentence was read, the tragic farce was over. The condemned prisoner was led back to the Tower by Sir William Kingston, 'a tall strong and comely knight, Constable of the Tower, and his very dear friend'.

'Who, when he had brought him from Westminster to the Old Swan towards the Tower,' wrote William Roper, 'there with a heavy heart, the tears running down his cheeks, bade him farewell. Sir Thomas More, seeing him so sorrowful, comforted him with as good words as he could, saying, "Good Master Kingston, trouble not yourself, but be of good cheer: for I will pray for you and my good lady your wife, that we may meet in heaven together, where we shall be merry for ever and ever."

'Soon after, Sir William Kingston, talking with me of Sir Thomas More, said: "In good faith, Mr. Roper, I was ashamed of myself that at my departing from your father I found my heart so feeble and his so strong, that he was fain to comfort me that should rather have comforted him." '[1]

More's family, waiting anxiously for the end of the trial soon heard the dreaded tidings. The story of Margaret's pitiful farewell is told with moving simplicity by her husband.

'When Sir Thomas More came from Westminster to the Tower-ward again, his daughter, my wife, desirous to see her father, whom she thought she should never see in this world after, and also to have his final blessing, gave attendance about the Tower Wharf, where she knew he should pass by, before he could enter into the Tower.

'There tarrying his coming, as soon as she saw him, after his blessing upon her knees reverently received, she, hasting towards him, without consideration or care of herself pressing in among the midst of the throng and company of the guard that with halberds and bills went round about him, hastily ran to him, and there openly in the sight of them all, embraced him, and took him about the neck and kissed him. Who well liking her most natural and dear daughterly affection towards him, gave her his fatherly blessing, and many godly words of comfort besides. From whom, after she was departed, she, not satisfied with her former sight of him, and like one that had forgotten herself, being all ravished with the entire love of her dear father, having respect neither to herself, nor to the press of the people and multitude that were there about him, suddenly turned back again, ran to him as before, took him about the neck, and divers times together kissed him most lovingly; and

[1] Roper, p. 90.

at last, with a full heavy heart, was fain to depart from him; the beholding whereof was to many of them that were present thereat, so lamentable, that it made them for very sorrow thereof to weep and mourn.'[1]

While she made her last farewell, Margaret could say nothing, but 'oh, father, father!' then clung to him with love and sorrow too deep for words. More, steadfast and firm, spoke to her in tender consolation, bidding her submit with patience to the will of God, who knew his innocence and the inmost secrets of his heart. But when she broke again through the guard, and once more embraced him in an ecstasy of grief, More himself could scarcely speak for unshed tears, as he made his last request—that she should pray for her father's soul.

Margaret's husband must have been standing by in self-effacing sympathy, though he says no word of himself. More's only son John, knelt at his father's feet as he passed on his way, and with tears begged for his blessing. Margaret Clement, too, was with them, and shared in the last scene of farewell.

More's last letter was written on the day before his death, to Margaret Roper, to whom his chief confidence was always given and whom he loved more tenderly than any one besides. It is full of little, practical directions, with a loving appreciation of the last proof of his children's affection. Apparently he was interrupted in the writing, or there surely would have been a word, as usual, for his 'shrewd wife', and a final blessing and prayer from the 'tender loving father' whose last earthly thought was for the children who were so dear to him. Roper tells the end of the story in few words.

'The day before he suffered, he sent his shirt of hair, not willing to have it seen, to my wife, his dearly beloved daughter, with a letter written with a coal, plainly expressing the fervent desire he had to suffer on the morrow.'[2]

The letter was as follows:

'Our Lord bless you, good daughter, and your good husband, and your little boy, and all yours, and all my children, and all my God-children, and all our friends. Recommend me when ye may, to my good daughter Cecily, whom I beseech our Lord to comfort. And I send her my blessing, and to all her children, and pray her to pray for me. I send her an handkercher: and God comfort my good son her husband. My good daughter Daunce hath the picture in parchment, that you delivered me from my lady Coniers, her name is on the back-side. Show her that I heartily pray her that you may send it in my name to her again, for a token from me to pray for me. I like special well Dorothy Colley, I

---

[1] Roper, pp. 90-1. Other details are taken from Stapleton (Hallett's ed.), pp. 200-1.     [2] Roper, p. 91.

pray you be good unto her. I would wit whether this be she that you wrote me of. If not yet I pray you be good to the other as you may in her affliction, and to my good daughter Joan Aleyn too. Give her I pray you some kind answer, for she sued hither to me this day to pray you be good to her. I cumber you good Margaret much, but I would be sorry, if it should be any longer than to-morrow. For it is Saint Thomas even, and the octave of Saint Peter: and therefore to-morrow long I to go to God: it were a day very meet and convenient for me. I never liked your manner toward me better, than when you kissed me last: for I love when daughterly love and dear charity, hath no leisure to look to worldly courtesy. Farewell my dear child, and pray for me, and I shall for you and all your friends, that we may merrily meet in heaven. I thank you for your great cost. I send now my good daughter Clement her algorism stone, and I send her and my godson and all hers, God's blessing and mine. I pray you at time convenient recommend me to my good son John More. I liked well his natural fashion. Our Lord bless him and his good wife my loving daughter, to whom I pray him to be good as he hath great cause: and that if the land of mine come to his hand, he break not my will concerning his sister Daunce. And our Lord bless Thomas and Austin and all that they shall have——'

here the letter breaks off abruptly, the sentence unfinished. It was the last thing he ever wrote.[1]

Early the next morning, the 6th of July, a message was brought to him by Sir Thomas Pope from the King and council, that he was to prepare himself to die before nine o'clock. In deference, perhaps, to public opinion, the horrible sentence reserved by law for traitors was commuted to beheading, for Henry knew that More was loved by Londoners, who saw his death with pity and regret.

He thanked Sir Thomas Pope for his 'good tidings', and spoke of his gratitude to the King for many past benefits and honours: 'and yet more bounden am I to his grace for putting me into this place, where I have had convenient time to have remembrance of my end. And most of all am I bounden to his highness that it pleaseth him so shortly to rid me out of the miseries of this wretched world.'

[1] *English Works* (1557), p. 1457–8.
Allusions in the above letter have been explained as follows. Dorothy Colley was Margaret Roper's maid and friend. She married More's secretary, John Harris; she was living at Douai when Stapleton wrote, and supplied him with many details about More. Joan, or Jane, Aleyn: another maid of Margaret Roper's. 'Saint Thomas even and the octave of Saint Peter', i.e. the eve of the feast of the Translation of St. Thomas of Canterbury (7 July), and octave-day of the Feast of SS. Peter and Paul (29 June). Margaret Clement's 'algorism stone' was for arithmetic: apparently a slate. The 'natural fashion' of John More was his manner of asking his father's blessing. 'Thomas and Austin' (Augustine) were the two sons already born to John More. (Stapleton, Hallett's ed., p. 203.)

He was told that at his execution he must not use many words, and accepted the command. He requested that his daughter Margaret might be present at his burial, and heard that the permission was already accorded.

Sir Thomas Pope, on taking leave of him, could not refrain from tears, and More comforted him with the words he spoke so often to his friends: 'I trust that we shall in heaven see each other full merrily.'

To a number of people who importuned him on his way to the place of execution, he replied very patiently and collectedly. When he arrived at the scaffold, it was found to be so weak that it was ready to fall, and he said 'merrily' to Sir Edmund Walsingham: 'I pray you, Master Lieutenant, see me safe up, and for my coming down, let me shift for myself!'

He spoke a very few words to the people, asking them to pray for him, as he would for them in the next world; he begged them to pray to God to give the King good counsel, and said, 'I call you to witness, brothers, that I die in and for the faith of the Catholic Church; the King's loyal servant, but God's first.'[1]

He knelt down and said aloud the fifty-first psalm, *Have mercy upon me, O God*'; then turned to the executioner and said to him cheerfully: 'Pluck up thy spirits man, and be not afraid to do thine office; my neck is very short, take heed therefore thou strike not awry, for saving of thine honesty.' The man wished to bind his eyes, but he said, 'I will cover them myself', and did so. He had intended that his long grey beard should 'suffer the same fate as his head', but now he removed it from the block so that it should not be cut off, 'for it at least had committed no treason'.

Quietly and cheerfully, as he had lived, so he died, and all might see his prayer was answered, that the grace of God would give him strength to the end, whatever suffering might come, 'to take it patiently and peradventure somewhat gladly too'.

The little homely jests upon the scaffold, which seemed to some of his critics so inappropriate and so undignified, were surely intended for the consolation and encouragement of those who were most dear to him. Margaret Clement was present at his death, and he may have seen other friends and relatives among the crowd. Long before this, he had said to them that 'if his wife and children would encourage him to die in a good cause, that it should so comfort him, that for very joy thereof it would make him merrily run to death'. The next world had always seemed

---

[1] Roper, p. 94; Stapleton, *Tres Thomae* (1588), pp. 341–2; cf. Hallett's ed., pp. 210–11; *Letters and Papers*, viii, no. 996; *Cal. S. P. Spanish*, v, pt. i, p. 510.

very near to him, and very real; the saints in heaven he regarded
as his friends, just as much as if they were on earth; his own
children, and Margaret most of all, would gain comfort from the
simplicity and naturalness of his manner of dying, believing that
death for him was in truth, 'not altogether death, but the door
to a happier life',[1] and that he passed through it 'well witting by
his faith that his death taken for the faith, should cleanse him
clean of all his sins, and send him straight to heaven'.[2]

In the little chapel of Saint Peter *ad vincula* in the Tower,
More's body was laid to rest. The burial was the tragic task of
two brave and devoted women, Margaret Roper and Margaret
Clement. With them, as they hastened to the Tower, on that
summer day, was Margaret Roper's friend and maid, Dorothy
Colley, whom More 'liked well'.

The announcement of the execution was brought to the King
as he sat at dice with Queen Anne. 'Is he then dead?' he asked;
and turning to Anne he exclaimed: 'You, *you* are the cause of
that man's death!' Rising abruptly, he left the room. Stapleton,
who tells the story, adds the improbable statement that he 'shed
bitter tears'. It may be, indeed, that a momentary regret stirred
his complacency, as he thought of the gay and gentle friend and
loyal servant of so many years, but conscience never made
coward of a Tudor; Henry was no Crouchback, to be haunted by
a vain remorse; he was incapable of true affection for man or
woman; resentment took the place of grief, and without hesitation
he ordered that the head of his friend should be exposed shamefully as that of a traitor, on a stake on London Bridge.

With courage equal to her love, Margaret Roper, watching her
opportunity, came at nightfall, nearly a month later, when she
knew that the head of her dearly loved father would be thrown
into the river to make room for another, and bribed the executioner to let her take it away, that she might give it fitting burial.

It has been thought, but never certainly known, that she
afterwards obtained leave to transfer her father's body to the
tomb which he himself had prepared in his parish church of
Chelsea, and on which is inscribed the epitaph he composed,
when he retired in 1532.[3] More's first wife, Jane, was buried there,
and so was Margaret Roper, who died in 1544.

[1] More's epitaph, composed by himself.
[2] *English Works* (1557), p. 1250.
[3] The epitaph is transcribed in Harpsfield's *Life of More* (1932), appendix iv,
pp. 279–81.
'The tomb is of grey stone, consisting of a plain base or sarcophagus, upon
which rests a four-centred arch forming a recess of moderate depth, flanked on
either side by a slight octagonal buttress supporting a foliated cornice. On each
spandrell or space between the spring and apex of the arch and the horizontal

The 'Great House' at Chelsea was confiscated and dismantled. Immediately after More's death, Cromwell came down to ransack the large and valuable library, taking his choice, not only of books but of other objects, for 'Mr. Secretary' had a nice taste in matters of art, and found much to interest him in More's collections, though their intrinsic value was not great.

Dame Alice More was reduced to comparative poverty, having even been obliged to sell her treasured gowns to pay for her husband's maintenance in the Tower. The King, however, allowed her a pension of £20 a year of her husband's money, and with this and the help of her family she lived in a small house in Chelsea. Property devised by More to his wife and children, even before his attainder, was confiscated, but he had made all possible arrangements for the comfort and welfare of those who had been dependent on him. The Daunces and Herons were settled in homes of their own before his arrest; the Ropers and Alingtons owned considerable property. Many times did More discuss the family affairs with Margaret Roper, and he said to her, near the end: 'My good child, I pray you heartily be you and all your sisters and my sons too, comfortable and serviceable to your good Mother my wife. And of your good husbands' minds I have no manner doubt.'

It is a striking paradox that although More and Fisher died, for the sake of conscience, martyrs in the cause of the Catholic Church,[1] yet they were not the victims of religious persecution. Their death was planned from motives of statecraft, not of religion; their execution was a political crime. More, the man of many friends, had three powerful enemies—Cromwell, Anne, and Henry VIII. Anne's hatred was the personal spite of a woman who feels herself to be despised. Cromwell felt for him the cold impersonal hostility of the scheming statesman who saw an obstacle on his path which must be swept aside. He had planned to make the King supreme in a strong, united State; his own

moulding above is an heraldic shield, the remainder of the spandrell being filled by foliage. Above this . . . are three large shields, that in the centre being surmounted by More's crest, a blackamoor's head. The back of the recess, up to the spring of the arch, is filled by a slab of polished black marble bearing the inscription, the date "Anno 1532" being cut in the stone immediately above it.' (Randall Davies, F.S.A., 'Chelsea Old Church' (London 1904), pp. 96–7).

More described himself in this epitaph as 'furibus autem et homicidis haereticisque molestus'. It has been stated that Erasmus, to whom he sent the draft, objected to the word, 'heretics', that it was consequently omitted, but the blank space left in silent, half-humorous protest. It seems more probable that the word haereticisque was omitted in some post-Reformation restoration of the inscription.

[1] Their Beatification was decreed by Pope Leo XIII in 1886.

fortune and life depended on his success, and More must acquiesce
or die. It was Cromwell who tried again and again to drive him
to say 'precisely one way or precisely the other'; it was he who
persuaded Henry of More's obstinacy and ill will. In religious
matters, Cromwell followed the King; his own convictions were
doubtful, though policy sometimes caused him to be counted
a friend to reformers. He feared the influence of More and
Fisher, and without scruple he worked for their destruction.
He attempted to justify their execution by affirming that they
'intended and endeavoured to stir dissension and sow sedition,
to destroy the King and subvert the realm'.[1]

Henry knew that the charge was untrue. He at least knew
that there was no danger of sedition to be feared from More,
who was so resolutely silent in his loyalty. The ultimate responsibility for More's death rests with Henry VIII. He was influenced
by Anne and by Cromwell, but he never was influenced against
his wish. Neither wife nor minister ever ruled him: he cast them off
when he chose; only a year later the headsman's blade was to fall
on the slender neck of Anne Boleyn, and Cromwell followed her to
the block in 1540. One day, in his prison, More had asked his daughter 'how Queen Anne did?' 'In faith father, never better', she replied. 'Never better, Meg?' he said: 'alas Meg, alas! It pitieth me
to remember into what misery, poor soul, she shall shortly come.'

The English government was not yet absorbed in the questions
of religious doctrine which in later years became acute, but Henry
was determined to be supreme in his own country, over State and
Church alike. Accustomed, from his early manhood, to flattery
and subservience, the very hint of opposition enraged him. The
lion had learned his strength indeed, and neither honour, affection,
nor pity restrained his resentful fury.

It was during his first year in prison that More wrote his beautiful *Dialogue of Comfort against Tribulation*.[2] In this, as so often in
deepest trouble, he set himself to cheer and console his friends and
family, and to encourage them to seek divine support in their
sorrow on his behalf. He felt assured that death was imminent;
the long mental struggle was over, and his spirit arose once more,
serene and gay, or serious and tender, to remind his school of the
precepts of former days.[3]

[1] Merriman, op. cit. i. 416.
[2] *A dialogue of Comfort against Tribulation, made by an Hungarian in Latin
and translated out of Latin into French and out of French into English.* More's
*English Works* (1557), p. 1139. He wrote also an unfinished *Treatise upon the
Passion of Christ* (*English Works*, p. 1272).
[3] Cf. Joseph Delcourt, *Essai sur la langue de Sir Thomas More* (Paris 1914),
p. 52.

The dialogue between 'Anthony' and 'Vincent', an 'uncle' and 'cousin', supposedly speaking of a foreign country, is easily imagined to be taking place between More himself and his nephew William Rastell, or John Clement, or another of his 'young men'. He wrote in the preface to this work:

'I well allow your request in this behalf, that would have store of comfort aforehand ready by you to resort to: and to lay up in your heart as a triacle against the poison of all desperate dread, that might rise of occasion of sore tribulation. And herein shall I be glad, as my poor wit will serve me, to call to mind with you such things, as I before have read, heard, or thought upon, that may conveniently serve us to this purpose.'

In this work may be found many 'merry tales'; a number of passages which would recall to his own family homely incidents familiar to them all: a friendly mockery of Dame Alice's sharp temper—an allusion to her charity—a reminiscence of the medical knowledge of Margaret Clement—above all, they would find a return to his favourite themes of the folly of pursuing riches, the evils due to pride, and the wisdom of seeking comfort only from God. He contends that tribulation is no evil, if it makes the soul feel its own dependence on divine strength and help.

'And this may be of comfort to all good men in their night's fear, in their dark tribulation that though they fall into the claws or the teeth of those lions' whelps, yet shall all that they can do, not pass beyond the body: which is but as the garment of the soul. For the soul itself which is the substance of the man, is so surely fenced in round about with the shield or the pavise of God. . . .'

In another consolatory passage he wrote:

'He that so loveth God that he longeth to go to him, my heart cannot give me but he shall be welcome, all were it so that he should come ere he were well purged. For charity covereth a multitude of sins, and he that trusteth in God cannot be confounded.'

Among these reflections, he gives an example of his own method of offering counsel to a man tempted to some evil deed, such as suicide, 'by illusion of the devil'.

'It is soon seen, that therein the sum and effect of the counsel must in manner rest in giving him warning of the devil's sleights.
'And that must be done under such sweet pleasant manner, as the man should not abhor to hear it. For while it could lightly be none other, but that the man were rocked and songen asleep by the devil's craft, and his mind occupied as it were in a delectable dream, he should never have good audience of him, that would rudely and boisterously shog him and wake him, and so shake him out thereof. Therefore must you fair and

easily touch him, and with some pleasant speech awake him so, that he
wax not wayward, as children do that are waked ere they list to rise.'[1]

In another passage he speaks of the duty of providing not only
for children, but for servants also and other dependants, in sickness or old age, as he himself had already done, as far as he was
able.

'Meseemeth also that if they fall sick in our service, so that they
cannot do the service that we retain them for, yet may we not in any
wise turn them out of doors, and cast them up comfortless, while they be
not able to labour and help themself. For this were a thing against all
humanity.'

He speaks of business:

'This devil that is called business, busily walketh about, and such fond
folk as will follow him . . . verily they walk round about as it were in
a round maze, when they ween themself at an end of their business, they
be but at the beginning again. For is not the serving of the flesh,
a business that hath none end, but ever more from the end cometh to
the beginning again? goe they never so full fed to bed, yet ever more on
the morrow, as new they be to be fed again, as they were the day before.'

In his long days in prison, he wrote the beautiful and little-
known *Godly Meditation*,[2] so revelatory of the loneliness of his
steadfast soul.

'Give me thy grace, good Lord,
To set the world at nought.
To set my mind fast upon thee
And not to hang upon the blast of men's mouths.
To be content to be solitary.
Not to long for worldly company.
Little and little utterly to cast off the world
And rid my mind of all the business thereof.
Not to long to hear of any worldly things.
But that the hearing of worldly fantasies may be to me displeasant.
Gladly to be thinking of God,
Piteously to call for his help.
To lean unto the comfort of God.
Busily to labour to love him.
To know mine own vilitie and wretchedness.
To humble and meeken myself under the mighty hand of God.
To bewail my sins passed,
For the purging of them, patiently to suffer adversity.
Gladly to bear my purgatory here.

[1] *Second Book of Comfort against Tribulation*, More's *English Works*, p. 1189.
[2] *A godly meditation written by Sir Thomas More, knight, while he was
prisoner in the Tower of London in the year of our Lord 1534*. More's *English
Works*, pp. 1416–17.

To be joyful of tribulations.

To walk the narrow way that leadeth to life.

To bear the cross with Christ.

To have the last thing in remembrance.

To have ever afore mine eye, my death, that is ever at hand.

To make death no stranger to me.

To foresee and consider the everlasting fire of hell.

To pray for pardon before the judge come.

To have continually in mind, the passion that Christ suffered for me.

For his benefits uncessantly to give him thanks.

To buy the time again, that I before have lost.

To abstain from vain confabulations.

To eschew light foolish mirth and gladness.

Recreations not necessary to cut off.

Of worldly substance, friends, liberty, life and all to set the loss at right nought, for the winning of Christ.

To think my most enemies my best friends.

For the brethren of Joseph could never have done him so much good with their love and favour, as they did with their malice and hatred.

These minds are more to be desired of every man, than all the treasure of all the princes and kings Christian and heathen, were it gathered and laid together all upon one heap.'

More stands between the Renaissance and the Reformation; he belongs, not wholly to either, but in part to both. In letters, as in life, he forms a link between the old and the new, between the devotional prose of an earlier age, and the dramatic literature of the Elizabethan era. He saw truth and beauty in the teaching of Greek sages and of Christian saints, in the reason of the ancients, and in the faith of the Church. He was a fine scholar, a great lawyer, a perfect friend; a loyal servant to the King, but 'to God first'.

It was above all for his character and example that he was loved and revered. Erasmus lived to mourn his loss, and his memory was treasured by his children, his scholars, and many who were influenced by his teaching. The tributes of his friends, and his own writings, form a lasting memorial to one of the most lovable of men, and as long as English literature endures, his name will hold an honoured place in the annals of his country.

# INDEX

Abingdon, co. Berks., 97, 122.
Abyssinia, 137.
*Adagia*, by Erasmus, 38.
Aegidius, Petrus, *see* Peter Giles.
Aldington, co. Kent, 53.
Alexander VI, pope, 226.
Aleyn, Jane or Joan, 229, 229 n. 1.
Alington (family), 232.
—, Alice, *see* Middleton.
—, Sir Giles, second husband of Alice Middleton, 46 n. 2, 145 n. 1, 213, 232.
Allen, Dr. P. S., 1 n. 2, 14 n. 4, 32 n. 1.
Amaurote, capital of Utopia, 78 n. 1.
Ambrose, St., 99.
Amiens, 163; treaty of, 164–5.
Ammonius, Andreas, Latin secretary to Henry VIII, 38 n. 2, 42, 45, 52, 63, 75, 76 n. 1, 83; death, 82–3; letters from, 45, 52, 63.
Anne, queen (Boleyn), 162, 164, 168, 202, 208, 225, 231–3; marriage, 184, 201–2, 207, 226; coronation, 201, 213; execution, 233.
*Annotations on the New Testament*, by Erasmus, 100.
*the Answer to the Poisoned Book which a nameless heretic hath named the Supper of the Lord*, by Sir Thomas More, 191 n. 3.
*Antimorus*, by Germain de Brie, 101.
Antwerp, 60–4, 67, 67 n. 3, 84, 88 n. 2, 197; senator of, 80; town-clerk of, *see* Peter Giles.
'Anyder', the river of Utopia, 78 n. 1.
*Apology*, by Erasmus, 62.
*Apology*, by Sir Thomas More, 191 n.3, 197.
Aragon, 53.
Aristotle, philosophy of 10, 63 n. 2; works of, 11, 22; Erasmus's edition of works of, 137.
Arnold, Nicholas 19, 19 n. 2.
Arthur, eldest son of Henry VII, 18, 161, 201.
Arthur, Thomas, servant of William Roper, 145 n. 1.
Arundel, [Henry Fitzalan, 12th] earl of, 105.
*de Asse et Partibus ejus*, by Guillaume Budé, 114.
*Assertio septem Sacramentorum adversum Martinum Lutherum*, by Henry VIII, 120, 120 n. 3, 121, 188, 203.
Attorney-general, the, 168.
Audley, Sir Thomas, Lord Chancellor,

184, 195, 202–4, 206, 213, 213 n. 2, 219, 223 n. 2, 224–5.
Augustine, St., 99, 120, 164; *de Civitate Dei*, by, 24, 66 n. 3; Vives's edition of, 117.
Augustinian Canons at Oxford, 20.
Axholme, Charterhouse of, 46 n. 1.

Bainham, [James], 195 n. 3, 196 n. 4.
Baldwin, Sir John, Chief Justice of Common Pleas, 223 n. 2.
Barcelona, treaty of, 166.
Barnborough, co. Yorks., 137 n. 3.
Barneston, Sir Thomas, house of, 213.
Barton, *see* Mrs. Bowes.
—, Elizabeth, the holy maid of Kent, 202–3, 207.
Basel, 23, 63, 78 n. 3; printing-press at, 76; museum at, 147.
Bath, bishop of, *see* Clarke.
Batirsay or Batirsey [Battersea], 144, 172, 172 n. 2.
Bayfield, [Richard], 195 n. 3.
Baynton, Mr. 173.
Beatus of Rheinau, *see* Rhenanus.
Beaufort, Margaret, *see* Richmond and Derby.
Belknap, Sir Edward, 44.
Bellamy, Richard, 223 n. 2.
Benson, William, Abbot of Westminster, 206, 208.
Beraldus [Nicholas], 189.
Bernard, St. 120.
*Bible*, Authorized Version of (1534), 193 n. 1.
Bilney, [Thomas], 195 n. 2.
Blount, William, *see* Mountjoy.
Blunt, Reginald, 140 n. 1.
Boccacio [Giovanni], 145.
Boëtius, 22, 126.
Boleyn, Anne, *see* Anne, Queen.
—, George, *see* Rochford.
—, Thomas, *see* Wiltshire.
Bon accorso, 6.
Bonvisi, Antonio, of Lucca, 48, 139 n. 1, 209, 221 n. 3.
Bordeaux, 44.
Bosworth, battle of, 2.
Bouge, John, 46 n. 1.
Bowes, Mrs., *née* Barton, 3rd wife of Sir John More, 1 n. 2.
Brabant, 61 n. 3.
Bramber, co. Sussex, M.P.s for, 170 n. 2.
[Brandon, Charles], *see* Suffolk.
Brewer, Dr. A. H., 107, 121, 171.

242                                    INDEX

Granger, Thomas, grandfather of Sir Thomas More, 1 n. 2.

Grapheus, see Schreiber.

Graunger, see Granger.

Gravelines, 61, 106.

Gravesend, co. Kent, 157 n. 2.

Gray's Inn, 14.

Greenwich, 93, 106, 122; Sir William Say's house at, 18 n. 2; Observant Friars of, 217 n. 1.

—, East, 40 n. 6, 157 n. 2, 169.

Grocyn, William, 10, 11, 20, 22, 26, 42, 52, 206; rector of St. Lawrence, Old Jewry, 24; visit to Italy, 10; lectures at Oxford, 10.

Grynaeus, Simon, 137, 145–6, 146 n. 1; professor of Greek and Latin at Heidelberg, 145–6; his edition of Plato, 137; of the *Commentaries* of Proclus, 137; letter from, 146.

Gubbins, see Gobions.

Guildford, co. Surrey, 122.

Gunnell, William, tutor to Sir Thomas More's children, 128, 128 n. 1, 129; rector of Conington, 128 n. 1; his school, 128 n. 1; his brother, 128 n. 1.

Hackett, Master John, 165 n. 4.

Hackney, vicar of, see Ursewick.

Hall's *Chronicle*, 81, 170–1.

Hale, John, vicar of Isleworth, 219 n. 1.

Hampshire, Commission of Peace for, 40 n. 6.

Hampton Court, 122, 164.

the Handbook for a Christian Prince (*Institutio Principis Christiani*), by Erasmus 68.

Handcombe, —, of Holliwell, co. Beds, 1 n. 2.

—, Jane, 2nd wife of Sir John More, 1 n. 2.

the Hanseatic League, 58 n. 2, 106.

Harpsfield, Nicholas, biographer of Sir Thomas More, 136 n. 1, 172.

Harris, John, secretary to Sir Thomas More, 145–6, 146 n. 1, 212; marriage with Dorothy Colley, 145, 229 n. 1.

Hart, see Hyrde.

Heidelberg, University of, 145.

Henry VI, 2, 4.

Henry VII, 4, 19, 25, 25 n. 2, 34 n. 1, 35, 35 n. 2, 37, 49, 58, 58 n. 5, 113, 124 n. 1; his death, 39; his children, 18.

Henry, Prince, see Henry VIII.

Henry VIII, 19 n. 3, 36–7, 37 n.1, 38, 38 n. 2, 44, 57, 60–2, 62 n. 1, 81–3, 86, 93, 94–5, 104, 122–3, 124 n. 1,

127, 136, 141, 150, 157 n. 1, 163, 168, 171–3, 193 n. 1, 203, 220–1, 232–3; marriages, 161, 201, 206–7, 225–6; divorce, 95 n. 1, 161, 161 n. 2, 162–5, 168–9, 175 n. 7, 181–2, 201–3, 225; foreign policy, 52–3, 58 n. 4 and 5, 83, 104–7, 111–13, 154–6, 164, 166–7; relations with Parliament, 150, 153, 170–1, 180–1, 184, ecclesiastical policy, 168, 180, 184, 200, 216–18, 221, 223–4, 226; attitude towards heresy, 119–21, 165, 184 n. 3, 188, 190, 196, 226; attitude towards the New Learning, 52, 89, 97–8, 117; relations with Sir Thomas More, 62, 68, 86, 89–92, 92 n. 3, 94, 96–7, 103–4, 107 n. 3, 108–9, 111, 113, 119, 134, 137, 149, 152–3, 156–8, 164, 169–71, 179, 182–8, 203–4, 208, 210, 213–14, 216–18, 229–33, 236; *Assertio septem Sacramentorum adversum Martinum Lutherum* by, 120, 120 n. 3, 121, 188; letter from, 190.

—, court of, 52, 82, 89–90, 92, 96–7, 103–4, 106, 109, 116, 122–3, 126, 134, 136, 143, 146, 161, 164, 184–5, 187, 200.

Herde, see Hyrde.

Heron, family, 232.

—, Cecily, see More.

—, Giles, son-in-law of Sir Thomas More, 148, 177, 228, 232; marriage with Cecily More, 136; M.P. for Thetford, 170 n. 2; execution, 136.

—, Sir John, treasurer of the King's chamber, 136.

Hewster, John, governor of the Company of English Merchants, 106 n. 5

Heywood, family, 142.

—, Joan, see Rastell.

—, John, dramatist and epigrammatist, 43, 43 n. 4, 143–4; marriage with Joan Rastell, 143; plays attributed to: *the Four P's, a new and very Merry interlude of a Palmer, a Pardoner, a Poticary and a Pedlar*, 43 n. 4, 144 n. 1; *the Pardonere and the Frere*, 43; *Johan and Tib*, 43.

—, Richard, protonotary of the court of King's Bench, 144.

Hilary, St., 120.

Hilton, [Walter], 119.

Hindley, co. Lancs., 159.

Hirtius, see Hyrde.

the History of King Richard the Thirde, by Sir T. More, 2, 48, 48 n. 4, 50, 51 n. 1.

Holbein, Hans, the younger, 146–7; portraits by, 16–17, 45 n. 3, 146–7.